Five Irish women

Manchester University Press

Five Irish women

The second republic, 1960–2016

EMER NOLAN

Manchester University Press

Copyright © Emer Nolan 2019

The right of Emer Nolan to be identified as the author of this work has been asserted by her in accordance with the Copyright, Designs and Patents Act 1988.

Published by Manchester University Press
Altrincham Street, Manchester M1 7JA
www.manchesteruniversitypress.co.uk

British Library Cataloguing-in-Publication Data
A catalogue record for this book is available from the British Library

ISBN 978 1 5261 3674 9 hardback

First published 2019

The publisher has no responsibility for the persistence or accuracy of URLs for any external or third-party internet websites referred to in this book, and does not guarantee that any content on such websites is, or will remain, accurate or appropriate.

Typeset in Sabon by
Servis Filmsetting Ltd, Stockport, Cheshire

For Iseult Deane

Contents

List of figures	viii
Acknowledgements	ix
Introduction	1
1 Edna O'Brien: writing sex and nation	13
2 Sinéad O'Connor: the story of a voice	49
3 Bernadette McAliskey: speechifying	80
4 Nuala O'Faolain: an emotional episode in public life	118
5 Anne Enright: taking the Green Road	163
Afterword	198
Bibliography	208
Index	217

Figures

1 Edna O'Brien on 'The Person in Question' (1966). Image courtesy of RTÉ Archives. 13
2 Sinéad O'Connor (May 1988) © Andrew Catlin / National Portrait Gallery, London. 49
3 Bernadette Devlin, anti-internment rally, London (26 March 1972). Photo by P. Floyd, Daily Express, Hulton Archive / Getty Images. 80
4 Nuala O'Faolain (1971). Image courtesy of RTÉ Archives. 118
5 Anne Enright, Cologne (2008). INTERFOTO / Alamy stock photo. 163

Acknowledgements

I am grateful to Maynooth University for the award of a period of sabbatical leave during which this book was drafted. My thanks to the Head of the English Department at Maynooth, Colin Graham, to my departmental colleagues, and particularly to Amanda Bent and Tracy O'Flaherty for their kind assistance during my term as Head of the School of English, Theatre and Media Studies. It has been an education in itself to work with the research students, past and present, in Irish and twentieth-century literature at Maynooth, especially Thomas Connolly, Daniel Curran, Bridget English, Matthew Fogarty, Francis Lomax and Eoghan Smith. The staff at the University Library at Maynooth and at the National Library of Ireland have been unfailingly helpful. An earlier version of Chapter 2 appeared in *Field Day Review* 6 (2010). It profited from the skilful editing of Ciaran Deane of Field Day Publications, who also advised on the illustrations for this volume. Lelia Doolan lent me a copy of her remarkable film, *Bernadette: notes on a political journey* (Digital Quilts, 2011). I am grateful for the critical engagement of many colleagues and friends in the field of Irish Studies and beyond, including Richard Bourke, Seamus Deane, Jo George, Luke Gibbons, Declan Kiberd, Liam Lanigan, David Lloyd, Breandán Mac Suibhne, Michael McAteer, Conor McCarthy, Barry McCrea, Denise Meagher, Chris Morash, Catherine Morris, Rachel Potter and Kevin Whelan. Joe Cleary, Michael G. Cronin and Sinéad Kennedy all found time to read drafts and gave excellent advice. Warm personal thanks are due to my mother, Eileen, and my brothers Lorcan, John, Victor and

Peter Nolan. Orla Nolan was enthusiastic about this project at an important moment. The book is dedicated to my wonderful daughter, Iseult Deane, with love.

Matthew Frost, Commissioning Editor at Manchester University Press, oversaw the process of publication with care and patience. My gratitude to him, to my anonymous reviewers, and to all at the press for their hard work in bringing this book into the light of day.

Introduction

This book is comprised of five portraits of Irish women from various fields – literature, journalism, music and politics – who have achieved outstanding reputations since around 1960: Edna O'Brien, Sinéad O'Connor, Bernadette McAliskey, Nuala O'Faolain and Anne Enright. This is not offered as a representative sample of accomplished Irish women but neither is it a merely random selection. For they are, all of them, quite exceptional in their achievements: all are or have been famous abroad as well as in Ireland, and several could claim at some point of their lives to have been among the most recognisable Irish people in the world. It is quite a homogeneous group in sociological terms: one – McAliskey – is from a working-class Northern Irish Catholic background, but the others all come from the southern Irish Catholic middle class. However, this book does not aim to be a comprehensive record of the successes of modern Irish women or Irish feminism. Numerous, diverse Irish women have had remarkable careers, sometimes in even more heavily male-dominated realms; there are many other extraordinary women, including important feminist campaigners, who may not have attracted the same level of international media attention as the women considered here. Rather, my focus is on the ways in which these particular distinguished women make sense of their formative experiences as Irish people and how they in turn have been understood as vibrant figures in whom certain liberating aspects of modernity in Ireland have been realised. Their creative work and their broader careers raise particularly compelling questions about women's emancipation, the legacies of modern Irish history and the possibility of radical social transformation in contemporary society. In my view, these are among the most important themes in academic and public debate in Ireland over the last sixty years or so.

In her classic work of 1949, Simone de Beauvoir described women as members of the 'second sex'. While there is no perceived contradiction between a man's humanity and his masculine identity, women have been defined as the 'other' of men – that is, they have usually been regarded as human beings of a different and secondary order. In philosophical terms, Beauvoir described women as confined to 'immanence': close to nature, passive, responsible for the reproduction of people and culture. Men (or at least privileged men) could far more easily aspire to 'transcendence' and to becoming creative innovators. A woman interested in the arts or science or politics was obliged to confront all kinds of preconceptions about her capacities, often including her own internalised ideas about feminine identity. Perceived primarily as a woman, rather than as a person who happens to be female, she was burdened with always having to think about her femininity. Beauvoir wrote that 'it is very seldom that woman fully assumes the anguished tête-à-tête with the given world';[1] yet, this was necessary if the female artist or thinker was to claim her freedom to express or challenge the human situation. In other words, it was difficult for her to confront the universe directly, leaving gender entirely aside. Beauvoir believed that in her time 'the free woman is just being born'.[2]

Beauvoir's *The second sex* has been much discussed and sometimes criticised by feminists in succeeding decades, especially since the emergence of the 'second wave' women's movement at the end of the 1960s. To some, her analysis seemed too dismissive of certain traditional dimensions of women's lives, such as motherhood. Further, in holding women to standards of 'universal' achievement that are in practice defined by men, Beauvoir could herself be accused of being 'masculinist' in her values. She is certainly no separatist and she does not regard women as fundamentally different (or superior) to men. But despite all the inevitable disputes about Beauvoir's legacy, some feminist theorists including Toril Moi argue for the continuing importance of Beauvoir's theory of women's freedom for feminism today. As Moi suggests, every woman has the right to speak about her experiences as a woman: it is oppressive to reduce women to their 'humanity' in a way that takes no account of their female bodies or their social experiences. But by the same token, feminism

> does not have to be committed to the belief that sex and/or gender differences always manifest themselves in all cultural and personal activities, or that whenever they do, then they are always the most important features of a person or a practice. Women's bodies are human as well as female. Women have interests, capacities, and ambitions that reach far beyond the realm of sexual differences, however one defines these.[3]

In other words, women do not always speak just *as* women.

I will look at this chosen group of five women in the light of Beauvoir's feminist philosophy in particular. All of them to a greater or lesser degree are influenced by but also resistant to stereotypes of feminine identity; other questions arising from Irish history and contemporary society in Ireland preoccupy them too. Yet they are heroic exemplars of the free woman, still perhaps just being born in modern Ireland. All of them are famous in their own right and not because of their connections to prominent families or male partners. Their careers were facilitated by the emergence of the Irish women's movement and several have also made key contributions to the feminist analysis of Irish culture. Yet they are all singular or even, in some cases, at times apparently lonely individuals. This is no doubt mainly due to their willingness to break with standard expectations of women's lives. It is also in part an impression created or heightened by press or media attention and one which at times may have suited the purposes of these women themselves. Indeed, we may sometimes be more comfortable hearing from a solitary, supposedly exceptional woman, especially if she is young and conventionally attractive, rather than contending with the questions posed by feminist or radical politics more generally. However, ultimately I am most interested in what the uncommon lives of these women tell us not just about themselves but about our common life – in general, but specifically in Ireland.

Anyone who considers the history of women in Ireland confronts a key question: compared to other Western European countries, was (or is) Ireland an especially dreadful place for women? For centuries, Ireland had been imagined as a woman in legend and poetry: Róisín Dubh, Cathleen Ní Houlihan, Mother Ireland. Such images also became associated with the Virgin Mary as an icon of passive suffering and sexual purity. The 1937 Constitution of the Irish Republic acknowledged the special position of the Catholic Church in the state and the importance of a woman's 'life within the home' for the common good of the nation. Feminists and liberal campaigners in favour of liberalising the country's laws on contraception, divorce and other issues of sexual morality have endured long and bitterly contested struggles from the 1970s on. In Ireland, feminism could not but seem threatening to the traditional life of the country as that had been moulded by the teaching of the Church.

It is unsurprising that for many of the generations emerging after the mid-century, Ireland's historic struggle for political independence seemed to have little to do with the freedom of Irish women. In her memoir, the novelist Edna O'Brien recalls her first sight of Dublin's O'Connell Street:

> Opposite [Nelson's] pillar was the General Post Office, where the men of the 1916 rebellion proclaimed the Irish Constitution, raised the Irish flag, but were soon overwhelmed and summarily executed in Kilmainham Yard. Further along, a statue of Daniel O'Connell, the Catholic emancipator, an iron man in a black iron coat with iron angels guarding him. But I was finished with all that, with history and martyrs and fields ... being, as I believed, on the brink of daring emancipation.[4]

Mary Robinson, on her election as the first female President of Ireland in 1990, hailed the women of Ireland in particular – 'mná na hÉireann' – who, in choosing a liberal, feminist candidate, 'instead of rocking the cradle [had] rocked the system'; Irish people, she said, had 'stepped out from the faded flags of the Civil War and voted for a new Ireland'.[5] Some thirty years after O'Brien, Robinson too associates the liberation of Irish women – and of the citizens of Ireland generally

– with a willingness to lay aside earlier conflicts in and through which the definition of the twentieth-century nation had been drawn.

However, feminism has not consistently been simply uninterested in or hostile to nationalism and republicanism in Ireland. A proportion of women in Northern Ireland, for example, took a different view of supposedly archaic disputes about the partition of Ireland in 1922. And as scholars have turned to the project of recovering the neglected histories of Irish women, it has become clear that many early twentieth-century 'first wave' Irish feminist thinkers were as profoundly committed to nationalist anti-imperialism as they were to campaigns for female suffrage and the equality of the sexes. Republican women have been caricatured as the diehard, ultra-conservative widows or other relatives of the lost martyrs of the Irish Revolution. In fact, female nationalist activists and artists were often daring and unconventional. They consistently criticised the independent Irish state for what they saw as its failure to live up to the radical political ambition of the 1916 Proclamation of the Republic.[6] Louise Ryan and Margaret Ward point out that while Irish nationalism has certainly been sexist, this has not necessarily precluded the involvement of women in nationalist movements. They argue that we must

> distinguish between how women have been represented in national histories and cultural and symbolic repertoires [and] how they have actually negotiated and challenged their roles and contribution to nationalism ... While nationalist symbols, images and texts have continued to depict women within a narrow range of cultural stereotypes, women's roles within nationalism have been, and continue to be, diverse, multifaceted and dynamic.[7]

This point is most directly relevant to one of the women I write about here: politician Bernadette McAliskey (formerly Devlin), one of the founders of the civil rights campaign in Northern Ireland and a Westminster MP at a pivotal moment in Northern Irish history. Yet the distinction drawn here by Ryan and Ward is important in a more general sense for Irish feminism. When women artists and scholars began to look into the history of their female precursors, especially in the early twentieth-century period, they did not tend to find individuals who would have declared with Virginia Woolf: 'As a woman I have no country. As a woman I want no country. As a woman my country is the whole world.'[8] Some of the most impressive of these women were prepared to work for and even fight over issues of sovereignty, empire and nation, alongside their commitments to suffragism and other campaigns for gender equality. As the republican leader Constance Markievicz put it in 1909: 'No one should place sex before nationality or nationality before sex.'[9] Even when contemporary Irish women may have felt no particular emotional connection to politicised women from the time, it still remains the case that, in the words of Margaret O'Callaghan, 'the story of Irish women is part of the complex story of partitioned Ireland's self-fashioning, and the relationship of cohorts of people within that society with their own pasts and the pasts of their parents; it is at the heart of that story and not an addendum to it'.[10] For example, O'Brien's fiction and memoirs clearly show that she was never, in fact, to be finished with Ireland and its 'history, martyrs and fields'. Among the women I discuss here, another celebrated memoirist, Nuala O'Faolain, dwells in most detail on how the Irish patriarchs of her childhood, including her own father, were intensely conscious of being the inheritors of a new state that the previous generation had struggled to create. She believed that this helped to shape nearly every dimension of her early experience: sexuality, family life, politics. For various reasons – some of them biographical – O'Faolain was also preoccupied with the question of Northern Ireland to a degree that was highly unusual for a southern Irish feminist. This was a concern shared with O'Brien and musician Sinéad O'Connor. The latter, as a female performer who has engaged with the traditional Irish musical repertoire and with received images of Irish femininity, has from the outset of her career been understood to be experimenting with and expanding the received idea of the female voice as expressive of the suffering Irish nation. In their various works of fiction, journalism and social commentary, O'Brien, O'Faolain and Anne Enright have all explored the specificities of Irish landscape, speech and sensibilities (which is not to say that such interests necessarily correlate with any particular political stance on the question of nationalism). But while O'Connor challenges aspects of the role of the female singer that in itself was understood to be a conventional one for an Irish woman, in their fiction O'Brien and Enright (and O'Faolain too in her two late novels) take up the position of national storytellers in an art form that had been dominated throughout the twentieth century in Ireland by James Joyce, Samuel Beckett and other male writers.

All the women considered here are strongly associated with what has come to be thought of as the liberal critique of Ireland. This is especially true of the women from the Republic, who have spoken out in opposition to aspects of the Catholic-dominated independent Irish state in particular. But in the late 1960s, McAliskey, as a young woman whose rhetoric chimed with that of student and youth protest movements of the time across Europe and America, was also seen as galvanising and modernising a previously ineffectual political resistance to the sectarian Northern Irish state in the late 1960s. But each of these women also frequently articulates a strong sense that while they are criticising Ireland as it is, *by* that very action they are also creating and revealing a more positive and more authentic sense of what 'Irishness' could mean or what it could become. However inescapably oppressive their own complex identifications with Ireland can be for them, at times, they also suggest that Irishness itself, understood as an historically determined condition, is in fact fundamentally hospitable to such values as diversity, equality and tolerance. Robinson herself struck exactly such a note at the conclusion of her inaugural speech. She declared that as President she hoped to sing the 'joyous refrain' of a medieval Irish poem adapted by W. B. Yeats: 'I am of Ireland … come dance with me in Ireland.'[11]

Robinson's message about change, then, was also one about revival. She said that she hoped that her presidency could become a kind of symbolic 'fifth province'.[12] She was drawing here on the notion that ancient Ireland had recognised a spiritual space, beyond the four provinces of the real Ireland, which represented empathy and reconciliation. It surely must have seemed particularly appropriate for a woman leader – even a campaigning barrister and professor such as Robinson – to draw on such imagery. This is especially true in the case of Ireland, where associations between the national territory and femininity remain familiar and resonant. But her inauguration also provided a striking visual image of a modern feminist challenge to masculine power. Television footage and photographs of the ceremony memorably show the new head of state dressed in vivid purple seated in front of rows of almost exclusively male politicians in dark suits. For many, this imagery almost immediately became a classic representation of a less hierarchical and a less repressive Ireland: its first definition was a political and social synthesis embodied in this female figure who had just emerged with such éclat from the pallor of the political system. This is just one example (although a central one) of how the enormous impact of many prominent female figures in Ireland in recent decades has depended on their capacity to draw on both archaic and contemporary ideas about women and on their having found the means to express these through media images as well in their own more specialised fields.

We can shed light on these conjugations of sex, tradition and change by exploring the question posed by Rita Felski: does modernity as such have a gender? Felski suggests that in fact the modern era can be understood as having both a 'masculine' and a 'feminine' face. Becoming modern is evidently the achievement of people who are rational, daring and transgressive and such qualities are primarily associated with men. By contrast, women may seem to be inherently traditional: as life givers and nurturers, they are more concerned with preserving stability than plotting revolutions. But while the advent of the modern is associated with, for example, images of industrialisation or machinery and of masculine ingenuity and strength, we think of women as in some senses better suited than men to a later capitalist era of consumerism with all its cultivation of the pleasures of self-adornment and mass culture. They are perhaps more at home in what Walter Benjamin calls the 'phantasmagoria' of the modern.[13] Through certain key representative figures, including the shopper, the feminist, the hysteric and the prostitute, who feature so recurrently in popular culture, cinema, literature and journalism, woman becomes 'a powerful symbol of both the dangers and promises of the modern age'.[14]

In some of the widely disseminated images of the women celebrated here, modern Ireland has produced its variants on such figures. There are good historical reasons why – in Felski's phrase – the feminine face of modernity in Ireland was particularly important. Outside Belfast and some other Northern urban areas, Ireland was not heavily industrialised. When the southern Irish economy did achieve growth, during the late 1960s up to the Oil Crisis of 1972 and during the 'Celtic Tiger' boom from around 1995 until the crash of 2008, its expansion was due mainly to foreign direct investment, high-tech industries, financial services and a property boom. Not much muscle or sweat there. And while women in Ireland may long have been considered the very embodiments of tradition, they also came to be regarded as the most salient victims of old Ireland (especially in the decades between the rise of the women's movement and increased public consciousness of other major issues such as child abuse and discrimination against gay people). The biggest battles between liberals and Catholic Ireland were concerned with sex and reproduction. Of course contraception, divorce and abortion were not just matters of relevance to feminists. They were also bound up with a more permissive attitude to sexuality in general and thus feminist campaigns in part represented an extension of earlier protests against the puritanical regime of the independent state. Although they may have been dismissed by many people as members of an unrepresentative elite, feminist journalists and activists were at the forefront of these debates, entertaining and scandalising a wide audience with their fearlessness, wit and flamboyance.[15] The five women considered here were not part of this specific grouping; however, both their work and its reception were shaped by this new awareness of women's experience and interests. The feminist herself became one of the paradigmatic modern figures in the Irish imaginary. And traces of stereotypes of the legendary 'wild Irish girl', from the warrior queen Grace O'Malley down to the red-haired Hollywood colleen, were also seen to cling to 'feisty' Irish women. This is true even when the latter are being most 'modern': 'strident', candid about sexual matters, taking on unconventional roles as spokespeople or public representatives. Of course, not all perceptions of 'women's libbers' were positive. As well as representing a defiant rebellion against the past, the feminist could shade into the hysteric: another modern type, but one whose rejection of social norms supposedly took the pathological forms of anarchy or promiscuity. Nevertheless, a previously marginalised section of the population had apparently found its authentic voice for the first time: here was a more spectacular emergence than (for instance) that of the Northern Catholic minority at roughly the same moment, or of any group representing the economically disadvantaged throughout the entire history of the state.

The women considered here are deeply committed to significant artistic and political values and were never just interested in becoming celebrities. Nevertheless they were all highly visible in the media during key episodes in their public lives. McAliskey's youth and gender inevitably meant that she was able to attract increased press attention to the movement for civil rights. A powerfully telegenic Edna O'Brien became a literary star in Ireland and the United Kingdom even as her local parish priest in Co. Clare was publicly burning copies of her banned first novel. Sinéad O'Connor's tearing up of a photograph of Pope John Paul II live on US television in 1992 was probably the pivotal moment of her entire career. Nuala O'Faolain is perhaps better remembered for two viscerally powerful interviews in the Irish media than for any of her works in print: the first on television with Gay Byrne on *The late late show* the day before the publication of her memoir in 1996, and the second with Marian Finucane on RTÉ radio a few weeks before her death in 2008. Only Anne Enright, as a more securely 'literary' figure, inhabits a world where the public relations is less sensationalist. Indeed, with the exception of Enright, the artists here (O'Brien, O'Connor and O'Faolain in her career as a novelist) all have affinities with 'light' or commercial forms, especially pop music and romantic fiction. At the same time, these artists are by no means ignorant of the immensely seductive and sometimes damaging power of manufactured fantasies. Women still belong to the second sex, so any assessments of the notable achievements of these individuals must involve consideration of how they have dealt with inherited, commodified and contested notions of feminine identity.

I will investigate here what we might call the genealogies of the media images and events involving these figures: their origins in the lives and ideas of the women, the ways in which they were received by people more generally, their crystallisation of certain key ideas about gender at a time of conflict and transition in the culture. For better or worse, late twentieth-century Ireland needed its unconventional or feminist women, as mavericks who nevertheless seemed to dramatise the possibility of major, far-reaching change. To paraphrase Freud's question about the supposed enigma of 'feminine' desire, in these five cases we might ask: 'What did these women want?'[16]

Notes

1. Simone de Beauvoir, *The second sex*, trans. H. M. Parshley (London: Vintage, 1997), p. 721.
2. Beauvoir, *The second sex*, p. 723.
3. Toril Moi, *What is a woman? and other essays* (Oxford: Oxford University Press, 1999), p. 8; in this book Moi offers a superb account of Beauvoir's thinking about gender and of later feminist debates about *The second sex*.
4. Edna O'Brien, *Country girl: a memoir* (London: Faber & Faber, 2012), p. 81.
5. Mary Robinson, 'Acceptance speech', 9 November 1990, www.president.ie/en/media-library/speeches/president-robinsons-acceptance-speech (accessed 21 June 2018).
6. Among other recent accounts of women in this period, see Senia Pašeta, *Irish nationalist women, 1900–1918* (Cambridge: Cambridge University Press, 2014) and R. F. Foster, *Vivid faces: the revolutionary generation in Ireland, 1890–1923* (London: Allen Lane, 2014).
7. Louise Ryan and Margaret Ward, *Irish women and nationalism: soldiers, new women and wicked hags* (Newbridge, Co. Kildare: Irish Academic Press, 2004), p. 3.
8. Virginia Woolf, *Three guineas* (New York: Harcourt, 2006), p. 129.
9. Constance Markievicz, writing in the nationalist-feminist paper *Bean na hÉireann*, quoted by C. L. Innes, *Woman and nation in Irish literature and society, 1880–1935* (Hemel Hempstead: Harvester Wheatsheaf, 1993), p. 138.
10. Margaret O'Callaghan, 'Women and politics in independent Ireland, 1921–68', in Angela Bourke et al. (eds), *The Field Day anthology of Irish writing: Irish women's writing and traditions* (Cork: Cork University Press, 2002), vol. 5, p. 134.
11. Mary Robinson, 'Inaugural speech', 3 December 1990, www.president.ie/en/media-library/speeches/address-by-the-president-mary-robinson-on-the-occasion-of-her-inauguration (accessed 21 June 2018).
12. Robinson, 'Inaugural speech'.
13. For Walter Benjamin's classic account of the 'dreamworld' of modern commodity culture, see *The arcades project*, trans. Howard Eiland

and Kevin McLaughlin (Cambridge, MA: Harvard University Press, 1999).
14 Rita Felski, *The gender of modernity* (Cambridge, MA: Harvard University Press, 1995), p. 3.
15 There is a growing literature on the history of Irish feminism: see, for example, Bourke *et al.* (eds), *The Field Day anthology*, vols 4 and 5; Linda Connolly, *The Irish women's movement* (London: Palgrave Macmillan, 2002); and Clara Fischer and Mary McAuliffe (eds), *Irish feminisms: past, present and future* (Galway: Arlen House, 2014).
16 Sigmund Freud's remark 'What does a woman want?' ('Was will das Weib?') is recorded by Ernest Jones, *Sigmund Freud: life and work* (London: Hogarth Press, 1955), vol. 2, p. 468.

I
Edna O'Brien: writing sex and nation

From the early nineteenth century, when Irish writers began to focus on the creation of a new kind of Irish writing in the English language, the country's cultural prestige has been intimately bound up with its great literary achievements. A consolidated national resistance to British civilisation was created through journalism and through historical, political and other works. However, this found a particularly powerful form in literature. Associated with W. B. Yeats and other artists of the Irish Literary Revival during the decades leading up to the achievement of partial independence and the partition of the island in 1922, this literature was romantic in its origins. It asserted Ireland's spiritual superiority to capitalist materialism and claimed that the Irish could provide an alternative to the soulless modernity embodied by Britain. This vision survives to some extent in contemporary Irish writing and in the culture generally.

But such romantic and nationalist strains in Irish literature exist alongside disenchantment and pessimism; indeed, the former may even provoke the latter.

Since the foundation of the independent state, the anti-heroic strain has dominated. Ireland may have been the home of a glorious ancient civilisation, but where was its greatness now? The struggle for political independence had not produced the promised equality nor had it overcome the economic and sectarian heritages of imperialism. Many Irish citizens were still condemned to poverty or emigration. A whole generation of leaders had been lost to execution and war; the counter-revolution effectively closed down the prospect of a radical alternative to the colonial condition. Indeed, many of the latter's worst features were actually sharpened in the new dispensation, most of all the clerical conservatism that threatened the secular identity of the state and degraded it almost to the status of a theocracy. This was calamitous for women in almost every respect. Ireland, the only English-speaking Catholic country in the West, was a vital territory for the Church. The Catholic diagnosis of modernity had placed a particular emphasis on the importance of the family for the consolidation of traditional society. In Rome's eyes, this was a 'war' against a promiscuous modernity that had to be won. Thus, the war was waged in Ireland with a particular ferocity and women – above all, 'fallen' women – were the particular focus of its sexual ideology and victims of its strict policing. Writers interested in producing an unflinching, honest appraisal of modern Irish life took their bearings from the early works of James Joyce, especially the chilly brilliance of *Dubliners* (1914), which had captured, with deadly understatement, the confessional and provincial sexual reality of Irish colonial society.

Of course, Joyce initially shocked his native audience. But Ireland eventually came to terms with his critical vision of the country, although it learnt to do so in part by commodifying him (and all its important writers). Indeed, the belated inclusion of such a writer into the Irish pantheon seemed to indicate that Ireland could – albeit after a struggle – absorb its artistic dissidents as a stage in its own dawning maturity or modernity, after the late 1960s especially. The great Author – Yeats, Joyce, Samuel Beckett and a few others – was and still is a key figure in Irish society. In him (no woman was in competition for the position), we could observe the island's dual existence. Ireland was simultaneously a refurbished, heroic culture and a dilapidated colonial remnant: sometimes it seemed that fantasies about the resurgent nation had themselves produced economic and political failure. And images of women are crucial to both romantic and realist versions of modern Ireland.

In the former tradition, female figures often feature as embodiments of the oppressed nation. For example, Thomas Moore's beautiful lyric 'The song of Fionnuala' (1808) is based on the old Irish legend of the Children of Lir, who were condemned to spend hundreds of years as swans wandering the lakes and seas of Ireland. When the children heard the Christian Mass bell ring out for the first time in Ireland, they were changed back into human form only to die of old age. Fionnuala, Lir's only daughter, alludes to Ireland's suffering as she pleads for her own release:

Sadly, oh Moyle, to thy winter-wave weeping,
Fate bids me languish long ages away;
Yet still in her darkness doth Erin lie sleeping,
Still doth the pure light its dawning delay.
When will that day-star, mildly springing,
Warm our isle with peace and love?

When will heaven, its sweet bell ringing,
Call my spirit to the fields above?[1]

In Irish realism, we find that the prevailing representations of women are quite different. Women and girls suffer greatly at the hands of men within their own families and society. They are often exploited and unloved. This can be taken as an indictment of the emotional and sexual repression apparently so pervasive in Irish Catholic culture. They may be able to survive and to display remarkable endurance and pragmatism, but more often women in such stories are defeated by their horrible circumstances. We might think, for example, of the mothers in rural, mid-twentieth-century Catholic society depicted in John McGahern's early fiction. *The barracks* (1963) offers this description of a woman's work in a rural home:

> There was the shrill alarm clock at eight ... and the raking of the ashes over the living coal close to midnight: between these two instants, as between tides, came the retreating nights of renewal and the chores of the days on which her strength was spent again, one always unfinished and two more eternally waiting, yet so colourless and small that only on a reel of film projected slowly could they be separated and named; and as no one noticed them they were never praised.[2]

Like the author's own mother as she is lovingly recalled in his *Memoir* (2005), these women have deep spiritual resources but they are ultimately destroyed. Rather than being victims, like Fionnuala, who share that condition *with* Ireland, such women are victims *of* Ireland. But since all such accounts are inevitably mediated through male writers' experiences of and fantasies about mothers, lovers and wives, it is not always possible to distinguish between the romantic and the actual. For example, is Joyce's Molly Bloom in *Ulysses* (1922) a mythicised or a realistic figure?[3] And can we then look instead to Irish women writers for accounts of women's lives that are not so determined by the projections or idealisations of men?

It is reasonable to expect that women writers will be more sensitive to the experiences of women in general. But keeping in mind

Beauvoir's point that women are not simply 'born' but rather produced by social conditioning, it seems inevitable that women as much as men may absorb assumptions about gender roles that are not easily set aside.[4] Many Irish women have embraced the myth of Mother Ireland: Yeats's friend and patron, Augusta Gregory, was the co-author with him of the play *Cathleen ni Houlihan* (1902), perhaps the most famous dramatisation of the nation as a woman. In general, twentieth-century Irish realist women novelists, such as Mary Lavin or Maura Laverty, were if anything generally rather less bleak or ferocious in their critique of Irish society than Joyce of *Dubliners* or the young McGahern. It is predictable that factors other than gender will determine the political and cultural interests of women writers, including class and religious affiliations. For example, Irish Protestant women novelists had pioneered the genre of the Big House novel, beginning with Maria Edgeworth in the early nineteenth century. In a late masterpiece in this lineage, Elizabeth Bowen's *The last September* (1929), the main concern is with the fate of the young Anglo-Irish heroine in the context of the decline of her own class. But no woman was considered a major innovator in either of the traditions of modern Irish romantic revivalism or counter-revivalism and none had won the status of the heroic Irish writer alongside Yeats or Joyce. Those were artists who in discovering their own sacred vocations were deemed also to have discovered a people.

Edna O'Brien, who was born in Co. Clare in 1930 and won widespread attention with her best-selling first novel *The country girls* (1960), is far from being the first Irish woman writer, although rural Catholic women writers were certainly rare before her time. Many more Irish women writers have emerged over the last sixty or so years. The poet Eavan Boland was probably the first explicitly to associate her work since the 1970s with the feminist critique of national myths and the recovery of occluded women's traditions.[5] In recent decades, many women writers have appeared who are generally highly sensitive to feminist perspectives and who themselves have been read with serious attention to issues of gender and sexuality. Anne Enright is this generation's best-known exemplar. But O'Brien's career – the sheer fact of it – makes her an exceptional figure in Irish cultural history. She is the first iconic Irish Woman Author.

A woman from a fairly standard rural background, O'Brien could herself be taken as an incarnation of the Irish colleen: red-haired and green-eyed, she was beautiful, fey and eloquent. Caithleen (or Kate) Brady is O'Brien's autobiographical counterpart in her first book and in the two subsequent novels that make up *The country girls trilogy*; O'Brien's 2012 memoir is called *Country girl*, underlining the association between character and creator. Like O'Brien, Kate is a child of the west of Ireland, and although she finds her way to London (via Dublin), she always yearns for 'that scene of bogs and those country faces'.[6] Her name recalls one of the allegorical figures for the country. A doting older local man recites poetry about the suffering of Ireland to her; when a lover pronounces her name she hears 'the bulrushes sighing ... the curlew, too, and all the lonesome sounds of Ireland'.[7] In O'Brien's work, then, we can trace the formation of a girl or woman who has been encouraged to identify herself with the national territory and who successfully internalises – even embraces – such an identification. It helps to make sense of her enduring attachment to a specific place (the west of Ireland) and it is associated too with the capacity of her heroines to arouse tender and protective feelings in men. Thus, O'Brien's self-understanding is deeply rooted in an essentialism. Irishness is for her a mode of identity; she takes it to be, or to have been, inaugurated by violence and thereafter conditioned by a primal and almost predestined violation. The history of the country and of the self is assimilated to the natural evolution of the landscape; all is of a piece – landscape, history, consciousness, and the abiding threat of violence, which is itself natural or determined. As she writes in *Mother Ireland* (1976), a volume that (perhaps significantly) combines travelogue and memoir: '[Ireland] has been thought to have known invasion from the time when the Ice Age ended and the improving climate allowed the deer to throng her dense forest ... It was inevitable that Ireland should be invaded by the powerful Saxons, her neighbours across the Irish Sea.'[8] This notion of identity is reinforced by images of the agony of Christ and of the sorrowful Virgin Mary that exercised a powerful influence over the imagination of the young O'Brien (as with Kate in her convent school in *The country girls*). As a national destiny, this condition of woundedness is shared by Irish women and men: both are victims of a tragic history.

O'Brien offers historical explanation of a kind ('It was inevitable') but this occasionally languid writing exposes stereotypes not by analysis but mainly by the excess of their production. There is a mild but persistently erotic undercurrent.

At the same time, her portrayals of the Irish family place O'Brien in the tradition of the grim social realism of the early works of Joyce and – fifty years later – of her contemporary McGahern. Kate, like many other women in O'Brien's later fiction, is exceptionally or even oppressively close to her mother. As this mother is constantly subjected to her husband's alcoholic rages and sexual predations, another kind of victimhood is therefore intimately close to hand and keenly felt by the young girl. O'Brien's representations of violence and abuse quickly evolved to become far more pronounced than in *The country girls* and considerably more explicit than (for example) McGahern's. Instead of adult women, girls are more often presented as the sexual victims. A relatively early novel with an Irish setting, *A pagan place* (1970) includes graphic description of the sexual exploitation of the young heroine by a priest. Of course, it is curious to think that, at the time, O'Brien may have been considered 'daring' simply to be writing about sex in this way: 'He opened his buttons, wrenched them open and presented himself and said to touch it. It was grotesque. The flesh all around it pained and raw. He said to touch it.'[9] Such a passage may have been considered as an audacious experiment in literary obscenity or even – for example, perhaps by the Irish Censorship Board, which banned her work – as salacious pornography. By the time, say, that O'Brien wrote *Down by the river* (1996), Irish circumstances had radically altered. The plot of this novel was based on the 'X' case of 1992, when a fourteen-year-old rape victim was prevented by a High Court injunction from travelling from Ireland to the UK for an abortion. The ensuing controversy dramatised for many the unacceptably cruel consequences of the 'Pro-Life' constitutional amendment of 1983. In O'Brien's book, the pregnancy is the consequence of the sexual abuse of a young girl by her father. Her early detractors would presumably have seen such a story merely as evidence of O'Brien's interest in illicit or perverted sex. In the changed conditions of the 1990s, she was instead regarded by many as someone who had been amazingly honest and accurate about Irish sexual pathologies and indeed as an artist in the vanguard of those who had exposed the mistreatment of women and children. In this context, her consistent belief in an essentialised Irish feminine identity – her dedication to *being* an Irish woman – did not appear to be so salient or important as her candour about the consequences of that condition.

But there is another element in O'Brien alongside the romantic and the realist. This is one that had no place in the work of the writers such as Yeats and Joyce that she venerates: the popular. Yeats in particular wanted to save Irish literature from what he considered to be the kitsch and sentimentality he so disdained in much nineteenth-century writing; he was committed to inventing an inspiring national art, informed by folk tradition, rather than to entertaining a mass audience. O'Brien readmits the mass cultural element: she comes to maturity at a much later point in the development of celebrity culture during the 1960s, and herself rapidly becomes something of a media star. The scandal attached to her name and image in Ireland only enhanced her glamorous image in Britain and America. And the works themselves have an affinity with popular romance forms that would generally have been understood as mainly of interest to women readers. Despite the grim representation of sex between men and women in O'Brien, most of the women she writes about are invested, above anything else, in their romantic relationships with male partners. In the early stories, they hope to escape from inept and brutal Irish men and seek happiness with more sophisticated, usually foreign, lovers. To do this, they beautify and commodify themselves, including by exploiting their soulful, melancholic Irishness – which in fact eventually irritates their lovers and is understood to contribute to these women's ultimate abandonment. In typical romance style, these plots often allow O'Brien to depict much more opulent and glamorous worlds than those to which her heroines originally belonged. Her awareness of the conventions of women's popular culture of her era in cinema and magazines is clear; her own career in print began with a weekly magazine column in Dublin, designed to be 'light-hearted, and of interest to women'.[10] As she remarks, 'it was a long way from James Joyce'.[11]

Thus, there is a tension in O'Brien between her attachment to popular women's culture and her sense of affiliation with early twentieth-century experimental or modernist Irish literature. While she has been somewhat dismissive of her own generation of Irish writers, she has consistently expressed admiration for the artists of the early twentieth century ('A great literary endowment, true, but lean offerings over the past thirty or forty years', as she wrote of the Irish literary scene in the 1970s.[12]) O'Brien wrote a biography of Joyce in 1999 and he is for her the key Irish literary figure. She has described the impact that reading Joyce for the first time had on her as a young woman, as she copied out his sentences over and over.[13] In her work – as in his – close connections are drawn between women, modernity and consumer culture: Molly Bloom, for example, who loves shopping, represents among many other things a fairly affirmative portrayal of the modern woman as consumer. But this is just one element in the epic structure of *Ulysses*; Joyce also frequently parodies consumerism and romance.[14] But owing to her closeness to the styles and patterns of romance, the taint of the 'merely' popular clung to O'Brien's reputation for a long time. This of course at the same time served to enhance her widespread appeal.

Indeed, Nuala O'Faolain has suggested that 'Edna O'Brien has had a more immediate and sustained impact on her native audience than any other writer of the twentieth century.'[15] O'Brien's presence in the media and the authority ceded to her on Irish affairs made her the forerunner of later Irish women artists and commentators who have since emerged both as exemplary victims of independent Ireland and as newly articulate critics of the Irish state and the Catholic Church. Her idea of Ireland was the first to which women, not men, had privileged access. Overnight, she became a herald of the new Ireland that seemed to be overcoming its joyless, misogynist repressions; her taboo-breaking narratives about sex, marriage and women's lives were nourished by the old, but still painfully alive experiences of exile which independent Ireland had intensified rather than alleviated. O'Brien introduced a new sensibility and idiom into the national narrative. It was the very fact that these exiles or escapees were women that resonated. In addition, they were members of that group that had been most policed by the Church; now, astonishingly, it was they who were negotiating the modern sexual culture of the metropolis, the London of the 'Swinging Sixties'. O'Brien's portrayals of luxury consumerist gratifications were part of the attraction of such stories for a curious Irish audience fed up with puritanism and poverty. Sex was included as one of those gratifications; in the eyes of many of her readers and of her heroines, it was the defining experience. Ireland had been only marginally affected by the changes in the status of women that the Second World War had produced and so the emigration of these women, especially to England of the 1950s and later, was in effect a kind of time travel.[16] Born into a world of colleens, they suddenly found themselves among increasingly self-aware women for whom such liberation was the necessary first step in what was to become feminism. That sexualised world would also become the new world of gender.[17] O'Faolain argues that 'because Edna O'Brien existed, we are able to imagine a certain kind of Irish girl and Irish woman, one of exceptional and vigorous melancholy, one of terrible dependence on love, but a woman, nevertheless, from a recognisable landscape'.[18] That is to say that O'Brien invented a world that was inescapably associated with an author (as in 'Joycean' or 'Yeatsian'), yet that was also, as with her illustrious predecessors, a communal world ('Ireland') – and in this case, with impeccable historical timing, a woman's Ireland.

The story of Kate Brady and of her best friend Baba Brennan in *The country girls trilogy* is probably the single most influential and celebrated twentieth-century account of Irish women's lives in fiction. For example, Eimear McBride, in her introduction to the most recent edition, describes *The country girls* as an 'era-defining' symbol of 'the struggle for Irish women's voices to be heard above the clamour of an ultraconservative, ultrareligious and institutionally misogynistic society'.[19] O'Brien's explorations of family and of Ireland in the *Trilogy* are revisited and developed in other stories and in her autobiographical writing. For some women readers, her takes on such key topics as Catholicism, nationalism and romance are distinctive but idiosyncratic; for example, O'Faolain concluded that O'Brien 'is entirely unique; a lone and obsessed wanderer of the wider shores of love'.[20] Indeed, an apparent masochism may well seem to pervade O'Brien's representation of spirituality, politics and sexuality. She is focused to an almost obsessive degree on the sorrows of romance and the figure of the abandoned, desolate woman. So, is she a representative Irish female voice but also in some senses a pre-feminist writer? Here is a woman artist who was granted a hugely significant role as a writer who could speak for generations of silenced Irish women. What account does her work then give of women's real desires? It is mainly thanks to feminism that we now have quite a few successful but less 'colourful' Irish women writers, whose reception is not so closely bound up with appearance and personality – although they have not, of course, had the electrifying effect on Irish society that a pioneer such as O'Brien produced in her heyday. But later writers may traverse the same territory as O'Brien, including the question of how a traumatic national history figures in the imagination of Irish women writers or Irish women in general. They may negotiate such material with what may appear to be greater critical distance or irony. O'Brien's identification with Ireland might seem like a troubling, archaicising element, the more so if we consider the prevailing feminist views of the political effects of such a tactic. But in her persistent attachment to ideas of national community and to aspects of conventional femininity – dimensions of being a woman that many second-wave feminists expected that 'free women' would quickly jettison – O'Brien certainly represents a key challenge and case study for contemporary Irish feminist criticism.

Most of the women considered in this book have spoken or written about the houses and families in which they grew up in astonishing detail. O'Brien's account of Kate's home in *The country girls* is echoed in her autobiographical works and in many of her stories. As in other cases as well, the marriage of the parents furnishes a powerful and enduring model of heterosexual relationships and of the possibilities of family life in general. The house (along with the family farm, for O'Brien) also remains imprinted on the young mind as a microcosmic version of the national community. Sinéad O'Connor states straightforwardly of her suburban family home in Glenageary in Co. Dublin: 'I grew up in that house, which was Ireland.'[21] Nuala O'Faolain too says of one of her family's houses by the sea at Clontarf (on the north side of Dublin city) that it was a precise symbol of what Ireland was like for her: in stormy weather, the house seemed to cower beneath the waves crashing on the sea front and 'the atmosphere inside the house ... could be as menacing'.[22]

O'Brien did not hail from a thatched cottage or the landscape of little fields and dry-stone walls that we might associate with the Atlantic coast of Ireland. At the beginning of the *Trilogy*, Kate tells us that her father was in the process of letting 400 acres of the old local Anglo-Irish estate that he had inherited from his family go to ruin.[23] O'Brien's memoir offers further detail on her own family's situation. While her father had taken part in an attack on the Big House during the War of Independence in the 1920s, his grandmother bought the estate with money sent from emigrant relatives in America. So the property had been acquired through considerable enterprise and ambition. O'Brien's own parents' house, Drewsboro, was built from sandstone salvaged from the partial destruction of the Big House. However, the house was constructed according to a 'modern', American-inspired design that had been created by O'Brien's mother, who had lived in the United States as a young woman. While his grandmother had been a 'lady' who dressed for dinner every evening and wore a white lace ruff, O'Brien's father was a drinker and a gambler who failed to look after the land.[24] Neither his grandmother's canny and acquisitive instincts nor his wife's good taste – both such promising indicators for an emerging Irish Catholic bourgeoisie – could prevail over O'Brien's father's incompetence. He should have been part of a newly powerful Catholic landowning class. But he could not provide the comfort in which women (in particular) might thrive and was fixated on asserting his authority over them with violence instead. Just as the Anglo-Irish had failed to win the hearts of their tenants and so to naturalise their rule, so the new Irish patriarchy evidently failed to impress its own women who craved the domestic comfort and romantic intimacy they associated with higher social worlds. Even though as a child she is fascinated by the ruins of the Big House – 'The rungs of a staircase dangled into what had once been a ballroom, feeding the various fantasies that I had contrived, of balls, carriages along the black avenue and footmen rushing out with lit sods of turf to help the visitors down'[25] – O'Brien evinces no nostalgia for the Anglo-Irish dispensation, echoing what would have been the verdict generally in the neighbourhood on the burning of this mansion as 'another notch of victory over the invader'.[26] But what she does demonstrate is an investment in an idea of gentility that seems to her to be particularly important for women. In this context, it is revealing that Kate's first romantic interest in *The country girls* is a rather elderly married French man known in the district as 'Mr Gentleman'. However, he is no Gallic romantic or rebel but thoroughly bourgeois in his lifestyle: the young girl is enchanted by the thought of his opulent house where he and his wife drink sherry and dine on roast venison.[27]

Such luxury appears immensely desirable to O'Brien's young protagonists who are acutely aware of women's despairing submission to the trials of marriage, childbearing and work in the house and on the farm. Just as the house is permeated for the child by her mother's anguish, so too out in the countryside, 'even on the best of days with the sun shining, the bees buzzing, the cattle drinking down by the waterside, a kind of terror lurked'.[28] The world of the farm is dominated by the same masculine and sexualised violence that afflicts the females of the family. For example, O'Brien recalls how 'a clutch of chickens, usually canary-coloured, would be in the yard, screeching one minute and lying dead the next, like bits of rag. The fox had been. Mr Reynard. Always Mr which in itself must have coloured one's considerations about the male sex.'[29] So instead, Kate's mother tries to make the house pretty with humble knick-knacks and decorations. These objects represent crucial gestures of defiance and sources of pleasure. Such kitsch becomes infused with the presence and – after her death by drowning – the daughter's memory of the lost mother. In a later story, O'Brien imagines such treasures as actually contained within the mother's body and by virtue of their association with her, ordinary household objects are raised to the same sacred status as the communion host or the treasures hidden in the land of Ireland: 'Her mother was the cup, the cupboard, the sideboard with all the things in it, the tabernacle with God in it, the lake with the legends in it, the bog with the wishing well in it.'[30] Compare this to the brutally disenchanted evocation in the same story of the actual paraphernalia that surrounds mothers – including that associated with maternity and babies: 'the baggy napkins, the bottle, and the dark-brown mottled teat'.[31]

So, the mother cleans the kitchen, feeds the animals and dreads her husband's sexual advances, while all the time dreaming of more beautiful images and things. The latter involve fantasies about femininity in which the daughter, in *The country girls*, shares from early on: high-heeled shoes, pretty dresses, make-up, sweets and fine food, and the pleasure of being oneself admired as an alluring object. Beauvoir would probably diagnose such 'narcissism' as a crucial and prevalent defence against a full acknowledgement of oneself as 'inessential': a way of psychically investing in one's own objectification. 'Woman,' Beauvoir writes, 'will only accept herself as inessential if she rediscovers herself in the act of abdication. Allowing herself to be an object, she is transformed into an idol proudly recognizing herself as such.'[32] Thus, this is a strategy for preserving a sense of self-worth in a society that denies women opportunities to transcend the self in more productive or creative ways. However, in mid-century rural Ireland women must struggle mightily to attain access to the myriad accoutrements of femininity that are required by modern, fashionable women. They need to have these things bought for them by rich lovers and husbands, as it is unlikely that they could ever have the opportunity to earn the money to buy them for themselves. It is also to be hoped that these men will display a more gentle and tender sexuality than that associated with the father and other (Irish) men. The young girl's sexual desires indeed go no further than a kiss: 'Nothing more ... Mama had protested too agonizingly all through the windy years.'[33] However, such dreams are doomed to be disappointed as generally men seek to penetrate women, causing them pain and inflicting on them all the horrible consequences of pregnancy, childbirth and so on.

In many ways, Kate Brady responds enthusiastically to the inherited religious and political culture around her as a child. O'Brien vividly recalls the history and the legends that she was taught as a child in *Mother Ireland* and elsewhere; in a similar way, images, songs and stories help Kate to aestheticise or soften the harsh realities she observes. Kate enjoys lessons in the village classroom and wins a scholarship to a convent boarding school; she hears the news of her academic success on the day her mother drowns. She leaves for the convent shortly after her mother's death, where Baba joins her as a fee-paying pupil. Religion and art help her to cope with the loss of her mother and with her grief for the tender dimensions of life at home and on the farm. She listens to the nuns singing to the Virgin Mary in the chapel: 'One nun sang like a lark. Her voice was different to the others, singing, "Mother, Mother, I am coming", and I cried for my own mother. I thought of the day when we sat in the kitchen and saw the lark take the specks of sheep's wool off the barbed wire and carry it to build her nest.'[34] But while O'Brien herself successfully passed her examinations, Kate is expelled – but only because she reluctantly participates in her friend Baba's plan to scandalise the nuns and have them both sent home so that they can move to Dublin.

From the outset, Baba is impatient with what she sees as artistic or religious mystifications of brutal realities. She sees Kate's need for such stories only as so much melancholic self-pity: 'Mary of the Sorrows telling you a lot of drip about her awful childhood.'[35] Thus she is an early critic of Kate's passivity, anticipating the later complaints of her husband and lovers. In school, she persuades Kate that they should both sign their names to an obscene message about a priest and a nun scrawled on a 'Holy Picture' – an image of the Virgin Mary – that they leave in the chapel. The nun who unknowingly begins to read out the message has to be carried away in deep shock by another sister.[36] While Baba boldly recalls the message ('Father Tom stuck his long thing ...'[37]), Kate is deeply ashamed of the incident – although she is eager enough to accompany Baba to Dublin afterwards and never really laments the abrupt termination of her formal education. The nun who reads the obscene words is not a despised figure but a person who was a favourite of Kate and who was always smiling as 'if she had some secret in life that no one else had. Not a smug smile but ecstatic'.[38] Baba's inscription on the picture is in keeping with O'Brien's early reputation as a 'bawdy' writer who above all else broke taboos by writing so outrageously about sex. But it is interesting to note that in many regards Holy Pictures remain as important to O'Brien as dirty words. The shock of transgression is both intense and repeatable over and over again, because the sanctified images it is intended to deface remain as sacred as ever. The rebelliousness and the willingness to talk openly about sex are ascribed to her friend (in effect the motor of the plot, as Baba also later instigates the move to England) – although ultimately these attitudes fail to bring her much more happiness than Kate is destined to enjoy.

However, what is remarkable in the *Trilogy* and elsewhere is the extent to which O'Brien's representation of a mature sexuality and feminine sensibility are entirely recognisable variations on the structure of feeling associated with certain strains of Irish Catholicism and popular Irish nationalism. She is keenly attentive to the libidinal investment in wounding and martyrdom that can be transferred from one realm to another. As she states in *Mother Ireland*: 'The spiritual food consisted of the crucified Christ. His Passion impinged on every thought, word, deed and omission.'[39] She remembers the history of Irish political rebellions being taught as a series of heroic but bloody acts of self-sacrifice – of 'honour cursed with defeat'.[40] O'Brien underlines the sexual aspects of the prevalent religious devotions: 'To be good was to be pure and yet the prayers had the glandular desperation ascribed to human love.'[41] In her more recent memoir, O'Brien also recounts how after losing her virginity (only following much fear and resistance) in a field on the outskirts of Dublin, she contemplates going to confession to a priest in the 'Church of the Most Precious Blood' in Cabra: she thought too 'of my own blood on the bit of field that cows would sniff at'.[42] This is perhaps an irreverent comparison of herself to Christ, to be sure, but poignant nevertheless. O'Brien got over her fear of God's punishment, but the accession to sexuality brought with it plenty of suffering in any case. Modern commodified romantic love offers new kinds of stimulants and new kinds of fetishised objects, but the threat of sexual penetration threatens to return the girl to a reliving of the old violations: 'the first thrust broke the phantasm'.[43] O'Brien writes of her own time as an adventurous young woman in Dublin, recalling a young man's attempt to seduce her on a horsehair sofa:

> Yes, you were going downhill. You had strayed far from the memory of the reality of the ellipse-shaped wounds of Christ, you found yourself living for these weekly delights where on screen you could witness 'the dallyings of divorcees and the lurid radiances of eroticism in bold Technicolour'. Not only that but you allowed yourself to relive the swoon of the horsehair sofa and the complete unconsciousness of the body up to the dreadful moment and his prophecy of being able to go through you like butter.[44]

She forsakes Jesus only to live out another version of his 'Passion' – the very word, indeed, combining ideas of desire, sacrifice and suffering. O'Brien as a girl thought of romantic stories as messages from another world and that 'sex the forbidden fruit was the glass coach in which to do a flit'.[45] But this proves not to be the case. It is little wonder, given those expectations, that the drama of her sexual 'initiation' (as such might have been understood at the time) is such a protracted and fraught affair in the *Trilogy*. In the end, Kate only actually has sex with Eugene Gaillard, the man whom she will shortly marry, at a point over halfway through the second volume.

According to Beauvoir, the narcissism of the femininity into which women are traditionally inculcated is poor preparation for the shocking experience of 'deflowerment': '[A woman] would like to be a fascinating treasure, not a thing to be taken. She loves to seem a marvelous fetish, charged with magical emanations, not to see herself as subject to seeing, touching, bruising.'[46] Beauvoir describes the woman's coming to terms with her sexuality, while also achieving freedom as an individual, as 'an enterprise fraught with difficulty and danger, and one that often fails' (this can also be perilous for men, but less than for women).[47] One danger is that pain itself might become a kind of pleasure for women. Of course, most feminists would dismiss as biologically essentialist the view that all contentedly heterosexual women must be sexual masochists; however, O'Brien does come quite close to such a view at moments.[48] Indeed in the *Trilogy*, Baba most clearly articulates the view that women are destined to pain by virtue of their biology. During a visit to an obstetrician, she muses:

> I was thinking then of women and all they have to put up with, not just washing nappies and not being able to be high-court judges, but all this. All this poking and probing and hurt. And not only when they go to doctors but when they go to bed as brides with men that love them. Oh, God, who does not exist, you hate women, otherwise you'd have made them different.[49]

Indeed, O'Brien stated in a 1984 interview that she believed that women's difference from men was 'fundamentally biological'; she expressed pessimism about any amelioration of conditions between the sexes: 'I would like women to have a better time, but I don't see it happening: people are pretty savage towards each other, be they men or women.'[50] Or as Jacqueline Rose declares (based not in her case on her view of biology but of the unconscious), while it must certainly be one of the goals of feminism for women to be freer in their sexual life, feminists 'must be careful not to exchange an injustice for an illusion': 'We are nowhere more deceived than when we present sexuality not as the trouble it always is but as another consumable good.'[51]

Shortly after the attempt by her father and men from her home village to save Kate from Eugene – a character closely modelled on O'Brien's former husband, the novelist Ernest Gebler, although Eugene is a filmmaker rather than a writer – she agrees to have sex with him. Eugene states that he does not want to force her and wonders whether some 'traumatic experience' caused her to be so terrified (Kate has never heard the word 'trauma' before).[52] But she believes that she owes him her virginity. As O'Brien wrote of her decision to live with Gebler: 'The early mortifications, the visions, endless novenas, the later "crushes" on hurly [sic] players, the melting glands at the cinema, the combined need for, and dread of, authority had all paved the way and it was in a spirit of expiation and submissiveness that I underwent that metamorphosis from child to bride.'[53] Kate does not feel any pleasure but merely 'some strange satisfaction that I had done what I was born to do. My mind dwelt on foolish, incidental things. I thought to myself, So this is it; the secret I dreaded, and longed for ... All the perfume, and sighs, and purple brassieres, and curling pins in bed, and gin-and-it, and necklaces had all been for this.'[54] As Michael G. Cronin comments, it is as if all the preparation and fetishisation of clothes and the body turns out to *be* the experience itself – there is no other revelation or transformation.[55] But in fact the sexual relationship with Eugene, although always unequal and ultimately cruel, is the most rewarding depicted in the *Trilogy*: 'Eugene guarded me like a child, taught me things, gave me books to read, and gave pleasure to my body at night.'[56] The real crisis comes for Kate after the break-up of her marriage, the loss of her child to the custody of her husband, her subsequent failed relationships, and her sense that – young though she still may be – she cannot play the childlike role she had with Eugene again, having 'lost the girlish appeal that might entice some other man to father her'.[57]

When Kate has a meeting with Eugene at Waterloo Station after their separation, she realises that their break-up is final. She is in these moments filled with nostalgia for childhood and Ireland. She passes by some nuns that remind her of how 'unscathed' she had been at the convent and keeps walking to escape the 'terror' of her fate, 'the danger of being out in the world alone'.[58] Distressed and hallucinating, Kate then imagines that she hears the 'Speak Your Weight' machine talk to her in a 'rich Irish country accent': 'A gray cloth map on the school wall, long forgotten, rose before her eyes, a map with names that were once names and now which had the intrigue of legend – Coleraine, Ballinasloe, and Athy. Places that she'd never visited and never wanted to visit but were part of a fable summoned up by this now familiar voice.'[59] She tries to talk back to the machine and when she gets no answer, she smashes the glass, injures herself and is taken away in an ambulance.[60] In her much later memoir, O'Brien recalls a similar scene in the station on the night she left her husband, remembering the voices as belonging to working-class Irish men:

> I went to Waterloo station, the place I had first seen when I arrived in London ... The men around me were mostly Irish ... They had a bottle of drink which they passed around. Another man got a coin for the weighing machine and had the others in stitches as the machine spoke his weight back to him ... I was not afraid there that night, or rather, I was less afraid than in the house I had vacated.[61]

The sense of recognition and fellowship is here with real people, rather than imagined ghosts as in the novel. But even in her more profound distress, the schoolroom map of Ireland reoccurs for Kate as a comforting image of belonging. Here, there is a realisation that while a successful heroine of romance (for example, a Jane Eyre) who manages to marry and keep her man then retreats into domestic contentment, the spurned lover is forced to re-examine the other relationships that she has repudiated and the history attached to them – in this case, all that pertains to Ireland. Nationality may be just as bound up with fantasy and pain as romantic love, but it involves a crucial, shared mapping of the world and a different kind of intimacy. As O'Brien states in *Mother Ireland*: 'Hour after hour I can think of Ireland, I can imagine without going far wrong what is happening in any one of the little towns by day or by night, can see the tillage and the walled gardens, see the spilt porter foam along the counters, I can hear argument and ballads, hear the elevation bell and the prayers for the dead.'[62]

There is in fact very little hostility in O'Brien to discourses of Irish national identity. These are, indeed, what Kate falls back on in a moment of despair (rather than potentially – for example – a deeper feeling of solidarity with other women concerning the failings of men). Like other women considered here (such as Nuala O'Faolain in particular) what we might call the psychogeography of Irishness proves to be a crucial and saving resource in a moment of profound personal crisis. For O'Brien, as an artist, this is evidently best negotiated from outside the country:

> I live out of Ireland because something warns me that I might stop if I lived there, that I might cease to feel what it has meant to have such a heritage, might grow placid when in fact I want yet again and for indefinable reasons to trace that same route, that trenchant childhood route, in the hope of finding some clue that will, or would, or could, make possible the leap the would restore one to one's original place and state of consciousness, to the radical innocence of the moment just before birth.[63]

No relationship with any man could entirely resolve or compensate for what has happened *in* Ireland or what happened *to* Ireland. But the project of an exogamous romance has definitely failed. Kate's imaginative turn to Ireland is not followed by any physical journey back (until after her death). However, there is a notable return to Irish terrain in O'Brien's later fiction. For as she puts it elsewhere, her writing arises from 'acute longing' for a place – in this instance, Clare: 'The church steeple, the hawthorn bushes, the clotted velvet roses on the chenille cloth and the by-roads that led nowhere made me want to write about them as if their existence was incomplete, otherwise. My own existence too.'[64]

Of course, O'Brien's most celebrated heroine, Kate, has no literary vocation to take up and cannot explore memory and her own history in this way. Her life continues unhappily until she dies by drowning (in a repetition of the fate of her mother) – possibly having taken her own life after a romantic break-up. In the Epilogue to the *Trilogy*, Baba awaits the arrival of Kate's coffin at Waterloo Station for her final journey back to Ireland, unable to find any consoling reflections about the life her friend has endured and dreading the funeral: 'Nothing for it but fucking hymns.'[65] O'Brien, by contrast, triumphantly survived the divorce from Gebler. In real life, the split was in any case more to do with writing than (as in the novel) adultery. Her husband found it difficult to accept that she was to be a published author and later claimed in court, during the custody dispute, that passages from her fiction showed that she was a 'nymphomaniac' who would turn their two sons into 'emotionally sick homosexuals'.[66] But it may seem frustrating that none of O'Brien's own talents and successes are reflected in the lives of her women characters – and that when she writes about herself, she seems always to emphasise the 'woebegone'.[67] In this sense, O'Brien lived the revolution, but did not write about it.

For many readers of O'Brien, her receptivity to religious and political images of passive female suffering, as well as to popular cultural discourses of commodified femininity and sexual submissiveness, are indications of false consciousness. In this view, O'Brien had internalised ideas about gender that are restrictive and damaging; as a writer she is simply too enmeshed in inherited ideologies to offer any real critique of them. As Peggy O'Brien puts it, she remains 'embedded in the flesh of her female protagonists' in order to avoid 'the terrors of separation, emergence and action'.[68] By contrast, for a group of later feminist critics, which includes O'Brien's most attentive and sympathetic scholarly readers to date, her work offers an unsurpassed depiction of a consciousness colonised by regressive notions of femininity, especially those propagated by Irish Catholicism and nationalism, as well as more general delusions about the joys of romance and marriage that pervade modern consumerist culture. Thus, merely to give voice to some of the most negative dimensions of an imposed feminine subjectivity is an achievement of major significance, especially in a country still heavily dominated in the 1960s and 1970s by Catholic sexual codes.[69] But O'Brien's position in relation to feminism is perhaps best captured by a joke from the 1979 Monty Python film *Life of Brian*. Confronting a huge crowd of followers, the unfortunate Brian, who has been mistaken for the Messiah, tries to persuade the crowd that has gathered around his house to abandon the belief that he is a special person. 'You've got to think for yourselves,' he roars. 'You're *all* individuals.' 'Yes, we're all individuals,' comes the response in perfect unison. 'You're all different,' Brian tells them. 'Yes, we *are* all different,' they answer. After a pause, one small voice is heard from the crowd reflecting sadly: 'I'm not.' The joke hinges on the mismatch between the meaning of the statement and the style in which it is made. The member of the crowd who declares himself not to be 'an individual' shows that in fact he is actually thinking for himself. In relation to feminism, in her obsession with love and nation, O'Brien too answers back that she is 'not an individual', but a person formed by inherited and conventional ideas and content to be so.

These issues are just as pertinent in the current, later phase of O'Brien's career, a period in which she has written a series of novels, set once again mainly in the Irish countryside, tackling the topic of masculine violence with greater intensity than ever and encompassing some quite extreme material including incest, abortion and paramilitary violence in the North. An indication of how her work has developed in this regard can be illustrated by the contrast between Kate in *The country girls*, who is sexually harassed (as we would say now) by several fairly unpleasant but essentially timid older men in her home town, and the fate of the central figure in O'Brien's 2015 novel, *The little red chairs*, Fidelma, who gets pregnant after an affair with a fugitive war criminal hiding in the quiet Irish village of Cloonoila – a figure based on Radovan Karadžić, 'The butcher of Bosnia'. The pregnancy is ended during an appalling act of gang rape. This evolution in O'Brien's fiction unfolds in the context of an Ireland in which feminism is far more influential than in the earlier decades of her career. In addition, O'Brien herself has been awarded belated but extensive acknowledgement in her home country through unprecedented scholarly attention, prizes, awards and public events; for example, in 2015 she was awarded the title of saoi of Aosdána by the President of Ireland (the highest honour attainable in this state-sponsored association of creative artists).[70] This suggests that she is now a figure of considerable cultural authority – as well as being famous, which was always the case. While being censored and marginalised in Ireland did in itself have a kind of boomerang legitimising effect, she is now accorded respect of a different order. Yet the significance of certain aspects of her literary contribution is still being debated.

She has been praised by some commentators for the ferocity of her exposure of Ireland's sexual and emotional dysfunctions in unsparing, horrifying passages in which she recounts the anguish of women and children (including of boys who go on to be killers, such as the main character in *In the forest* (2002), based on a real-life case of triple murder in Co. Clare). Heather Ingman, for example, seeking to 'leave aside the romance themes in her work' (although this is a hardly possible ambition), describes O'Brien as self-consciously and programmatically challenging 'her nation's brand of gendered nationalism' in such works.[71] Passages in O'Brien detailing or exposing violence are juxtaposed with narrative interludes in which such cruelty is contextualised in Irish history and especially in relation to the issue of the possession of the soil or land. Hostile critics have read this as anachronistic, rather than revealing any real analytic interest in the past – an infusion of an impassioned, nationalist, melodramatic rhetoric that illustrates that O'Brien has not 'moved on' – that is, taken serious note of developments in contemporary Ireland. Hence, the same novels that are celebrated by some liberal critics as fearless disclosures of dark Irish realities are criticised by other, equally liberal critics for their regressive obsession with old myths of Ireland, and thus regarded as consistent with O'Brien's 'romantic' take on the Northern conflict, in such novels as *The house of splendid isolation* (1994). (For example, she conducted extensive face-to-face interviews with INLA (Irish National Liberation Army) leader Dominic McGlinchey for that novel; in reward for such efforts, she was described in the *Guardian* as 'the Barbara Cartland of long-distance republicanism.'[72])

In the opening pages of her novel *Wild Decembers* (2000), the

Great Famine of the 1840s is presented as necessary to understanding the community depicted and the tale of hereditary hatred and vengeance. The novel is thus ostensibly predicated on the historical explanation of the sexual politics of Ireland by reference to material conditions rather than by the ready-made method of racial stereotype. It therefore avoids presenting possessiveness towards land or women as *sui generis* aberrations, unique to that community:

> The enemy is always there and the people know it, locked in a tribal hunger that bubbles in the blood and hides out in the mountain, an old carcass waiting to rise again, waiting to roar again, to pit neighbour against neighbour and dog against dog in the crazed and phantasmal lust for a lip of land. Fields that mean more than fields, fields that translate into nuptials into blood; fields lost, regained, and lost again in that fractured sequence of things.[73]

However, the commitment to history may not in fact survive the reifications of '*the* enemy', '*tribal* hunger', '*that* fractured sequence of things'. Women are also particularly subject to the random operations of romantic passion – libido, repeatedly compared to a force of nature in the vividly described landscape of the west of Ireland, seems more irresistible and potentially ruinous than ever. As the main character, Breege, says of her calamitous affair:

> Bugler opened up some vein in me, and it is not his fault any more than it is mine ... You can go years and years of normal life, all day, every day, milking, foddering, saying the given things, and then one day something opens in you, wild and marvelous, like the great rills that run down the mountain in the rain, rapid, jouncing, turning everything they touch into something living; a mossy log suddenly having the intent and slither of a crocodile.[74]

Men may also experience love in this way, but for them this is a temporary state. But in a different way, they are also victims of other large, impersonal forces, subject to the imperatives of 'honour and land and kindred and blood',[75] which often kill them. In the worst cases, there is something ferocious in them that cannot be explained. For example, Vlad (the Karadžić character) in *The little red chairs* is a kind of nationalist, declaring that different peoples 'have something that flowers have ... a distinct scent of their own'.[76] His Irish lover, Fidelma, follows him to his trial at the International Criminal Court in The Hague, desperate to understand 'what goes on inside him ... the inner footage',[77] that might account for his need to kill. But he remains an enigma to her. The cost of the violence this monstrous figure has unleashed is registered mainly through the many tales of loss of life and forced displacement, especially of women and children, narrated in the novel. Nevertheless, O'Brien ends with a chorus of migrants in London all chanting the word for 'home' in their own languages: 'You would not believe how many words there are for *home* and what savage music there can be wrung from it.'[78] Despite the horrors of 'ethnic cleansing' detailed in the book, there is not much countering endorsement here of multiculturalism or globalisation.

So, there is surely considerable evidence here of O'Brien's enduring attachment to unfashionable and arguably regressive notions of national and gender identity. And of these, the former appears to take priority. So how might we make sense of this 'free woman' who does not reject traditional femininity or the identification of women with the national territory? We could suggest that, as long as such ideas retain real force, it is important to understand them 'from the inside' of women's conscious and indeed unconscious experience. Laura Kipnis has made a convincing argument that femininity, or the issue of the 'female psyche', remains a key issue in women's lives and relationships, suggesting that we are on some 'seriously conflicted inner terrain' in contemporary feminism: 'social change goes whizzing past your ears, with the backwardish psyche – not always quite so amenable to change – bringing up the rear'.[79] And specifically in relation to Ireland, Clair Wills has proposed that because of the understandable hostility among feminists in particular to the trope of woman-as-nation, it has fallen to creative artists to explore 'the hidden forces within Irish culture which find expression in these symbolic ideals and fantasies'.[80] She argues that it is thus Irish women's creative, rather than critical work, that has most extensively explored the symbolic meanings of the female body and 'the covert aspects of sexual, cultural and political identification'.[81] O'Brien would surely occupy a leading position among such Irish artists. Thus, Wills urges us to be wary of the argument that in making 'representation secular and enlightened it is possible to dissolve the realm of fantasy and myth. But there is no simple division between fantasy and a core of experience, because events and experiences are themselves bound up with fantasy.'[82]

And of course, some straightforwardly positive consequences, in political terms, have resulted from O'Brien's particular conjugations of sex and nation. Any early accusations that female artists (including much younger artists such as Sinéad O'Connor) in some way exaggerated or luridly overstated the kind of abuse that went on in Irish families and institutions sadly by now has been utterly discredited. The criticism they faced is certainly a classic instance of 'shooting the messenger' (as Patricia Coughlan puts it in relation to the reception of O'Brien's work more generally[83]). O'Brien's engagement with Northern Republicans, including Sinn Féin's Gerry Adams (she published a cautiously sympathetic interview with Adams in the *New York Times* in 1994, which was widely criticised in Ireland), looked quite different after the Peace Process and the Belfast Agreement of 1998.[84] She was always dubious about modernisation in Ireland, and about whether the place was really so different to the traumatised post-colony that she left in 1950s. She still referred to Ireland as 'Godot land' – regardless of the accession to the European Economic Community and other changes – two decades later.[85] But this also assumed new significance in the wake of the economic crisis of 2008. For example, when O'Brien appeared alongside journalist and academic Ruth Dudley Edwards in a BBC *Newsnight* debate on the International Monetary Fund/European Union (EU) bailout of Ireland in 2010, many might have anticipated an unequal contest between the romantically inclined novelist and the staunchly anti-nationalist intellectual. But while Dudley Edwards dismissed Ireland as 'an adolescent nation' that 'blew it' with the excesses of the Celtic Tiger years, O'Brien refused to blame the Irish for the humiliation of the bailout, wondering what alternatives there would have been to EU membership and the financialisation of the economy. As she declared:

'the world is financial'. For one who has regularly been denounced for supposedly proposing easy generalisations about Irish psychology, O'Brien's scepticism here about Ireland's economic options in fact produced the more coherent explanation of the crisis in terms of the historical situation of late twentieth-century Ireland.[86]

When Irish critics came to look at O'Brien afresh in the 1990s and afterwards, there were inevitably some attempts simply to gloss over what might appear to be some of the more problematic political implications of her works, in well-intentioned efforts to applaud her achievements instead. But the most compelling commentaries were nuanced in their responses to the material and its history. (However, it is interesting to consider if O'Brien herself took much regard of such critical subtleties. As late as the 2012 memoir, she still numbered 'feminists and academics' among those hostile readers who were 'tearing into her'[87] without mentioning any later responses; in the same book, she tells of an episode of severe depression, apparently brought on in part by dwelling on how her work had so often been deemed 'wanton', 'irrational', 'narrow' and 'obsessional'.[88] One wonders if the sense of being beleaguered and vulnerable has become an ineradicable feature of O'Brien's creative process?) Lisa Colletta and Maureen O'Connor, in particular, have investigated the ambiguities of O'Brien's public persona and of its reception. They insist that O'Brien's is an 'operatic performance' of Irish female identity and they enumerate the various feminine and national stereotypes that she has 'inhabited to parodic excess'; in their view, such 'deliberate, stylized, highly theatrical stagings of the self' are essentially playful, but they also lay bare the 'constructed nature of national and sexual identities'.[89] However, such readings can run the risk of reviving other, less sympathetic, dismissals of O'Brien as merely 'stage Irish' – and as cannily aware of the commercial appeal of such images to audiences outside Ireland.[90] But more importantly, this is also perhaps to underestimate O'Brien's obviously sincere and long-held convictions about questions of national belonging: 'Irish? In truth I would not want to be anything else. It is a state of mind as well as an actual country. It is being at odds with other nationalities, having quite different philosophy about pleasure, about punishment, about life, and about death.'[91]

Patricia Coughlan concentrates on another aspect of O'Brien's work – the way in which the author dwells on women's bodies in their biological reality as debased or 'disgusting'. (In *Night* (1972), for example, the narrator offers the following brutally reductive self-definition: 'I am a woman, at least I am led to believe so. I bleed et cetera.'[92]) Coughlan emphasises that the emphasis on the abject condition of the female body in the fiction does not arise from women's pre-given biology. Rather, O'Brien reflects a general cultural ambivalence about women as mothers and one that was especially pronounced in Catholic Ireland. This argument leaves aside the question of whether the author is caught up in, or critical of, such ideologies: Coughlan suggests that O'Brien instead 'chronicles, analyses, and mourns over' the condition of women in Ireland.[93] Indeed, O'Brien's aesthetic accomplishment in capturing this melancholic abjection is in effect the only demonstration of a woman's agency – of the possibility of resistance to these circumstances – that emerges from her work. In other words, the very fact that O'Brien is *writing* about generally repressed dimensions of Irish women's lives necessarily involves a progressive and liberating distance from the historical experience that she describes.

To consider this involves returning to the question of 'writing Ireland' with which this chapter began. O'Brien admires and seeks to emulate what she sees as the grand traditions of Irish letters. In accepting the appointment as saoi of Aosdána, she spoke about the distinguished history of Irish writing and commented: 'Language is something we have inherited and if we have a collective and an individual responsibility ... it is to retain that language, not corporate language, not glib language but the language that we've been handed down that is singular testament to Ireland's humanity and to that precious jewel, Ireland's imagination.'[94] She seeks to distinguish 'corporate' and 'glib' language – the language of commerce and cliché – from 'great writing', and perhaps also from the common speech of ordinary people in their distinctive communities. The modernist generation in Ireland turned the clichés of nationalism (sad songs, militant ballads, bad verse) into high art (Yeats first, then in a different style, Joyce). O'Brien affirms this modernist claim for Art, but in an era when such claims in Ireland have themselves become clichéd. In addition, she re-embraces the popular and romantic in their standardised forms as well. From the beginning, there were hostile readers who found her combination of the Great Irish Author and the Woman Writer incongruous or impossible. But there is a sense in which this sense of incongruity belongs not just to the reception of O'Brien, but is a constitutive anxiety in the writing itself.

From the outset, O'Brien understands writing as being about sadness and failure. It arises directly out of romantic rejection. O'Brien states that after her first big romantic disappointment in *Mother Ireland*, she waited for the man involved long after he could have been expected to appear, 'the better or the most excruciatingly to live out the pain of the first conscious jilt'. She claims that later she came more fully to understand 'the triumph that can attend rejection', as those 'who feel and go along with the journey of their feelings are richer than the seducers who hit and run'. As she lingered on the street, O'Brien claims that she composed her 'first mawkish poem'; repeating this aloud was 'some sort of solace and an inducement to go on'.[95] O'Brien's reputation as a writer was formed out of the link between intimate vulnerability and a blaze of publicity. Writing exposes the secret self, always at risk of being mockingly denigrated and spurned. An Irish woman's writing, especially, can expect to be criticised but hope to be loved. O'Brien makes claims for Ireland's specificity and grandeur, and also offers significant social critique, but does not in her writing imagine or create a community where either colonial or emotional damage could be overcome. To remember is to relive a traumatic wounding, while modernity promises only an equally damaging deracination or amnesia. Writing reveals but does not relieve the predicament.

Several commentators have commented that, instead, O'Brien's writing seems to make a special plea to the reader for sympathy or understanding. As Peggy O'Brien remarks: 'the prose unquestionably makes this powerful gesture of appeal to us, demanding reaction, either to affirm or reject the author'.[96] The point is reminiscent of Beauvoir, who lamented rather harshly in the 1940s that the woman artist, intimidated in 'the universe of culture, because it is a universe of men', will tend narcissistically to identify her work with her own ego:

the book and the picture are merely some of her inessential means for exhibiting in public that essential reality: her own self ... She gives literature precisely that personal tone which is expected of her, reminding us that she is a woman by a few well-chosen graces, affectations and preciosities. All this helps her to excel in the production of best-sellers; but we must not look to her for adventuring along strange ways.[97]

But O'Brien has in fact won the approval and affection of both popular and more literary audiences – from the days of her early scandalous notoriety in Ireland, when the books were so sought after by all kinds of readers, to today's more highbrow fans and academic critics. But yet she does not appear to feel an intense connection with these readers. (As we shall see, there is a strong contrast here with Nuala O'Faolain – an even more directly confessional writer than O'Brien.)

Perhaps the range of O'Brien's aesthetic and political stances can be illuminated by reference to the philosopher Judith Butler. Several commentators agree that O'Brien's work and career are characterised by styles and performances that variously seem to pay tribute to, parody or subvert received ideas of Irish and feminine identity. In an essay on the politics of drag performance in Jennie Livingston's celebrated documentary film *Paris is burning* (1990), Butler considers the way in which mainly working-class African American and Hispanic transgender women and gay men perform roles in their drag balls that are clearly derived from the dominant culture that surrounds and oppresses them (for example, 'walking' as rich white women, or straight male 'executives'). Butler notes that sometimes such performances are 'subversive' and sometimes they are uncritical appropriations of mainstream culture. They can in fact be both at once. The received norm may not be displaced; it can even be reiterated as 'the very desire and the performance of those it subjects'.[98] Thus the film 'documents neither an efficacious insurrection nor a painful resubordination, but an unstable coexistence of both'.[99] In a similar way, O'Brien's work perhaps conveys 'a sense both of defeat and a sense of insurrection'.[100] She continues to dwell under the shadow of the clichés that she does not entirely wish to escape.

This linkage, this to-and-fro between the elite and popular, canonical and 'feminine', is O'Brien's peculiar territory. But we should certainly respect that O'Brien wants to be what she says she wants to be, even if this appears to keep her within what Butler might call 'the traumatic orbit'[101] of her injuries: a 'fallen' woman honouring Mother Ireland.

Notes

1 Thomas Moore, 'The song of Fionnuala', *Irish melodies* (London: Longmans, 1873), p. 39.
2 John McGahern, *The barracks* (London: Faber & Faber, 1963), p. 21.
3 I explore the sexual and national politics of Joyce's representations of women in *Joyce and nationalism* (London: Routledge, 1995), ch. 6.
4 See Beauvoir, *The second sex*, p. 295.
5 See, for example, Eavan Boland's prose memoir, *Object lessons: the life of the woman and the poet in our time* (London: Vintage, 1996).
6 Edna O'Brien, *The country girls trilogy* (New York: Farrar, Straus and Giroux, 1986), 137. The *Trilogy* comprises *The country girls* (1960); *The lonely girl* (1962), later retitled *The girl with green eyes* (1964); *Girls in their married bliss* (1964); and an epilogue (1986).
7 O'Brien, *The country girls trilogy*, pp. 12, 163.
8 Edna O'Brien, *Mother Ireland* (New York: Harcourt Brace Jovanovich: 1976), pp. 11, 15.
9 Edna O'Brien, *A pagan place* [1970] (Harmondsworth: Penguin, 1971), p. 177.
10 O'Brien, *Country girl: a memoir*, p. 97.
11 O'Brien, *Country girl: a memoir*, p. 98.
12 O'Brien, *Mother Ireland*, p. 33.
13 O'Brien, *Country girl: a memoir*, p. 98.
14 I explore Joyce's relationship with earlier Irish popular and nationalist fiction in *Catholic emancipations: Irish fiction from Thomas Moore to James Joyce* (Syracuse: Syracuse University Press, 2007), ch. 5.
15 Nuala O'Faolain, 'Edna O'Brien', in *Ireland Today* (Bulletin of the Department of Foreign Affairs) (September 1983), p. 10.
16 See Clair Wills's account of the perceived connections between women, commerce and modernity in mid-century Irish cultural debate and her discussion of O'Brien's fiction in this context in *The best are leaving: emigration and post-war Irish culture* (Cambridge: Cambridge University Press, 2015), ch. 2.

17 Wills describes O'Brien's characters as exhibiting the growth of a new kind of female subjectivity and as 'on the threshold of a new understanding of themselves'; *The best are leaving*, p. 99.
18 Nuala O'Faolain, 'Irish women and writing in modern Ireland' (1985), in Bourke *et al.* (eds), *The Field Day anthology*, vol. 5, pp. 1604–5.
19 Eimear McBride, 'Introduction', in Edna O'Brien, *The country girls trilogy* (London: Faber, 2017), pp. ix–x.
20 O'Faolain, 'Edna O'Brien', p. 13.
21 See O'Connor quoted in John Waters, 'Sinéad the keener', *Irish Times* (28 January 1995).
22 Nuala O'Faolain, *Are you somebody?: the accidental memoir of a Dublin woman* [revised US edition of *Are you somebody?: the life and times of Nuala O'Faolain*] (New York: Henry Holt, 1998), p. 203.
23 O'Brien, *The country girls trilogy*, p. 10.
24 O'Brien, *Country girl: a memoir*, pp. 6–7.
25 O'Brien, *Country girl: a memoir*, p. 8.
26 O'Brien, *Country girl: a memoir*, p. 6.
27 O'Brien, *The country girls trilogy*, p. 13.
28 O'Brien, *Mother Ireland*, p. 74.
29 Edna O'Brien, 'Co Clare', in 32 *Counties: photographs of Ireland by Donovan Wylie, with new writing by thirty-two Irish writers* (London: Secker & Warburg, 1989), p. 229.
30 Edna O'Brien, 'A rose in the heart of New York', in *A fanatic heart: selected stories of Edna O'Brien* (New York: Farrar, Straus and Giroux, 1984), p. 388.
31 O'Brien, 'A rose', p. 385.
32 Beauvoir, *The second sex*, p. 373.
33 O'Brien, *The country girls trilogy*, p. 145.
34 O'Brien, *The country girls trilogy*, pp. 66–7.
35 O'Brien, *The country girls trilogy*, p. 185.
36 O'Brien, *The country girls trilogy*, pp. 105–6.
37 O'Brien, *The country girls trilogy*, p. 105.
38 O'Brien, *The country girls trilogy*, pp. 104–5.
39 O'Brien, *Mother Ireland*, p. 42.
40 O'Brien, *Mother Ireland*, p. 68.
41 O'Brien, *Mother Ireland*, p. 42.
42 O'Brien, *Country girl: a memoir*, p. 102.
43 O'Brien, *Country girl: a memoir*, p. 99.
44 O'Brien, *Mother Ireland*, pp. 136–7.
45 O'Brien, *Mother Ireland*, p. 81.
46 Beauvoir, *The second sex*, p. 373.

47 Beauvoir, *The second sex*, p. 423.
48 See discussions of Helene Deutsch's notorious essay, 'The psychology of women in relation to the functions of reproduction' (1935), which argues that not just menstruation and childbirth but also penetrative sex are all inevitably painful for women, in Juliet Mitchell, *Psychoanalysis and feminism* (Harmondsworth: Penguin, 1974), pp. 126–7; and Laura Kipnis, *The female thing: dirt, sex, envy, vulnerability* (London: Profile Books, 2006), pp. 158–9. See also Shirley Peterson, '"Meaniacs" and martyrs: sadomasochistic desire in Edna O'Brien's *The country girls trilogy*', in Katherine Laing *et al.* (eds), *Edna O'Brien* (Dublin: Carysfort Press, 2006), pp. 151–70.
49 O'Brien, *The country girls trilogy*, p. 473.
50 Edna O'Brien, from an interview quoted by Jill Franks, *British and Irish women writers and the women's movement: six literary voices of their times* (Jefferson, NC: McFarland, 2013), p. 129.
51 Jacqueline Rose, *Women in dark times* (London: Bloomsbury, 2014), p. xi.
52 O'Brien, *The country girls trilogy*, p. 229.
53 O'Brien, *Mother Ireland*, p. 141.
54 O'Brien, *The country girls trilogy*, p. 316.
55 Michael G. Cronin, *Impure thoughts: sexuality, Catholicism and literature in twentieth-century Ireland* (Manchester: Manchester University Press, 2012), p. 189. In this, he contrasts *The country girls* to other Irish *Bildungsromane*, such as Joyce's *A portrait of the artist as a young man* (1916) or Kate O'Brien's *Mary Lavelle* (1936), in which scenes of sexual initiation are profoundly meaningful and liberating, even when, as for the young woman in *Mary Lavelle*, the experience involves pain.
56 O'Brien, *The country girls trilogy*, p. 323.
57 O'Brien, *The country girls trilogy*, p. 455.
58 O'Brien, *The country girls trilogy*, p. 445–6.
59 O'Brien, *The country girls trilogy*, p. 456.
60 O'Brien, *The country girls trilogy*, p. 457.
61 O'Brien, *Country girl: a memoir*, p. 151.
62 O'Brien, *Mother Ireland*, p. 143.
63 O'Brien, *Mother Ireland*, p. 144.
64 O'Brien, 'Co Clare', p. 230.
65 O'Brien, *The country girls trilogy*, p. 531.
66 O'Brien, *Country girl: a memoir*, p. 166.
67 O'Brien, *Country girl: a memoir*, p. 204.
68 Peggy O'Brien, 'The silly and the serious: an assessment of Edna O'Brien', *The Massachusetts Review*, 28:3 (Autumn 1987), p. 487.

69 For example, see Patricia Coughlan, 'Killing the bats: O'Brien, abjection, and the question of agency', in Laing *et al.*, *Edna O'Brien*, pp. 171–95.

70 See Anne Enright's review of the memoir *Country girl* in which she decries the misogyny that characterised many Irish responses to O'Brien; Enright goes so far as to hint that, having been the victim of so much sexist commentary, O'Brien should be excused from further criticism or analysis: 'O'Brien is the great, the only, survivor of forces that silenced and destroyed who knows how many other Irish women writers, and her contradictions – her evasions even – must be regarded as salutary', '*The country girl* by Edna O'Brien – review'; *Guardian* (12 October 2012). While Enright is keen to be properly appreciative of and generous to O'Brien here, any suggestion that O'Brien should not be as carefully analysed as any other major writer may run the risk of not taking her work with the seriousness that it deserves. Academic criticism of O'Brien, which began to emerge relatively late in her career, includes Amanda Greenwood's *Edna O'Brien* (Tavistock: Northcote, 2003); the essays collected in Laing *et al.*, *Edna O'Brien*; and Lisa Colletta and Maureen O'Connor (eds), *Wild colonial girl: essays on Edna O'Brien* (Madison, WI: University of Wisconsin Press, 2006). On O'Brien's Aosdána appointment, see Pamela Duncan, 'Imogen Stuart, Edna O'Brien and William Trevor elected saoithe', *Irish Times* (16 September 2015).

71 Heather Ingman, 'Edna O'Brien: stretching the nation's boundaries', *Irish Studies Review*, 10:3 (2002), p. 253.

72 Quoted by Greenwood, *Edna O'Brien*, p. 2. See also Greenwood's broader account of some of the hostile responses to O'Brien's Irish-set fiction of the 1990s. Fintan O'Toole, for example, wrote a highly critical article on *In the forest*, suggesting that only O'Brien's long enforced absence from Ireland could have rendered her so apparently insensitive to the pain of those who had been bereaved by the killings that inspired the plot. But this was nevertheless symptomatic, he suggests, of her loss of connection with contemporary Ireland. For a discussion of and response to O'Toole's article, see Greenwood, *Edna O'Brien*, pp. 102–3.

73 Edna O'Brien, *Wild Decembers* [1999] (New York: Houghton Mifflin, 2001), p. 2.

74 O'Brien, *Wild Decembers*, p. 211.

75 O'Brien, *Wild Decembers*, p. 259.

76 Edna O'Brien, *The little red chairs* (London: Faber & Faber, 2015), p. 269.

77 O'Brien, *The little red chairs*, p. 287.

78 O'Brien, *The little red chairs*, p. 297; emphasis in original.
79 Kipnis, *The female thing*, pp. xi, xii.
80 Clair Wills, 'Feminism, culture and critique in English', in Bourke *et al.* (eds), *The Field Day anthology*, vol. 5, p. 1583.
81 Wills, 'Feminism, culture and critique in English', p. 1583.
82 Clair Wills, 'Women, domesticity and the family: recent feminist work in Irish cultural studies', *Cultural Studies*, 15:1 (January 2001), p. 54.
83 Coughlan, 'Killing the bats', p. 182.
84 Fintan O'Toole remarked of the Adams interview that O'Brien 'knows a strong, flawed and emotionally unavailable hero when she sees one'. Quoted by Greenwood, *Edna O'Brien*, p. 2.
85 O'Brien, *Mother Ireland*, p. 37.
86 Edna O'Brien, interview with BBC *Newsnight* (November 2010), 'Irish writers on national shame and anger over bailout', news.bbc.co.uk/2/hi/9216037.stm (accessed 22 June 2018).
87 O'Brien *Country girl: a memoir*, p. 204.
88 O'Brien *Country girl: a memoir*, p. 304.
89 Colletta and O'Connor, 'Introduction', in *Wild colonial girl*, p. 5. Rebecca Pelan also analyses the mixed responses of audiences and readers to O'Brien's public persona – memorably described by one reviewer as 'this Connemara Dietrich'; see 'Reflections on a Connemara Dietrich', in Laing *et al.*, *Edna O'Brien*, pp. 12–37.
90 For example, see Peggy O'Brien's description of Edna O'Brien as 'an outrageous concoction of what foreigners expect an Irish person to be – mellifluous, volatile, wanton, irrational'; 'The silly and the serious', p. 474. Less critically, but in a similar vein, Colletta and O'Connor comment on how O'Brien's public self is 'knowingly and gleefully marketed'; *Wild colonial girl*, p. 5.
91 O'Brien, *Mother Ireland*, p. 144.
92 Edna O'Brien, *Night* [1972] (London: Faber & Faber, 2014), p. 3.
93 Coughlan, 'Killing the bats', p. 182.
94 See Duncan, 'Imogen Stuart, Edna O'Brien and William Trevor elected saoithe'.
95 O'Brien, *Mother Ireland*, p. 140.
96 P. O'Brien, 'The silly and the serious', p. 488; see also Nuala O'Faolain on Edna O'Brien's 'urgently inviting' writing, which commands attention to the creating self in the style of a 'narcissistic' European romanticism; 'Edna O'Brien', 10.
97 Beauvoir, *The second sex*, pp. 716–17.
98 Judith Butler, 'Gender is burning: questions of appropriation and

subversion', in Susan Thornham (ed.), *Feminist film theory: a reader* (New York: New York University Press, 1999), p. 389.
99 Butler, 'Gender is burning', p. 392.
100 Butler, 'Gender is burning', p. 386.
101 Butler, 'Gender is burning', p. 383.

2
Sinéad O'Connor: the story of a voice

Sinéad O'Connor is surely Ireland's best-known woman artist. In the late 1980s and early 1990s, her startling appearance and the extraordinary vocal performances on her first two albums brought her huge fame as an international rock star. From the beginning, she combined an ambiguous sexual appeal, a distinctive clarity of voice and an aura of intense personal anguish. Although she became an early icon of the Celtic Tiger era, her attitudes towards Ireland, Catholicism and the music business were at odds with many aspects of the upbeat, commercialised 'Irishness' so prevalent in the popular culture of the time. In various ways, O'Connor has been associated with 'trouble': dealing with an extremely difficult private life in public, drawing attention to female sexuality in its emotional and reproductive complexities rather than in its commodified forms, and retaining a stubborn attachment to an Irish identity that is often perilously close to stereotype.

Media discussion of O'Connor has been dominated by a longstanding fascination with her image and by criticism of her continuing engagement with the publicity industry of which she is also in many ways a casualty. But the main focus here will be on her astonishing singing voice. O'Connor is quintessentially a solo performer. She has never played the role of a member of a family group, such as Clannad or the Corrs, or of the female singer in front of a band. At the outset, that solo voice, in combination with her arresting beauty and considerable songwriting talents, created a career – pop music stardom. But even her best-selling work involved an unstable compound of the coolly commercial and the nakedly confessional. Her biggest hit was 'Nothing compares 2 U', a cover of a song by Prince. Its famous accompanying video – MTV Video of the Year in 1990 – depends for its dramatic effect on the shadings of grief and sorrow that pass over O'Connor's face in close-up as she sings; towards the end of the song, as her eyes meet the camera directly for the first time, she begins to cry. However, within a few years, O'Connor's large-scale commercial appeal, in such performances of 'feminine' suffering, had been largely destroyed – mainly by the outrage caused by her ripping up a photograph of Pope John Paul II on the American TV chat show *Saturday night live* in 1992 in protest against Vatican collusion in child sexual abuse. After this, the entertainment business itself became a contributor to O'Connor's ongoing experience of trauma. However, her voice was not silenced. Its stark loneliness intensified but she took this lyric quality that had always been natural to her voice and nurtured it to see how it would ramify and evolve; the development of her voice became an enterprise, an experiment. As a solo artist, she dwelt on the possibility of emotional autonomy, even autarky, but then embarked on a long voyage to discover a route towards communal feeling. This describes the contour of O'Connor's artistic project from the debut album *The lion and the cobra* (1987) and its follow-up, *I do not want what I haven't got* (1990), to the more introspective *Universal mother* (1994) and *Faith and courage* (2000). Arguably, it reaches full definition in her cover album of Irish traditional songs, *Sean-nós nua* (2002), where the solo voice becomes, by a sleight of genius, the collective voice. This process harbours the promise that, while trauma admits of no easy resolution, it can nevertheless be faced or even outfaced. O'Connor's career raises questions about musical 'femininity', especially in pop music and in Irish music. She is blessed with a voice that has all the potential for the erotic and the ethereal, so readily associated with solo female performance. She fully explores these dimensions, but she also seeks quite different effects, refusing to limit herself to celebrating romantic love or purveying serene 'wisdom'. In the process, she raises key questions both concerning the possibilities for women's or feminist art in Ireland and also, more generally, about the critical potential of Irish popular art in contemporary conditions.

In the years since the turn of the millennium, O'Connor has continued to perform and to record, albeit intermittently. This has been achieved despite lengthy periods of severe mental and physical ill-health. The story of O'Connor's survival – both as a person and as an artist – is in itself remarkable. In the last few years, she has also made a triumphant return to songwriting on two albums, *How about I be me (and you be you)?* (2012) and *I'm not bossy, I'm the boss* (2014). It is notable that the collectivist resolutions of trauma, celebrated in the work of her mid-career, have not survived into this subsequent phase (these albums were recorded when O'Connor was in her late forties). Musical or verbal references to Irishness are notably absent, even in those songs that denounce the crimes of Catholic priests. Instead, many of the songs narrate – in sometimes almost unbearably intense and direct detail – recurrently frustrated longing and sexual passion. But these albums are not just a testimony to the unending drama of human desire and its many pitfalls, but are also an oblique (and rather despairing) comment on developments in Ireland over the period of O'Connor's musical career.

O'Connor's long-unfolding exploration of trauma through the medium of the human voice is especially suggestive and compelling for a number of reasons. Among these are her own understanding of her childhood experience. After her parents separated when she was a young child, she and her siblings spent several years in the custody of their mother, who was depressed and addicted to alcohol and prescription drugs.[1] O'Connor claims that she was subjected to humiliating and sadistic abuse at her mother's hands. She has said of this period in her life that she 'was born and was murdered in that house'. She prayed to God for help and believed that she was in return granted 'a voice and a chance to be heard'; and yet she states that 'there was always a sound that I was trying to get from myself, which is the sound I made as a child ... The howling. That was the sound that I'd blocked off.'[2] The more adult, articulate voice promised self-expression and the opportunity to become an artist, while the immature, inarticulate voice represents the inchoate cry of the abused child.

O'Connor's voice, especially in her early work, typically modulates between pure, soaring power and angry yelping or screaming. This second voice, it could easily be assumed, is her way of recreating the pain of her childhood. While the first voice is dematerialised or transcendent, the second corresponds more closely to what Roland Barthes has described as a 'grained' voice – one that sounds as if it has come from 'the cavities, the muscles, the membranes, the cartilages' deep within the body of the singer.[3] Moreover, it is paradoxically in this grained, bodily voice, in its very inarticulacy, that we can hear more clearly the characteristically specific sound of an individual. In O'Connor's case, it more closely reflects the well-known qualities of her speaking voice, with its combination of a rather nonchalant suburban Dublin accent and a supposedly over-emotional 'stridency'. There is a dissonance that is peculiar to her, that is audible in the texture and cadences of her speaking or singing voice; it would be too simple to suggest that, in her public performances, the beautiful, impersonal voice ever fully absorbs the angry, personal one. She has herself advanced this interpretation, indicating that the historical or political importance of her work lies in her capacity to transform grief into the aesthetic form of the funeral song or 'keen' (from the Irish 'caoineadh', meaning a cry or lament) – to give voice to and so to assuage not only her own pain but that of others as well. Through remembering personal and collective suffering, her audience – and especially Irish people dealing with the legacies of colonialism, the Famine and an oppressive Church – will be 'healed'.[4] Such remarks have been met with some condescension from most of the academic critics who have given any serious attention to her work.[5] But an examination of her music leads us to the conclusion that matters are in any event considerably more complicated.

Cathy Caruth argues that

> trauma seems to be much more than a pathology, or the simple illness of a wounded psyche: it is always the story of a wound that cries out, that addresses us in the attempt to tell us of a reality or truth that is not otherwise available. This truth, in its delayed appearance and its belated address, cannot be linked only to what is known, but also to what remains unknown in our very actions and our language.[6]

Because trauma is an experience that cannot be assimilated as it occurs, it both 'defies and demands our witness', for the victim is haunted not just by the reality of a violent event in the past, but by 'the reality of the way in which its violence has not yet been fully known'.[7] O'Connor's voice registers such violence everywhere – in the relationship between mother and child, man and woman, the artist and the music industry, the individual and the institutional Church. In Caruth's terms, O'Connor's singing testifies to the inescapability of the belated impact of trauma, in its persistent witness to the voice that 'cries out from the wound'. The modulations of her voice between the melodic smoothness of its purity and the rasping jaggedness of its anger do not conform to any predictable pattern. Its 'stridency' is never far removed from its lyric or spiritual qualities. Even in its soaring mode, the voice has a 'catch' or flaw in its purity which comes not from any sense of muscular effort or strain, but from a refusal of the emancipatory seductions that a clearly struck high note, with its shine and finish, seems to offer. It is as if her voice finds the traumatic moments in the songs that she sings, but then searches behind or beyond the sometimes banal lyrics of her pop or traditional material for something more answerable to its desire. This lends a quality of restless, dissatisfied intelligence to almost all of her recorded work. She tests her voice against the limitations of her material, or even more desperately, tests its own limitations, asking if there is any sound or combination of sounds that can fully articulate feeling. Thus, the voice, the song, the performance can never shed its frustration; to the listening audience *this* is a characteristic vibration that hangs in the air after the performance has been completed: the aftermath of representation, its incompletion.

The lion and the cobra in 1987 announced the arrival of a major new talent in Irish popular music. While the Irish identity of some earlier rock stars such as Phil Lynott or Bob Geldof had depended more on their projection of a soulful or rebellious masculinity than on particularly 'Irish' sounds, O'Connor sang in an unmistakably Irish accent and in styles that often evoked traditional or folk modes. With its elements of rock, punk and hip-hop and arrangements involving a huge variety of instruments including acoustic guitars and Irish fiddles, her music offered a novel conjugation of traditional and international musical forms to set beside experiments by bands like the Horslips or the Pogues.[8] Yet there is little sense of camaraderie or 'craic' about O'Connor's version of Irish rock. The layering of her voice produces an eerie polyphony; the echoes of Irish ballads and laments in many of the songs are spooky rather than sentimental. Other Irish elements, such as the quotations from W. B. Yeats or the recitation of a biblical verse in Irish by Enya Ní Bhraonáin, are defamiliarised by the slick, ultramodern production. This attitude of cool detachment seemed unlike anything in the folk tradition. But there is a dissonance in her early work between such confident self-assertion and an angry, tortured self-consciousness. An impression of incongruity is created by the modish, minimalist packaging of music that is engulfed in the anguished sense of personal loss, itself haunted by the ghostly echoes of a national, communal tradition from which it is nevertheless quite distinct.

This clash was perhaps duplicated in the most recognisable and 'iconic' feature of O'Connor's appearance – her baldness. In many photographs, the starkness of her naked skull only serves to emphasise her large, pale eyes and the classical, sculptural beauty of her face. Any woman who shaves her head seems to announce her indifference to the dictates of fashion and her contentment with her own unadorned looks. Yet baldness can also suggest self-mutilation, the effects of cancer treatment or helpless infancy. For example, the cover of *The lion and the cobra* features an image of O'Connor in which her mouth is open and her face screwed up in a snarl of rage; in a softer but more melancholy version of the image used for the US release of the album, her mouth is a perfect Cupid's bow but her expression, with eyes downcast, is one of complete dejection. In these head-and-shoulders shots, she is dressed in a blue undershirt, redolent of the garb of an inmate of a prison or a concentration camp. Her thin arms are crossed defensively across her chest and her head and face are a chalky, spectral white. The visual presentation of O'Connor (videos, album covers, publicity shots) was bleached of any stereotypical suggestion of Irishness; despite this, her fans – Irish and non-Irish, male and female – seem to have embraced her as a startling new icon of modern Irish femininity. But a woman's bald head also recalls the horrible spectacle of communal punishment meted out to someone who has been guilty of sexual contact with the enemy. Such images recall photographs of shaven women who had consorted with Nazis being paraded through the streets in post-Liberation France, or of Catholic women in Northern Ireland, accused of consorting with British soldiers, who were shaved, tarred and feathered and left bound to church railings. In such images, the woman's bald head is a mark of belonging that reflects the brutality of the oppressed community itself.

In the songs on *The lion and the cobra*, the experience of rejection and isolation is explored in the fairly conventional format of songs about unhappy love affairs. While there are some raunchy or upbeat dance tracks such as 'I want your hands (on me)' and the hit single 'Mandinka', several other songs point more clearly towards O'Connor's future development. 'Jackie', the first track on the album, is a lament for a lover lost at sea. It opens quietly enough in the style of a folk ballad, but reaches a climax in anguished, blood-curdling screaming. Here we first encounter O'Connor's characteristic blend of rage, sorrow and defiance. The song 'Troy' is six minutes long and full of daring vocal pauses and swoops. The title is borrowed from W. B. Yeats's sonnet 'No second Troy', and in quoting from the poem, the singer identifies herself with Yeats's beloved Maud Gonne, a republican and feminist revolutionary ('There was no other Troy for me to burn'). The song begins in a fairly muted nostalgic register – recalling 'Dublin in a rainstorm / sitting in the long grass in summer / keeping warm' – but culminates in protracted howls of pain and fury. From the outset, she continuously challenges her voice's innate musicality, achieving a particularly appealing chromatic effect only immediately to cancel or annul it. It is clear from such early tracks that O'Connor is exploring not just rage, but a range of angered feeling. Anger has the peculiar effect of opening up her voice, stimulating a new sonar space, in which different shades of emotion unfurl like bands of colour.

The cover of *I do not want what I haven't got* also features a close-up photograph of O'Connor's face. But here, the dark background softens the impact of the bald head; her large pale eyes are spot-lit as she gazes ardently into the distance. The album opens with a recitation of a prayer for serenity and is full of references to the artist's supposed new-found maturity. Although the sound of her voice is generally softer and more closely miked than on the first album, nonetheless any sense of contentment is to some degree undercut by many of the songs. The video for the best-selling 'Nothing compares 2 U' – one of the most popular of the 1990s – also explores anguish through elements of its striking imagery. It features O'Connor's face, starkly pale against a dark background, for most of the song. Her skin appears to blush and pulsate as the voice appropriates, or negotiates, Prince's short narrative of loss and desolation. Her mouth trembles; finally, her eyes swell and overflow. (O'Connor said she had cried when reminded of her mother by the lines: 'all the flowers, Mama, that you planted in the backyard / all died when you went away'). Witnessing her tears in these moments feels almost like an act of voyeurism. The startlingly intimacy of the extended close-up is juxtaposed with outdoor scenes that show O'Connor, her naked head bare and dressed in a long, dark soutane-like coat, walking through a classical French garden (the Parc de Saint-Cloud in Paris) in deepest winter. The white and grey tones of stone walls and long flights of steps dominate; the camera lingers on the sombre, weather-eroded faces of statues. The video then cuts in the final seconds to a blue-green image (the first rich colour in the clip) of a statue depicting a hooded, female form, with her eyes closed and her hand raised to her face. So this exhibition of a woman's self-exposure concludes with the far more conventional image of Madonna-like grief memorialised by the classically inspired sculptor. O'Connor has injected Prince's pop song about a romantic break-up with an extraordinary sense of devastation which seems to elevate emotion to austere grandeur; this is in turn framed by the scenes of the frozen garden and the calcified human forms. But such intimate exhibitions of pain or loneliness would not easily achieve such ultimately decorous expression or resolution again.

'I am stretched on your grave' is an experiment with Irish traditional singing and hip-hop rhythm; the track is based on a translation by Frank O'Connor of an Irish poem, 'Táim sínte ar do thuama', set to a melody by Philip King. This version has been recorded previously, including a fine version by Sonny Condell of Scullion, but O'Connor's treatment is even more shockingly elemental and shatters established folk conventions. 'Black boys on mopeds' offers a spare, autobiographical version of a traditional emigrant's lament. In retrospect we can see – or rather, hear – decisively emerge in such tracks a conflictual relationship between the collective sound of traditional music with its piercing, elongated lamentations and O'Connor's anguished subjectivity.

O'Connor lived in England during the Thatcher era. She had gone to London to pursue her musical career, sharing this journey with many thousands of young Irish people forced to leave Ireland by the severe recession of the 1980s, including many graduates or people from middle-class, urban backgrounds like her own. This was a generation that at home had enjoyed membership of a liberal and relatively privileged elite, but which found that abroad it had much in common with an earlier Irish diaspora. In England, the young Irish took menial jobs or signed on the dole; many had their first encounter with anti-Irish prejudice, which had been greatly inflamed in the wake of IRA bombing campaigns in Britain. Her song resonated with this new group of emigrants, which had little reason to be grateful to Ireland but was not ready unconditionally to celebrate its new home either.[9] The album also extends O'Connor's affective range to include what appear to be enigmatic and disturbing addresses to her late mother (who had died in a car crash when O'Connor was eighteen years old) and strikingly unconventional songs about maternal feeling as such. 'You cause as much sorrow' contains a refrain that might sound like an adolescent tantrum – 'You've done nothing so far / Except destroy my life / You cause as much sorrow dead / As you did when you were alive' – were it not for the soaring beauty of the vocal delivery. O'Connor here carries off one of her characteristic feats of managing to appear both bitter and indifferent at the same time: at such moments, she sings as if she is as snarlingly dismissive of her own lyrics and her own vocal effects as she is of the person who has betrayed her. The ferocity of O'Connor's attacks on her mother were taboo-breaking, but so too were aspects of her account of her own motherhood. 'Three babies', for instance, has been interpreted as an address to infants who had been aborted. It seemed odd that someone like O'Connor, who had always been a strong supporter of abortion rights, should express these sentiments about the 'cold bodies' of the babies who will be 'returned' to her. But in its attempt to portray a state of confused maternal distress (the singer refers to herself as 'this thing that I have chosen to be'), the song presents motherhood as a realm of ambiguity and conflict. This is not just because of the prevailing mores of a patriarchal society, but also because of the primal passions maternity in itself involves. In this regard, the song neither sanitises nor repudiates abortion. Against a backing track of acoustic guitar and lush strings, O'Connor begins in a soft and lyrical register. As the song progresses, the tone of tender devotion is interrupted by moments of sudden yearning hoarseness. These suggest a struggle with violent, self-abnegating desire. For example, on their second occurrence, the stark lines 'the face on you, the smell of you' are tackled in a powerful, emphatic and unnerving style which expresses as much despair as affection. Yet on this occasion the clamant note surrenders to the melodic line and the song ends quietly with a sense of resolve or perhaps merely of resignation. 'Three babies' is neither a Gothic lament (of which O'Connor had already produced some disturbing examples) nor a touching celebration of a fulfilled, loving relationship; rather, it oscillates between the two possibilities. O'Connor's confessional impulse is at its most powerful in such work. This kind of material aroused some distaste and even derision.[10] For this and other reasons, her fame began to mutate into notoriety in the early 1990s.[11] After the incident involving the Pope's photograph, she began to spend more of her time in Ireland and gradually shed most of the conventionally 'sexy' aspects of her image. But she continued to talk incessantly to journalists and interviewers, assuming not just the right to defend herself against attacks, but also always seeking to appropriate a kind of cultural or political authority to which, as a young, female pop performer, she had no obvious access or claim.

O'Connor's next two albums represent the culmination of that phase of her work that deals explicitly with her personal trauma. Despite its title, *Universal mother* is about the necessity of *separating* from the mother and also about the notion of sisterhood – not primarily in the sense of feminist solidarity, but of sibling relationships, including males as well as females. In this regard, the remark from an interview by Germaine Greer which opens the album, that 'the opposite of patriarchy is not matriarchy but fraternity', has tremendous significance; it seems that the configuration and shared ordeals of her family of origin have had a permanent effect on her sense of political and national community as well. The album opens with a fierce and nightmarish vision of her childhood home, 'Fire on Babylon'; this is followed by the tender 'John, I love you', which gives another account of the same disturbing story in a completely different register. Using fairy-tale imagery and a waltzing rhythm, the song encourages 'John' – apparently O'Connor's brother – to believe that 'there's life beyond your mother's garden'. *Universal mother* also includes several of her most exquisite love songs, including 'A perfect Indian' and 'Thank you for hearing me'. The former contains allusions to the legend of the Children of Lir, an Irish legend about four royal children who are placed under a spell and transformed into swans by their wicked stepmother. They are condemned to wander the lakes and seas of Ireland for nine hundred years until they hear the Mass bell, announcing the arrival of Christianity in Ireland. At that moment, they are changed back into their human forms, only to wither with age and die. O'Connor has spoken of the significance of the story to her; in the song, she declares: 'too long have I wandered / like Lir's children / there's only one way to be free'.[12] The central character in the legend is Fionnuala, the sister who sings to comfort her three younger brothers. In implicitly associating herself with this figure (although O'Connor was in fact the third child and second daughter of five children), she assumes not the role of powerful mother, but of a sympathetic yet relatively helpless sibling. The image of the wronged child as a kind of childish, surrogate mother (or friend) is in fact more central to O'Connor's music as it evolves than any mythical image of matriarchal power – or 'the goddess' – to which she also occasionally refers. But before any happy relationship is possible, it is first necessary to become 'free' by achieving solitude. ('And real love requires you, give up those loves / Whom you think you love best', as she puts it in 'What doesn't belong to me' from *Faith and courage* – one of her last and most poignant songs about her mother.) 'A perfect Indian' opens with tender words about a man but then drifts away from the scene of sexual love. The lyrics dwell instead on a 'beautiful daughter' whose identity appears to merge with that of the singer herself. In this song, O'Connor counterpoints a soothing, slow-paced lyric against momentary exposures of dramatic anguish. For example, in the line 'sailing on a terrible ocean', the voice swerves on the syllables '-ing' and 'terr-', as though losing control of the melody that seems for those seconds to be no more than a mask for hidden feelings. Although the song ends with the firmly emphasised word 'free' and a resounding piano chord, the final impression is not of reconciliation or resolution. The singer longs for release or emancipation, but this is still merely an aspiration. 'Thank you for hearing me', the final song on *Universal mother*, appears to be a gentle, prayer-like love song, but modulates in the final verses into a valediction: 'Thank you for breaking my heart / Thank you for tearing me apart / Now I've a strong, strong heart / Thank you for breaking my heart'. There are no verbal or musical clichés here about the power of love: such easy sentiments are undercut by O'Connor's fidelity to the scene of her own trauma. When all the drama of accusation and entreaty on *Universal mother* is exhausted, we are left with the lonely voice which, finally withdrawing all its treacherous consolations, dissolves into a soundtrack of waves breaking on the seashore.

There was a six-year interval between *Universal mother* and O'Connor's next full-length solo album, *Faith and courage*, in 2000. The latter marked several new developments in her music, including a more explicit emphasis on religion. Elizabeth Cullingford notes that O'Connor kept 'her intense and paradoxical involvement with Catholicism in full public view' during the late 1990s.[13] However, the earnest spiritual quest of O'Connor's music seems in many ways at odds with the attitude to religion reflected in some of her other artistic ventures around this time. In particular, her cameo role as the Virgin Mary in Neil Jordan's film *The butcher boy* (1997) seemed to be a playfully irreverent and provocative gesture. Her participation in the film has generated a good deal of debate. For instance, Colin MacCabe praises O'Connor's 'erotic' performance and suggests that she embodies attitudes towards sexuality and the body which spelt the end of the 'masculine theocracy' which held sway in Ireland between the middle of the nineteenth century and the final years of the twentieth.[14] In other words, this is a thoroughly subversive and anti-Catholic representation of the Virgin. However, it is hard to see how O'Connor's Virgin, played in a blonde wig and voluminous blue and white robes, is deliberately sexual at all; even her profanity ('For fuck's sake, Francie!') is no more than an echo of the language of the unhappy young boy to whom she appears. Even though the style of Jordan's film was upbeat and zany, for some, O'Connor – who also made a further brief appearance as a harp-playing Irish colleen – had nevertheless remained too close to damaging fantasies about idealised Irish or Catholic mothers. From this point of view, the Virgin and the colleen are far from being agents of sexual liberation and cannot represent true alternatives to the boy's brutal, alcoholic father or the priests who punish and abuse him. Because they are symbols of 'the utopian, *ergo* impossible, national vision', these phantasmal women merely create further pain and trauma for Francie.[15] Only Cullingford argues that Jordan and O'Connor are drawing on powerful qualities of the Virgin as a traditional religious image. As Cullingford describes the role, the Virgin is beautiful and consoling even as she proves to be a useless adviser to the child: 'O'Connor's gentle performance establishes that, while all mothers are fallible, even the Mother of God, they are vastly preferable to fathers, lay or clerical.'[16] However we interpret O'Connor's Virgin, it is noteworthy that her appearance in *The butcher boy* was more warmly received by Irish audiences than were either her media 'stunts' or her records: perhaps women performers are regarded more positively if they seem to be flirtatious or ironic, as they are still being 'womanly'.

In some respects, *Faith and courage* represented a return to O'Connor's spiky but debonair rock persona, with the buoyant, self-assertive 'No man's woman' or 'Daddy I'm fine' and possibly the happiest love song in her oeuvre, 'Dancing lessons'. But religious themes are certainly prominent. Curiously, given that she continued to identify herself as a Catholic, her songs in this period make virtually no reference to Mary, Jesus or the Church. Instead, she dwells mainly on a mixture of ancient Celtic spirituality and Rastafarianism on this album. The Celtic spirituality which O'Connor ascribes to the Irish is 'lost': it is not some immutable feature or easily available current resource.[17] When religion appears, it comes in a political mode, as a form of spirituality that has been repressed or marginalised. Celtic spirituality is itself such a construct, musically given to the effects of ethereality and the disembodied echo of the solo voice which indicates an unworldly or metaphysical space. Similarly, she has experimented with the 'celestial' effects of Christian plainchant, as in 'Kyrié eléison' on this album. But O'Connor is also drawn to forms of religion that are militant, apocalyptic and millenarian. Reggae or Rastafarian music is not just a vibrant strand in West Indian and Western popular culture, but an expression of political protest on behalf of wretched people looking forward to deliverance from 'Babylon'. It also offers the mournful solo voice a means of experimenting with a group or national style of singing. *Faith and courage* has a similar interest in relation to Irish traditional music. For example, on the track 'In this heart', O'Connor harmonises with a group of traditional singers, producing quite ravishing effects that are, nevertheless, familiar in that context. However, this is not an experiment in ensemble vocal performance that she repeats in her solo work. In the cover albums which follow *Faith and courage*, she essays group styles in more subtle and ultimately more compelling ways. The juxtaposition of the Celtic note with Rastafarianism is an instance of combining the lonely voice of the lost and dispossessed with the choric voice of popular protest. I will glance briefly at the reggae album *Throw down your arms* (2005), before considering the earlier *Sean-nós nua* in more detail: O'Connor's encounter with Rastafarian music raised issues about authority, appropriation and mimicry which are also relevant to the national and gender politics of her turn to traditional Irish material.

Why would a white Irish woman singer record an album of reggae songs associated with male Jamaican artists such as Bob Marley or Burning Spear (Winston Rodney)? The apparent incongruity of the project is emphasised by the cover art for the album, which features a photograph of O'Connor as a young girl wearing her Holy Communion dress, displayed inside a Celtic border decorated in the Rastafarian colours of red, green and gold. For anyone familiar with O'Connor's biography, this doe-eyed child looking shyly at the camera, her fingertips pressed together in a gauche attempt at a prayerful pose, represents a disturbing image of Irish Catholic identity. O'Connor had already associated child abuse with Black historical experience when she sang a version of Marley's 'War', substituting the words 'child abuse' for 'racism' in several of the lines. This was just before she ripped up the picture of the Pope. She reprises 'War' on the final track on *Throw down your arms*. Yet what relationship exists between O'Connor's unhappy story and these powerful performances of well-known songs from a completely different musical culture? (It is notable, though, that she avoids covering any of Marley's commercial hits.) On this album, O'Connor neither radically changes the arrangements of the songs nor tries to imitate reggae-style singing. Her singing is not an attempt to 'adapt' the songs to different conditions, but seems designed to display a respect or reverence through recreating them in a just slightly different style. However, few things generate more consternation among commentators hostile to the colonial interpretation of Irish history than the notion that the Irish believe themselves to be 'virtually black': the fear is that Irish nationalists may associate Irish historical experience with the history of slavery or racism in an opportunistic and self-indulgent fashion.[18] But Michael Malouf asserts that O'Connor does not attempt to merge these discrete histories. He suggests that, on such reggae-influenced tracks as 'The lamb's book of life' on *Faith and courage*, O'Connor restrains the 'ethereal and inspirational' sound of her voice: she enters into dialogue with the reggae sounds, rather than dominating or being subordinated to them. This is consistent with her general insistence on emphasising what the Irish have to learn from Rastafarianism and from African culture, as part of what Malouf describes as her attempt to situate Ireland as part of a 'radical cosmopolitanism from below'.[19] Certainly, there is a strong contrast between O'Connor's interest in reggae and the much greater influence of African American musical forms on most Irish popular musicians, including major figures like Van Morrison and Bono. O'Connor resists the gospel-influenced line of American evangelical spirituality to which Irish musicians have accommodated themselves so readily. This is of a piece with her rejection of the easy relationship between Irish popular music and American culture. In songs such as 'Marcus Garvey' from *Throw down your arms*, there is a gesture of modesty in not departing too dramatically from Burning Spear's original interpretation. The song laments a betrayed leader and predicts that he will return to bring vengeance. With a hypnotic, ecstatic saxophone and horns backing, the singer is by turns tender and admonishing. Although he has 'no food to eat' and 'no money to spend', he entreats: 'Come, little one and let me do what I can for you / And you and you alone'. Then he threatens that 'He who knows the right thing / And do it not / Shall be spanked with many stripes, / Weeping and wailing and moaning, / You've got yourself to blame, I tell you'; the song ends with the triumphant incantation 'Catch them Garvey, catch them ... Hold them Marcus, hold them'. But in some senses, in taking on the prophetic role originally performed by the male singer as spokesman for his people, O'Connor places herself in the position of the representative 'speaker'. She also evokes a strong millenarian strain in Irish culture that goes back to the Jacobite political ideology of the 'aisling' poems of the seventeenth and eighteenth centuries. Such songs were often about a dream or vision of a sorrowful woman who tells the male poet of how she has been wronged and abandoned. It could be argued that in her reggae persona, O'Connor combines versions of both roles in the aisling. She is a beautiful woman whose voice can dramatise loss and yearning, but she avoids the passivity associated with the traditional allegory by bringing a strong sense of her militant anger and her notorious 'outspokenness' to 'Marcus Garvey', 'War' or 'Downpressor man'. Liberated from the melancholy undertow of so much Irish traditional music, she explores a new kind of rebellious feeling. Throughout the album, the voice takes an obvious delight in its discovery of solidarity.

O'Connor's interest in covering other artists' songs and her embrace of an Irish traditional repertoire evidently did little to enhance the appreciation of her work either among Irish feminist critics or academic commentators on Irish popular music. Simone de Beauvoir draws a contrast between 'expressive' women artists such as singers or actresses and those who attempted to become truly 'creative' artists. Only the latter seemed to offer women the possibility of overcoming their entrapment in femininity – the latter being defined as 'other' to a normative masculine identity (although Beauvoir believed that very few women artists in patriarchal society had in fact achieved this freedom or transcendence through their art).[20] In that light, O'Connor's retreat from songwriting after *Faith and courage* could be interpreted as a loss of creative nerve. In addition, her adoption of the role of traditional Irish female singer may have seemed to confirm what some would have described as her predilection for presenting herself as an allegorical representation of the suffering nation. As we have seen, second-wave Irish feminism, for good historical reasons, has proven particularly hostile to the identification of femininity with Irishness in nationalist discourse.[21] O'Connor was far more sympathetic to republicanism (as well as to Catholicism) than most major cultural figures in late twentieth-century southern Ireland.[22] So, despite the misogynistic treatment that she has often received in the media and her consistent protests on behalf of the victims of abuse (including her participation in demonstrations concerning the 'X' case in 1992, when the High Court granted an injunction against a fourteen-year-old rape victim to prevent her travelling to the UK for a termination of pregnancy), feminists in Ireland have not to date paid extensive attention to her career.[23] It has fallen more to critics of popular music to consider O'Connor's relationship with feminism.

International rock is a heavily male-dominated and often misogynistic cultural form, its rebelliousness often bound up with an aggressive assertion of male sexual freedom. There have been few opportunities for female performers to 'infuse rock with "feminine" qualities'.[24] In Ireland, the counter-cultural appeal of rock's hedonistic energy was especially attractive to young people who felt stifled by social and religious orthodoxies, north and south of the border. In addition, the fusion of rock with Irish influences produced hybrid forms of popular music that were among modern Ireland's most important cultural achievements. Hence, there was an understandable tendency to assume that the rock element in Irish popular musical hybrids was unquestionably positive and 'modern' – significantly so in the realm of sexual politics. While the Irish element also had value as a mark of local or regional creativity and resistance to Anglo-American cultural homogeneity, it could also suggest a regressive attachment to romantic stereotypes of Irishness that most young people in particular were anxious to escape. So any evidence of 'individuality', aggression or sexual candour from Irish women performers was regarded as a welcome contrast to the asexual passivity of nationalist and Catholic stereotypes of femininity. Thus, the argument goes that O'Connor is most progressive when she is loud and irate but most regressive when she is too indulgent of her 'soft' side or of nationalism and religion. In such accounts, she may play with inherited images of Catholic or Irish womanhood, but only in order to 'subvert' them. According to some critics, her fans were always in danger of misrecognising this project, especially as so many of them outside Ireland might be indifferent to the pitfalls of Irish nationalism. As Noel McLaughlin and Martin McLoone argue: 'As a performer and a star [O'Connor] is best understood as caught in a dialectic between unsettling pre-existing national imaginings and then reworking them on the one hand, while on the other she is critically praised for the manner in which she is seen to consolidate just such traditional imaginings.'[25] Responding to O'Connor's later work, Gerry Smyth writes that over the course of her career 'the radical force of her original "bolshy" identity began to be lost as she was increasingly co-opted for a traditional narrative of Irish femininity'; in particular, *Sean-nós nua* 'represented a further (and perhaps final) stage in O'Connor's negotiation of an Irish female musical identity'.[26]

Such assessments as Smyth's assume that the only progressive attitude to 'traditional narratives' is opposition. But even in O'Connor's early work we get a subtler composite of repudiation and retrieval of a notion of Ireland than can be found in the cruder reflections of previous Irish rock émigrés, such as Geldof. O'Connor's attitudes reflect not so much an inherited traditionalism as a self-conscious and provocative departure from the pervasive 'revisionism' of Irish youth culture and of urban culture in the Republic at that time – hers, we might say, is a species of anti-anti-nationalism. In general, her response to Irishness and Catholicism involves uncompromising critique but not disaffiliation. This is epitomised in her decision not to repudiate the Church in pursuit of her anti-Vatican campaign. Rather, in a sensational appearance on an Irish chat show (the famous *Late late show*) in 1999, she declared herself to *be* a Catholic priest – complete with soutane, clerical collar and crucifix. Since the Church is 'universal', in being a priest she is claiming to inhabit the universal dimension which the Church itself provincialises into its male, celibate form. As a woman and feminist, singing such standard Irish schoolroom songs as 'Óró, sé do bheatha 'bhaile' – and performing them in a remarkable style which somehow manages both to reproduce and yet transcend the bawling, rather masculine enthusiasm of the conventional renditions – she emancipates and universalises this musical material. It is even arguable that a woman artist is best placed to achieve this, especially given O'Connor's reputation for speaking up for the suffering of Irish women and children. And while she had invited the singer Enya to contribute lines in Irish to *The lion and the cobra*, she now lays new claim to the language herself and sings several tracks in Irish.

Yet the charge might persist that for O'Connor to celebrate Irish nationalist heroes is to be 'male-identified'. Feminists have long debated the place of gender solidarity in relation to other bonds based on ethnic or class identities.[27] But we could perhaps further consider this issue with reference to Toril Moi's account of Beauvoir's theory of women's freedom. The latter sheds light on the question of what it means for a woman artist such as O'Connor to speak (or sing) 'as a woman'. In O'Connor's work up to the late 1990s, we hear the solo 'aria' voice of spectacular purity and her violations of this in sounds that seem to express primal emotions in an uncensored fashion: on the one hand, femininity as an idealisation; on the other, a highly charged representation of the experience of being a daughter, a lover, a sister or a mother. Her negotiation between these voices is both a private drama and a public achievement. However, to confine O'Connor to this is to risk reducing her artistic identity to sexual difference: indeed, Beauvoir suggests that every generalisation about 'femininity' will inevitably produce a reified and clichéd view of women. Expanding on Beauvoir's point, Toril Moi suggests that 'investigations of the meaning of femininity in specific historical and theoretical contexts are indispensable to the feminist project of understanding and transforming sexist cultural practices and traditions. Yet any given woman will transcend the category of femininity, however it is defined. A feminism that reduces women to their sexual difference can only ever be the negative mirror image of sexism.'[28] While Beauvoir was strongly critical of feminine 'mysticism' and would scarcely have been impressed by O'Connor's religious commitments, she might perhaps have been sympathetic to her resolute quest for independence: indeed, this was essential if the female artist was seriously to address the human situation.[29] In the world of pop, O'Connor was obviously a sexualised commodity, so she adopted loose shirts and robes, flinched away from the camera, sang with downcast eyes and at times subdued some of her voice's angelic effects in order to avoid being heard only 'as a woman'. Hence the perceived asexuality of religious women also becomes to some extent an attraction for her, rather than something she inevitably wishes to subvert. However, attention to *Sean-nós nua* will demonstrate that the turn to the communal is neither a defeat nor a surrender to 'tradition'.

The album presents some extremely accomplished versions of well-known songs from the repertoire of Irish traditional music. For example, O'Connor's version of 'The parting glass' is distinguished by the characteristic intensity and decisive clarity of her singing. The young female voice is at odds with the bibulous conviviality evoked by the lyrics, creating a striking dissonance between the vocal personality associated with 'Sinéad O'Connor' and the male persona of the song. In such recordings, the singer is an actor who respectfully follows a script familiar to the audience. To a degree, this is conventional – the audience can accommodate some distance between the singer and the story. In the case of O'Connor, the dissonant effect is enhanced by her celebrity status and serves to remind us that she is not a 'natural' in this musical milieu. But when she sings material more in keeping with the styles typical of women traditional singers (as for instance in 'Her mantle so green'), her vigour and the emphatic charge of the singing is in marked contrast to the gentler delivery of a folk-influenced singer such as Mary Black. (O'Connor's style is in fact far closer to, say, Luke Kelly's – although his working-class Dublin tones would have sounded more 'authentic' to most traditional-music audiences than her more middle-class, 'southside' accent.) Thus, in many ways, this album highlights the singularity of her voice and the uniqueness of her musical approach to the traditional repertoire. However, in some of the numbers, O'Connor achieves something remarkable. *Sean-nós nua* was anticipated by her collaboration with The Chieftains on their album *The long black veil* (1995). There, on the track 'The foggy dew', as later in 'Paddy's lament' from *Sean-nós nua*, she intensifies the desolation and rage of her voice so that everything at risk of becoming hackneyed in the songs is revived as pain. Thus, O'Connor shocks the expectation of ready-made feeling, precisely by reviving it within its traditional frame. In such instances, the solo voice is supported by the presence of the collective, choric voice – the voice of political protest in the songs – and for this reason, the effect is exhilarating rather than desolating, despite the generic weight of lamentation.

'Paddy's lament' tells of an Irish emigrant recruited by Lincoln's army to fight in the American Civil War. The refrain goes:

Here's you boys
Now take my advice
To America I'll have ye's not be going
There is nothing here but war
Where the murderin' cannons roar
And I wish I was at home in dear old Dublin.

The sentiments are conventional enough: many songs warn against emigration and the perils of becoming cannon fodder for foreign states. But in O'Connor's declamatory performance, the words carry the weight of a personal as well as of a national history – the disdainfully articulated enunciation of the four syllables of 'America'; the heavy stress on 'war'; the almost imperceptible hesitation before the voice softens into 'Dublin', itself pronounced neither in the mid-Atlantic accents of a Bono nor the folksy 'Dubb-e-llin' of a Ronnie Drew. The sound of helicopters in the background evokes Vietnam and reinforces the message that the United States is itself an imperial oppressor. A nineteenth-century traditional idiom accommodates a contemporary political agenda: we should not over-idealise the US, nor renounce allegiance to home in a 'globalised' age. 'The foggy dew' strikes a balance between guttural contempt (as in the final syllables of the lines 'Britannia's Huns / with their long-range guns') and clear-voiced reverence ('But the Angelus bells o'er the Liffey swell / Rang out in the foggy dew'). This is not a song of triumph, but an elegy for the dead of the Easter 1916 Rebellion. During the first three stanzas, the singer is carried along by the energy of the rebellion; in the fourth, she mourns its failure. On *The long black veil*, the transition is marked by the return of O'Connor's voice after an instrumental interlude with The Chieftains playing pipes, bodhrán and fiddles. The opening phrase of the last stanza is stretched across three wailing, ascending notes but punctuated by a deliberate exhalation before the last and highest of them – isolating it by this gesture of anguish. It is as if language is consumed in the energy of the voice and we apprehend the trauma that is masked, not enunciated, by the words. The sound O'Connor produces at this pivotal moment expresses the piercing pain of violation and the loss of the utopian possibility that had animated the previous verses and the joyous concert of the instrumental sequence. But then the lapse into the final lines is delicately cadenced so that the spear-sharp moment is not so much extinguished as escorted back into the choric dimension. The singer-witness has survived, rides 'back through the glen' and prays for the fallen; the recording ends with her voice, now unaccompanied, but not isolated in privacy. Protest and aspiration have also survived, although in a quieter register. The realm of shared memory and recognition to which the genre of the political ballad appeals is here enriched by the intensity of the subjective feeling of traumatic loss which O'Connor explores. The song now gleams again with the pain of loss and the thrill of the strength that flows from overcoming it.

In 2009, the publication of the Ryan and Murphy reports – into child abuse in Irish institutions for children and in the Catholic archdiocese of Dublin respectively – generated unprecedented public distress and anger. The reaction confirmed that contemporary Ireland is still contending with the legacies of disgraceful and horrifying national scandals that were ignored or covered up during most of the era of independence. But while 'traditional' Ireland had never looked worse, 'modern' Ireland had also apparently lost its way after the banking crisis in late 2008. The subsequent crash represented the discrediting of the project of economic liberalisation or globalisation that had inspired Irish modernisers since the 1960s.

O'Connor has made a number of statements about the issue of clerical sexual abuse since the recent renewal of widespread interest in the scandal.[30] In the changed conditions of today's Internet culture, this has been an opportunity for some familiar charges against O'Connor to be revived and for other commentators to insist that she is owed an apology for the treatment she received in 1992.[31] Certainly, the anti-Vatican protest now seems prescient. And while Irish artists generally believe themselves consistently to have stood up for sexual enlightenment and liberal values, none since the days of official censorship has suffered so intensely for their insistence on exposing Ireland's secrets as O'Connor. Her persecution came through the medium of television and tabloid newspapers rather than from the traditional authorities. Further difficulty has arisen from her embrace of social media that, in obscuring the distinction between private and public communication, has exposed her to the perils of ill-advised self-exposure at times of great vulnerability.

Her two albums since 2012, *How about I be me (and you be you)?* and *I'm not bossy, I'm the boss* were proclaimed by almost every reviewer to be the most accessible and affecting work that O'Connor had produced for years. In some of these songs, she returns to the question of the Church and child abuse, crying vengeance on behalf of victims while at the same time continuing her own long quest for security and comfort. She decries the intensifying cult of celebrity in the music industry. There is little direct allusion to the economic crisis. But local conditions, such as the recession and the return of mass emigration, along with personal factors such as the apparent break-up of O'Connor's once stable domestic settlement with her children, may have contributed to the renewed problematisation of 'home' explored on both albums. ('Home' was in fact the original title of *How about I be me* – although as one of the song titles has it, the singer seems more often to consider herself 'Very far from home'.)

The cover image on the album is a painting by Neil Condron, entitled *Upon small shoulders*, of a barefoot, cherub-faced little girl wearing a white smock and perched on a rusty scaffold in an apparently derelict or abandoned building. An Irish tricolour is draped above and beneath her. The painter has stated that the appearance of the scaffold in the picture is an allusion to the Irish property crash and that the title of the work refers to the burden of debt imposed on future citizens of Ireland by the government's decision to bail out the banks. The picture also reminds us of the revelations about child abuse that had emerged around this time. Yet the girl's upward gaze does not appear fearful and she makes some kind of urgent gesture to the viewer with her tiny outstretched hand. Condron describes her posture as 'confident and defiant'. [32] O'Connor herself had owned this painting although she later had it auctioned for the benefit of the Penny Dinners – a Dublin charity that supplies meals for homeless people. The large Irish flag and the green of the album cover represent a far more direct use of conventional signifiers of Irishness than ever before in O'Connor's career – and certainly not on *Sean-nós nua*. The painting points to national failure, but the tricolour itself is vivid and bright – an enveloping shelter for the child, rather than an emblem of shame. This image seems to anticipate aspects of the commemoration of the centenary of the Easter Rising in 2016, during which the issue of women's involvement in revolutionary nationalism became a key theme in public and scholarly debate. Condron's ambitious painting (the original canvas is seven foot high) foregrounds a victim of the state against a utopian presentation of the flag as republican symbol. But this optimistic message about the legacies of the past and hope for the future is not in fact directly reflected in the songs that O'Connor sings.

In quite a different way, the cover photograph for *I'm not bossy* is also startling – O'Connor in a long wig and short PVC dress, holding a gleaming electric guitar. She has usually avoided such rock chick images. Yet this self-presentation seems quite low key and causal – a kind of joke. It is hard to imagine that O'Connor actually felt any anxiety about trying to conform to prevailing ideas of femininity in the music industry. This is in keeping with the apparently relaxed accomplishment of these songs that encompass a broad range of pop and rock styles. Her voice, now operating in a lower register and darker tonalities, still has its characteristic fire. Yet the idea of being self-confident or 'mature' – perhaps a little bit like being an Irish heroine, along the lines of the little girl in the painting – seem perhaps a little staged or notional on these albums. These things are hard won and of real value, but they are eclipsed for her as an artist by the importance of denouncing those who have betrayed the innocent and by her old despair about relationships – and about relationship itself. As she puts it in one exhausted-sounding moment during a classically furious O'Connor break-up song from *How about I be me*, her cover version of John Grant's 'Queen of Denmark': 'Don't know what to want from this world / I really don't know what to want from this world'.

It may seem that the bouncier pop and rock rhythms on these records (by contrast with, for example, the brooding Old Testament-inspired *Theology*, from 2007) also inspire or correspond to a late turn on O'Connor's part to themes of romance, sex, getting married and conventional families (for example, 'Dense water deeper down', from *I'm not bossy*, or '4th and Vine' and 'The wolf is getting married' from *How about I be me*). Elsewhere, in the buoyant 'Take me to church', from *I'm not bossy*, 'church' (but 'not the ones that hurt') is a redemptive place in a different sense – not just a venue for weddings (in fact, the singer asks 'What've I been signing love songs for? / I don't want to sing them anymore'), but also a place in which to celebrate forgiveness and renewal ('So cut me down from this here tree ... I'm the only one I should adore'). But the resurgence of such passionate feelings seems to involve some incongruity. In 'Old lady', from the 2012 album, a mature person deals with the indignities of unrequited love, which can turn anyone into a needy child or adolescent again: 'When I'm an old lady / I'm gonna be his baby'. But the most stunning paean to sexual love here is the beautiful 'The Vishnu room' (also the original title of the 2014 album).

Against a lush Indian-style backing, the singer's voice is full of longing and appeal, yet she also seems to have achieved perfect clarity and self-possession and a mode of address that is almost hypnotically lulling and reassuring. But the promise of perfect bodily and emotional reciprocity is hard to achieve or sustain. The breakdown of romantic dreams awakens primal, infantile feelings of abandonment and dread. Although the two kinds of experience are kept distinct, this also connects with the broader political theme concerning the abuse of children – hence the continuing experiments on these albums with songs that rage at religious corruption alternating with wistful, ruminative and lonely ballads.

In the apparently confessional 'I had a baby', O'Connor expresses sorrow that her son does not have a relationship with his father, because the precious child was born after a brief fling when she was 'crazy'; more indirectly, in 'Back where you belong', caring for another seems to involve them going 'home' while she remains alone – filled with tender concern, but having to surrender a beloved presence. In a completely different register, 'Take off your shoes' from *How about I be me* angrily warns about the fate of clerical sinners:

If you believed at all in your breviary
If you believed even in just the ghost of me
You wouldn't be so surprised to see me.

The speaker decries the "vanity" of those who claim to honour God and threatens a vengeful return. But rather than regarding the priestly abusers and their protectors as representative of an outmoded religious consciousness, O'Connor condemns them in the name of God. Their disregard of the spirit is denounced even in the title of the song: 'Take off your shoes, you're on hallowed ground'. Those who have desecrated the sacred precincts of the Church will be punished and the victims avenged.

The last song on *I'm not bossy* is 'Streetcars'. This is a track on which O'Connor's intimate, ballad-style voice is fully audible against a muted piano accompaniment. Here she announces a farewell to passion from a position of becalmed solitude. In the final verse – 'And I will, I must and so I will / Dwell beneath the desert still / For there's no safety to be acquired / Riding streetcars named desire' – she emphasises particular words that convey disappointment but resolution (especially in the first line, where she draws out the word 'will' twice, while briefly but firmly stressing the word 'must'). The final word 'desire' is whispered – almost suppressed, as if forbidden. The track ends with a single note struck softly three times. It would be a melancholic conclusion to her recording career to date, if not balanced by other moments during which 'safer' or more promising modes of relationship are essayed. An unexpected example is provided by the track 'Reason with me' from *How about I be me*, sung in the voice of an addict. Sadness and failure are recounted in the lyrics, but this junkie has not given up: 'Don't want to waste the life God gave me / Don't think it's too late to save me'. The refrain 'Reason with me', repeated three times as the song concludes, takes a standard phrase used about a supposedly over-emotional person ('I tried to reason with her'), and makes it into a request for dialogue. And she adds a further plea: 'Let's reason together'. The repetition of these phrases allows O'Connor to play with the word 'reason'. It becomes a kind of multi-syllabic puzzle before rising to an urgent appeal. The song is a moving experiment in giving emotional colour to the idea of 'thinking things through' – not as a solo enterprise, but as an act of communication and a collective project.

There was a fair deal of attention paid to the significance of the arts in the context of Ireland's most recent economic bust of 2008. But, for example, initiatives such as the discussions of the culture industry at the Farmleigh Conference on Irish recovery in September 2009 were founded on the idea of a fairly comfortable relationship between Irish artists and a government-led drive for economic regeneration. In many ways, this appears to be a perpetuation of the notion of Irish culture that prevailed during the boom years: commercially successful Irish cinema, literature, music or theatre could be both expressive of an essentially Irish spirit or character, and capable of being exported and of selling well elsewhere – especially in America. O'Connor's name was not mentioned at that time on the roll call of distinguished Irish artists who could continue to help out 'brand Ireland'.[33] This is primarily because of the tension in her work between music and commerce, individuality and mere 'personality'. But in her memorable voice we can hear a subtly-rendered history; if we have the ears to hear, we can long listen to the modulations of both.

Notes

1. For an account of O'Connor's childhood, see Dermott Hayes, *Sinéad O'Connor: so different* (London: Omnibus, 1991), especially pp. 12–17.
2. Quoted by John Waters, 'Sinéad the keener', *Irish Times* (28 January 1995).
3. Roland Barthes, 'The grain of the voice', *Image – music – text*, trans. Stephen Heath (London: Flamingo, 1977), p. 181.
4. See Waters, 'Sinéad the keener'.
5. For instance, Stuart McLean takes the example of O'Connor's 1994 rap 'Famine' as illustrative of the pitfalls of the 'trauma and recovery' reading of the Great Famine that came to the fore with renewed popular attention to the cultural legacies of the Famine around the time of the commemoration of its one hundred and fiftieth anniversary; see Stuart McLean, *The event and its terrors: Ireland, famine, modernity* (Stanford: Stanford University Press, 2004), pp. 154–5. David Lloyd also criticises a 'redemptive' view of the retrieval of historical memory, as opposed to a 'melancholic' view of Irish modernity as characterised by a constitutive and unresolved loss; see 'The memory of hunger', in Tom Hayden (ed.), *The Irish hunger: personal reflections on the legacy of the Famine*, ed. Tom Hayden (Boulder, CO: Roberts Rinehart, 1997), pp. 32–47. However, Lloyd discusses the sound of the howling dog at the beginning of 'Famine' and mentions O'Connor's understanding of herself as a keener as 'entirely apposite', but perhaps because this track features O'Connor's speaking voice only and apparently endorses 'remembering' as 'healing', he does not address the phenomenon of her music more generally; see Lloyd, 'The memory of hunger', pp. 32–3. Joe Cleary alludes in a more overtly sympathetic way to O'Connor's attempts to 'work through' her personal version of collective cultural trauma; see *Outrageous fortune: capital and culture in modern Ireland* (Dublin: Field Day, 2007), p. 185.
6. Cathy Caruth, *Unclaimed experience: trauma, narrative, and history* (Baltimore, MD: Johns Hopkins University Press, 1996), p. 4.
7. Caruth, *Unclaimed experience*, pp. 5–6.
8. For an analysis of O'Connor's music in the context of the 'hybrid' forms of Irish popular music, see Noel McLaughlin and Martin McLoone, 'Hybridity and national musics: the case of Irish rock music', *Popular Music*, 19:2 (2000), pp. 195–6.

9 The music of Dolores O'Riordan and the Cranberries in the 1990s may have had a comparable significance for slightly later Irish emigrants in London. In a tribute to O'Riordan, Helen O'Rahilly states that the Cranberries' hit song 'Linger' seemed to reflect Irish women's emotional experience of exile; see O'Rahilly, 'As an emigrant, "Linger" wasn't about love, it was about Ireland', *Irish Times* (19 January 2018).

10 For a mild version of this negative response to O'Connor, see the contrast drawn by some young Irish women emigrants between President Mary Robinson and O'Connor. It is arguable that Robinson was the only Irish woman with a higher international profile than O'Connor's in the early 1990s. But Breda Gray reports that for several women she interviewed, 'unlike Mary Robinson, who becomes a redemptive national figure in the women's accounts, Sinéad O'Connor is represented as a figure of pathological Irish femininity'; while Robinson is a stoical figure who 'kept up appearances' in presenting Irish modernity on a global stage, O'Connor unpatriotically exposed her hurt and vulnerability, thus letting the country down. See Breda Gray, *Women and the Irish diaspora* (London: Psychology Press, 2004), pp. 56–8.

11 Elizabeth Cullingford details the furore that followed the *Saturday night live* appearance in a pioneering essay devoted in large part to O'Connor. The network, NBC, received a torrent of protest calls and O'Connor was booed at a Bob Dylan tribute concert in Madison Square Garden a few weeks later; even the notably irreverent singer Madonna joined in the chorus of criticism. Cullingford goes on to suggest that 'the hysterical derision that regularly greets O'Connor's actions, especially from Irish journalists (one of whom describes her as 'a few wafers short of a mass'), seems out of proportion to her offences and suggests that she unfailingly hits a raw nerve'. See 'Seamus and Sinéad: From "Limbo" to *Saturday night live* by way of *Hush-a-bye baby*', in Cullingford, *Ireland's others: gender and ethnicity in Irish literature and popular culture* (Cork: Cork University Press, 2001), pp. 248–50, 256.

12 O'Connor also refers to the significance of the story as national allegory when she states: 'I have a friend who I argue with about this. And I say to him, "I am Ireland". I was born and live here. I've seeped in all these feelings that come from generations and generations. I watch what's going on and I see how it mirrors what's going on in my own life. I grew up in that house, which was Ireland. There were four children there. I feel a connection with the story of the Children of Lir, which also represents the four provinces of Ireland.' See Waters, 'Sinéad the keener'.

13 See Cullingford, 'Seamus and Sinéad', p. 251. In this essay, Cullingford defends O'Connor's 'critical Catholicism', comparing her stance on religion to that of other cultural figures such as Seamus Heaney and Neil Jordan, for whom Catholicism was a formative influence: despite their criticism of the Church they cannot simply ignore or repudiate Catholic or religious images.
14 Colin MacCabe, *The butcher boy* (Cork: Cork University Press, 2007), pp. 68–9.
15 Emer Rockett and Kevin Rockett, *Neil Jordan: exploring boundaries* (Dublin: Liffey Press, 2003), p. 184.
16 Cullingford, 'Seamus and Sinéad', p. 256.
17 See Waters, 'Sinéad the keener', for O'Connor's view that the Irish have experienced a 'massive loss of contact with any spirituality'. In an open letter written shortly after the notorious *Saturday night live* appearance, O'Connor blamed the suffering of the Irish and her own abuse on British colonisation, which occurred with the collusion of the papacy: 'The cause of my abuse is the history of my people, whose identity and culture were taken away from them by the British with full permission from the "Holy" Roman Empire.' See William Leith, 'The life of Saint Sinéad', *Independent* (29 November 1992).
18 R. F. Foster deplores this tendency in *Luck and the Irish: a brief history of change, 1970–2000* (London: Allen Lane, 2007), p. 149.
19 See Michael Malouf, 'Feeling Éire(y): on Irish-Caribbean popular culture', in Diane Negra (ed.), *The Irish in us: Irishness, performativity, and popular culture* (Durham, NC: Duke University Press, 2006), pp. 344–46; Malouf also quotes O'Connor's denunciation of prejudice against recent immigrants in Ireland, p. 353.
20 See Beauvoir, *The second sex*, pp. 711–24.
21 For example, see Gerardine Meaney, *Gender, Ireland and cultural change* (London: Routledge, 2010); for an analysis of the disputes about nationalism in Irish feminist theory, see Emer Nolan, 'Postcolonial literary studies, nationalism, and feminist critique in contemporary Ireland', *Éire-Ireland*, 42:1 and 2 (Spring/Summer 2007), pp. 336–61.
22 During the early years of her career, O'Connor made statements expressing sympathy with the aims of the Provisional IRA; in 1989, she sang the nationalist ballad, 'Irish ways and Irish laws', with the folk singer Christy Moore at a 'Troops Out' rally in Dublin. See Hayes, *Sinéad O'Connor*, p. 94.
23 Cullingford's essay 'Seamus and Sinéad' is the exception here, although it concentrates on O'Connor's TV and film appearances rather than her music.

24 Simon Reynolds and Joy Press, *The sex revolts: gender, rebellion and rock 'n' roll* (London: Serpent's Tail, 1995), p. 233.
25 McLaughlin and McLoone, 'Hybridity and national musics', p. 196.
26 Gerry Smyth, *Noisy island: a short history of Irish popular music* (Cork: Cork University Press, 2005), p. 109.
27 See, for example, Elleke Boehmer, *Stories of women: gender and narrative in the postcolonial nation* (Manchester: Manchester University Press, 2005).
28 Moi, *What is a woman?*, p. 8.
29 Beauvoir, *The second sex*, p. 721.
30 For example, see Sinéad O'Connor, 'To Sinéad O'Connor, the Pope's apology for sex abuse in Ireland seems hollow', *The Washington Post* (28 March 2010).
31 For example, see Eoin Butler's blogpost, 'Isn't Sinéad O'Connor overdue a massive grovelling apology from absolutely everybody?', www.eoinbutler.com/home/isnt-sinead-oconnor-overdue-a-massive-grovelling-apology-from-absolutely-everybody (accessed 29 June 2018).
32 See Neil Condron, 'Upon small shoulders', https://condron.ie/upon-small-shoulders (accessed 29 June 2018).
33 Joe Cleary notes the widespread failure of Irish artists after the economic crash to protest against the harsh regime of neoliberal austerity that followed or to seriously interrogate what economic 'recovery' – supported by the 'creative sector' – might actually mean for the society as a whole. See Cleary, '"Horseman pass by!": the neoliberal world system and the crisis in Irish literature', *Boundary 2*, 45:1 (February 2018), pp. 42–3.

3
Bernadette McAliskey: speechifying

At a few key points in modern Irish history, women have won particularly memorable electoral victories. In 1918, Constance Markievicz became the first woman elected to the House of Commons; in an especially famous victory, Mary Robinson was elected President of the Republic of Ireland in 1990. Another significant moment was the arrival at Westminster in April 1969 of a twenty-one-year-old student, Bernadette Devlin, to take up her seat as the new MP for Mid Ulster. Devlin was mobbed by journalists and photographers: one commentator mused that this long-haired, fashionably short-skirted young woman looked like an Alice in Wonderland ('a tiny little figure, demure, perhaps a little frightened').[1] Her furious and eloquent maiden speech, on conditions in Northern Ireland and on the emerging campaign for civil rights, was delivered just hours later.

In each of these cases, women, often figured in Ireland as timeless symbols of the nation, took up very different roles as representatives of particular political constituencies. They had varying views of nationalism. Markievicz and Devlin (later McAliskey) regarded themselves as republicans. Assuming office some seventy years after the Anglo-Irish Treaty of 1921 had instituted partition (a measure which Markievicz had resolutely opposed), Robinson sought to represent an Irish state that would not insist on its sovereignty over the six counties of the North: five years earlier, she had strongly criticised the Anglo-Irish Agreement, which granted the Republic a consultative role in the government of Northern Ireland. They each had affiliations with feminism – in Markievicz's case, this was the first-wave women's movement, focused mainly on the campaign for female suffrage. They were also all associated with socialism – or at least with left-wing politics (Robinson was a member of the Irish Labour Party). But in the cases of Markievicz and Robinson, their successes were thought of primarily as advances for separatist republicanism and feminist liberalism respectively. The popularity of Sinn Féin candidates in the aftermath of the 1916 Rising conferred legitimacy on the rebels' declaration of the Irish Republic, in contrast to the Irish Parliamentary Party's support for the violence of the British Empire and its Great War. Robinson's involvement in campaigns such as those for legal access to contraception and for the decriminalisation of homosexuality helped in presenting her election, against an establishment candidate mired in charges of corruption, as a major step forward for liberal opinion in Ireland. It is unlikely that either woman would have objected to such characterisations of their electoral success. But the politics of Devlin's victory are perhaps more ambiguous.

Devlin was no doubt seen by some, inside and outside the North, as an exceptionally idealistic young woman defending her people – the latter understood to be the beleaguered Catholics of Northern Ireland, who had been in effect abandoned by the independent Irish state. This was an image that resonated in religious tradition: named after a Catholic saint, Devlin was later dubbed 'St Bernadette of the Barricades' for her role in organising the defence of Catholic areas in Derry/Londonderry in August 1969. Some likened her to Joan of Arc.[2] But none of this was welcome to Devlin. As a socialist, she wanted to stand for the poor of Northern Ireland – the 'peasants' and the 'have-nots', as she put it in her maiden speech – and not for a group defined mainly by its sectarian identity. On the same occasion, she denied that the disturbances were just 'a Catholic uprising'.[3] Moreover, Devlin did not want to claim any special importance for herself – she was merely a spokesperson for ordinary people. However, it was undeniable that Devlin and the other leaders of the new People's Democracy movement at Queen's University Belfast had dramatically transformed the face of Catholic protest in the North. Their language (as in their statement of their key objectives, which was later adopted by the broader campaign for civil rights) was bracingly clear.[4] They displayed no timorousness in facing up to the unionist establishment or to moderates in the Catholic community. They drew on the rhetoric, tactics and imagery of the African American civil rights campaign, the US anti-war movement and student protest in Europe. Devlin and her colleague Eamonn McCann, in particular, looked as if they had wandered off the set of a French movie on to the streets of Derry: the break with the old style of nationalist politics in the North could hardly have been starker. Devlin certainly had an air of incorruptible innocence and was to some degree motivated by what some would describe as 'tribal' loyalties. But these traditional 'feminine' qualities were in tension with the obvious modernity of her attitudes and self-presentation. From the outset, more conservatively minded supporters advised her on how to behave properly in public and ordered that she should not be seen smoking, drinking or keeping company with boyfriends.[5] Devlin was famously described by one unionist politician as 'Fidel Castro in a mini-skirt'.[6] By contrast, Robinson projected an air of sobriety and gravitas. Somatically, she did not embody any threatening stereotype of sexual or of women's liberation. This was possibly an advantage in her battles against sexual hypocrisy and repression which were based on principle rather than on appearing to be particularly interested in claiming such liberties for herself.

Devlin made an extraordinary impact in Ireland and internationally, especially in the United States. She was the outstanding speech maker of the civil rights movement and indeed of late twentieth-century Irish republicanism. She is by far the most notable female contributor to the tradition of Irish political oratory. (In her memoir, *The price of my soul* (1969), she describes learning off by heart patriot speeches by Robert Emmet and Patrick Pearse from a recording by Michael Mac Liammóir; at the age of twelve, she won a talent competition in her home town of Cookstown for her recitations of these speeches.[7]) In Derry at the end of the 1960s and in the early 1970s, she was a folk hero. As McCann notes, the people of the Bogside or Creggan may not always have been in tune with her rhetoric, but supporting Devlin – as when she was imprisoned in June 1970 for supposedly inciting riots the previous August – was a way of standing by their own estimation of the action they had undertaken, in asserting themselves politically after decades of second-class citizenship.[8] However, despite all this, Devlin is not regularly recalled as a major figure in the history of Irish feminism.

The movement for women's liberation and the civil rights campaign in Northern Ireland emerged around the same time; both were newly visible groups that were achieving political articulacy in imitation of similar groups in the United States, France or Eastern Europe. However, in Ireland particularly the two movements had markedly different priorities. As the slogan went: for feminists, the personal was the political. Consequently, the key point of departure for the movement was women's private experiences of violence and misogyny; feminism then went on to protest against the confinement of women to the domestic realm and to make demands for economic equality and reproductive rights. Northern Catholics too complained of unequal and unfair treatment. But in their case, discrimination was a problem of the public rather than the private sphere. And while some – for example – criticised the Catholic Church for its cooperation with the unionist state as the price of maintaining its control of Catholic education in the North, Catholicism remained important to many as a key dimension of their identity. Opposition to the state in Northern Ireland could not but be, collectively speaking, Catholic, since anti-Catholicism was the principle and spirit of the state. By contrast, southern feminists were generally bitterly hostile to the Church because of what they regarded as its baleful influence on law, education and cultural attitudes in the Republic.

It is particularly interesting to compare McAliskey to mainstream Irish feminism in the Republic. McAliskey is a strong secularist who has always supported sexual freedom and reproductive rights. Of course, she is a political activist rather than a writer or a creative artist, so one might not expect her to have dwelt on her own formation in the style of Edna O'Brien or Nuala O'Faolain. But she did write a memoir early in her career and has been invited in numerous interviews over the years to discuss her childhood, her political awakening, her view of contemporary developments, or the interlacing of all of these. It is clear that McAliskey conceptualises family, community and nation in radically different ways to those of some of the other women considered in this book. Her worldview is that of an egalitarian socialist. Thus, she belongs to a strand of feminism far less focused on individual liberation, self-expression and social advancement than most of the versions of feminism that have been more prominent in Ireland and in Western feminism generally. This is not to say that the other women discussed here are not also highly aware of social injustice or critical of capitalism. But the varieties of feminism they represent are more vulnerable to being co-opted by the marketplace – freeing women to be autonomous workers and consumers, but little else.[9]

In addition, Devlin's heroic moment in Westminster in 1969 would eventually be seen by many to be overshadowed by the later history of violent conflict in Northern Ireland. Were the radical young protesters to be blamed for provoking the unionist state and the British government into the coercive measures that in turn led to the revitalisation of the Irish Republican Army (IRA)? This was the view of the highly influential politician and historian Conor Cruise O'Brien. In his book *States of Ireland*, O'Brien in effect cast Devlin in particular, 'the most conspicuous figure on the barricades', as an irresponsible female idealist – or, like other young protesters of the time in other countries, an 'Antigone' – who was indifferent to the suffering and chaos that might result from her own non-violent resistance to the law.[10] On Bloody Sunday, 30 January 1972, thirteen unarmed protesters were shot dead by British paratroopers in Derry and many others were wounded. When Devlin, who had witnessed the events, was denied the customary speaking rights in the House of Commons the following day, she crossed the floor and struck the Home Secretary, Reginald Maudling, across the face. At this point, the affection in which the British press held Devlin evaporated. According to the *Daily Mirror*, she was 'a girl whose only vision is calamity ... who unleashes but does not understand the destructive nature of violence'; the 'song of Bernadette' had become a 'dirge'.[11] (And these were not the least polite things said about Devlin: unionist leader Ian Paisley remarked that 'the murder in this young woman's heart boils to the surface and spills from her mouth as she screams ... [her] veins are polluted with the venom of Popish tuition'.[12])

For many feminists, too, in the Republic of Ireland during the Troubles, women identified with republicanism such as McAliskey – even though the latter has distanced herself from republican militarism, declaring that she is 'not a soldier in this war and never [has] been'[13] – seemed to be wedded to outmoded nationalist principles that promoted rather than combated male violence. For example, Nuala O'Faolain recalls speaking at a conference on nationalism and feminism at the Guildhall in Derry in the early 1990s: 'I said the armed struggle was one of the reasons there was no all-Ireland sisterhood – that Southern women, in my opinion, had little or no sympathy with Northern nationalist women. That the men of Sinn Féin were just another layer of patriarchs among the many in Northern Ireland that oppressed women.'[14] O'Faolain states that she was excoriated by McAliskey and spat at by other women as she left the conference. Of course, this anecdote does not adequately reflect the full range of the political views of either woman. McAliskey has never been reluctant to criticise Sinn Féin or the IRA, including their patriarchal attitudes, during her decades of political activism; O'Faolain spoke and wrote compellingly about Northern Ireland during her career in television and journalism. Indeed, O'Faolain lamented the censorship enforced under Section 31 of the Broadcasting Act that banned all representatives of Sinn Féin from the airwaves, as a result of an order issued by Conor Cruise O'Brien as Minister for Posts and Telegraphs in 1976. She has described what she considered to be the viciously paranoid and bigoted culture that prevailed in RTÉ during her time there, dominated by O'Brien's ally Eoghan Harris, ostensibly in order to protect the state from Northern republicanism.[15] (It is interesting that both Harris and O'Brien later became unionists.) But this account of the bitter stand-off between the two women reminds us of the intensity with which such issues were debated.

The centenary of the Easter Rebellion in 2016 was marked by a widespread interest in recovering the history of women of the revolutionary period, including combatants such as Markievicz.[16] However, the example of Markievicz highlights the fact that politically radical or 'extremist' women upset conventional ideas about women as essentially passive, caring beings. For example, it is difficult to read W. B. Yeats's poem 'On a political prisoner' – which depicts Markievicz in prison in the wake of the Rebellion – without feeling that the poet considers her incarceration in some ways to be a positive thing for her: at least when forcibly subdued, she might rediscover her lost femininity. In the first two stanzas, Yeats describes how the rebel is now so becalmed that a wild bird can feed from her hand:

> She that but little patience knew,
> From childhood on, had now so much
> A grey gull lost its fear and flew
> Down to her cell and there alit,
> And there endured her fingers' touch
> And from her fingers ate its bit.
>
> Did she in touching that lone wing
> Recall the years before her mind
> Became a bitter, an abstract thing,

Her thought some popular enmity:
Blind and leader of the blind.
Drinking the foul ditch where they lie?[17]

The woman (and especially the upper-class woman) is denatured by her contact with the 'foulness' of popular politics – a realm in which she also exercises a dangerous influence on the passions of men. However, it is important to ask whether feminists are interested in returning to 1916 in order merely finally to include female participants, witnesses or victims in a historiography previously dominated by masculinist bias. Does such a project of recovery remain disinterested or neutral when it comes to assessing the political choices of these women? Or would they wish to suggest that women had a stake in the Rebellion – or in republicanism more generally – *as* feminists? Such questions are also relevant to any consideration of McAliskey's life-long, self-reflective commitment to socialist republicanism and feminism in Ireland.

Few people can have survived with such apparent equanimity the degree of media stereotyping and caricature that McAliskey endured over the period of the civil rights campaign through the Troubles and up to the present, all across the spectrum from 1960s playgirl to bloodthirsty harridan: she has been 'a doll ... breathing fire and brimstone'[18]; a fallen woman (when she gave birth to her first child outside marriage in 1971); and – in the words of one supposedly sympathetic American writer – a 'minor, even quaint, figure ... a loser more than ever', entirely out of step with and isolated in the contemporary scene.[19] In 1981, she survived an assassination attempt by loyalist paramilitaries, probably acting in collusion with British soldiers, when she and her husband Michael were shot several times in their home in front of their three young children. The botched killing was one in a series carried out by the Ulster Defence Association (UDA) with the aim of exterminating the socialist leadership of the republican movement. An earlier victim, in June 1980, had been the university lecturer and socialist Miriam Daly, murdered in her home in Belfast. As McAliskey puts it, 'I wasn't missed, but I didn't die.'[20] That is also, perhaps, a fitting epigraph to her whole extraordinary story.

Devlin was born in 1947 in Cookstown, Co. Tyrone. She states in the first line of her memoir that 'socially my father was the bottom Cookstown could produce': John Devlin was of Traveller background and the son of a roadsweeper.[21] Bernadette's mother, Lizzie, came from a family that was highly conscious of their social respectability as they owned a small amount of land and a pub. Lizzie's parents were appalled by the prospect of John Devlin as a husband for their daughter. The rejection of Bernadette's father by her grandparents, who as people of influence persuaded many neighbours to ostracise the couple also, had enduring material and psychological ramifications. Her family would have been poor anyway but now they were also cut off from family and community support. Devlin was the third of six children, five of them girls. She was clearly deeply marked by her family's pariah status but she was also especially impressed by her parents' devotion to each other and their defiant pride in the face of such snobbery. There is certainly no romanticisation in her memoir of communal solidarities based on religion or class. Recalling how her parents were evicted from their lodgings in the middle of winter after their first child was born, she compares them to the Holy Family on its way into Egypt – 'one father; one mother; one child a couple of weeks old' – except that her family was living among people who called themselves Christians.[22] Her parents eventually rented two damp rooms in a rat-infested building, where Bernadette was born. She is concerned to point out that some of the only real help offered to the family came from across the sectarian divide: for instance, two Protestant councillors were the only people willing to sign the reference that finally enabled them to move to a Housing Trust estate.[23]

Here was a loving, self-reliant family unit pitched against the world. Her father was a skilled carpenter and a committed republican and socialist. He was blacklisted among employers in Northern Ireland as a 'Political Suspect' – the term was stamped on his insurance card – and he was forced to find work in England, travelling home to see the family at intervals. He was also a storyteller, who entertained the children with the legends and history of Ireland. Devlin says that she was surprised at school 'that you had to learn about Vinegar Hill or the decline of the Irish linen industry in formal history lessons. I hadn't realized this was history: it was something I had always known, from hearing it over and over again as a bedtime story.'[24] Her father shared willingly in all the domestic work. Her parents' marriage was a model of mutually respectful cooperation and the entire family 'a very democratic assembly'.[25] In the documentary film *Bernadette: notes on a political journey*, she recalls her of her childhood: 'Lies were not appreciated. Whingeing wasn't appreciated.' Her parents wanted the children to think for themselves and 'great store' was put on learning and education. Their basic principles were summed up by her mother: 'you were brought up to believe there was nobody better [than you] and you were also brought up to believe that there was nobody worse'. That is to say, self-assertion and equality were both stressed. When Bernadette was just nine, her father had a heart attack during one of his journeys back to England and died. He was forty-six years old. In the wake of this calamity, Devlin states that he became an idealised figure and his values, mediated through her mother, were simply 'part of your life'.[26]

This is an account of childhood and of Irish family life strikingly different from those of other prominent Irish women. In this case, deprivation and discrimination cause real damage but strengthen solidarity and resilience. This particular traditional family is based on emotional empathy and support. The daughter does not conceive of an individualistic escape from the suffering evident in the house or even from the damaged, prejudiced community. Irish history and mythology are associated with the loving and revered paternal figure but are archaic and at a remove. Any notion of a 'homeland' is hopelessly distant. In the meantime, this is a female-dominated family in which it is assumed that girls can manage everything that needs to be done.

Devlin joined another community of women and girls when she was admitted to grammar school, St Patrick's Academy in Dungannon. She was among the beneficiaries of the British Labour government's Education Act of 1947 which, despite unionist resistance that delayed it for a year, instituted free secondary education in Northern Ireland. This in turn helped many Catholic children to aspire to university. One of the consequences was the emergence of a newly assertive generation of Catholic students and graduates, including Devlin herself, in the late 1960s. But while the convent school relied on state support, in line with the Church–state educational arrangement, it was also a strongly republican enclave at odds with the unionist establishment. Devlin did well there, eventually becoming a prize-winning student of the Irish language and Head Girl of the school. In her memoir, she presents herself as neither uncritically absorbing the ideology of the convent school nor as rejecting it outright. Clearly, she personally did not find the school oppressive and nor does she seem to believe that it inculcated a particularly damaging view of women. She liked and respected the presiding nun, Mother Benignus, even though Devlin regularly challenged her on her 'fanatical hatred' for England and the English.[27] Just as at home, Devlin assumed unusual responsibility within the school. She considered that the management of the place was chaotic, so, together with some of her friends, she devoted herself to instilling more discipline in the younger girls. She reports that these senior girls discussed Northern Irish politics together in the breaks, while the nuns fretted about trivialities such as uniform inspections and whether the students' gym tunics were too short.[28] In all this, Devlin seems almost extravagantly attentive to the lessons of home and school: she was even more principled and more energetic than her elders. She just took the messages about standing up for yourself and for your community a little further than might have been intended. As she puts it: 'you missed the bit that said you were actually not supposed to be speechifying'.[29]

Devlin went on to Queen's University in 1965. To begin with, she was a committed and diligent student. After her mother's early death from cancer, the pressures on the family were even greater and she spent a period commuting to Belfast, in order to look after her younger brother at home. She began as a student of Celtic languages but switched to Psychology. She enjoyed learning Irish, but she was frustrated by the narrow, purist attitudes of the Irish-speaking students and the Gaelic Society. So, as at school, cultural identity was subordinated to practical considerations, and Psychology seemed to be a good option for someone who wished to 'improve some aspect of life in Northern Ireland' in education (she thought about becoming a teacher of Travellers) or in social work.[30] (As it turned out, she was eventually disciplined by the Vice Chancellor for 'bringing the university into disrepute' and never sat her final examinations.) But in the initial absence of what she considered to be meaningful organised politics at university, culture filled the gap. In Queen's, she was not impressed by any of the student political parties – they were endlessly fascinated by their own debates, 'but they weren't *real*'.[31] Devlin states that there was more 'real politics' in the Folk Music Society than in any of the parties: they sang American civil rights songs before anyone else in the university was interested in the cause, and songs about unemployment in Belfast before the emergence of a strong civil rights movement in Northern Ireland. Because of the interest in American music, there was a balance of influences – 'so you had the best of both American protest song and traditional Irish folk music'.[32] Devlin sometimes refers to her unreflective, instinctive political consciousness as 'republicanism' but for her it was ultimately 'socialism' that expounded the crucial political values of equality, fairness and solidarity across national boundaries. For example, she describes how she first turned against traditional republicanism at university in favour of working for social justice within the partitioned state. The real task was not to free the six counties, but to start the national revolution all over again: 'there were *no* free counties, anywhere in Ireland'.[33] But she ultimately concluded that while it was crucial to try to unite the people through socialism, this could only be realised on all-island basis. The still colonial dimension of Northern Irish politics was, for example, illustrated by the fact that no meaningful economic or political advances were made under a nominally socialist government in Westminster in the late 1960s.[34]

During summer 1968, Devlin joined some of the first marches of the campaign for civil rights; however, she was always uneasy with the idea of a movement for equality for 'Catholics'. This was especially the case as 'Mother Church' was, in her opinion, one of the 'greatest traitors' Ireland ever had, concerned above all else with preserving her own security and influence.[35] However, the protest marches had the almost immediate effect of underlining the sectarian nature of the Northern Irish state, as police and large numbers of Protestant civilians forcibly prevented the marchers from entering Protestant areas. In the view of Devlin and the other student leaders, the moderate leadership of the civil rights movement had little idea of how to proceed as these dramatic confrontations unfolded. In its place, the People's Democracy leaders strategised about how to respond to the banning, blockading and police charging of marches. Devlin witnessed police violence at a march in Derry on 5 October 1968 – but on this occasion, the scenes in the city were for the first time described in every newspaper in Ireland and Britain and seen on television screens all over the world.[36] This was a turning point for the movement. Derry was a frontier city, positioned on the mouth of the Foyle just a few miles from the border with Co. Donegal and the Irish Republic. The historic walled city had been defended from the forces of Catholic King James in 1688 and had been a symbol of Protestant resistance and supremacy ever since. The walls now overlooked the ghettoes of the Bogside, the Creggan and other overcrowded Catholic slum areas. Derry had an exceptionally high rate of unemployment and one of the worst records of police brutality, discrimination in the allocation of housing and of the gerrymandering of elections of any place in the North. As one writer put it in the early 1970s: 'more than anywhere else in Northern Ireland, Derry was the stage of the people's war'.[37] In January 1969, Devlin witnessed the Battle of Burntollet Bridge, a few miles from the city, when protesters on a 'Long March' from Belfast to Derry were attacked by hundreds of loyalist protesters with stones, bottles and cudgels, facilitated by police who stood by during the assault. She was among the small group of marchers that eventually arrived uninjured in the city, received by cheering crowds and a rally in Guildhall Square. The scene was set for her own remarkable career in the place she memorably referred to on that occasion as the 'capital city of injustice'.[38]

When Devlin describes the appalling conditions in the house where she was born, she nevertheless notes that her parents preferred to live there than as unwelcome lodgers in her mother's family home. And her father spent his free time trying to fix the place up and provide better conditions for the family. She comments: 'Rats or no rats, both my parents preferred living in independence and privacy to the comfort and servitude of my grandmother's house. At least the Molesworth Street rooms belonged to them. They paid the rent. My mother's favourite expression in life was: at least we can lock the door.'[39]

'At least we can lock the door': Devlin's political preoccupation with housing and homes was informed by early experience. Lack of fair access to housing for Northern Irish Catholics throughout the early period of Devlin's life was a major political grievance and this became a key issue for the civil rights movement. Inequitable practices in allocating social housing were more prevalent in areas where Catholics were numerous and threatened the 'security' of Protestants, as in Derry. Homes also brought political rights, as only those who owned property could vote in local elections: the very first demand of the People's Democracy programme was 'One Man, One Vote'. A protest against the unfair allocation of housing in Dungannon was the immediate 'spur to action' for the demonstrators who took to the streets in the autumn of 1968.[40] Devlin's own family had needed a home in order to shut out a hostile world and to preserve their own identity. Working-class Catholics needed houses to live in. But in addition, they needed homes in order to lay claim to political existence as a community – to be counted – and they also demanded that the franchise be extended to all those who did not own property. And if this community was under-represented and marginalised in the North, it could not claim a home in the rest of Ireland either. As noted above, Devlin at one stage believed that the Northern working class should accept Northern Ireland as their home and try to make it as fair as possible: an independent Ireland would not necessarily be any better for the poor and marginalised. But she did not ultimately shed her commitment to a better Irish republic as the best political home attainable. As she states at the end of a documentary directed by Lelia Doolan, she has not to date been 'disabused of the concept that the kind of society which allows human beings to survive and to prosper and to interrelate as human beings is a socialist republic'.[41] In the absence of any such home, when the Bogside came under continuous attack by the police during the protests in 1969, the community sheltered behind barricades and declared a 'Free Derry'. The slogan was painted on a gable wall as a way of marking the perimeter of an alternative political dispensation.

Thus, Devlin's role as one of the main organisers of the citizens' defences, especially during the Battle of the Bogside in August 1969 when the police mounted a sustained assault but were kept out of the area for more than two days, was in many respects a familiar one to her. In her own view, she was there to marshal and instruct people and to encourage them to stand up for themselves. She supervised the erection of barricades and the making of petrol bombs. She believed that the violence involved was purely defensive and she took no direct part in it herself. But she was a youthful, charismatic, female leader of what looked like a popular revolt. It was reported that Devlin was immune to tear gas and that she could 'walk with a bullhorn through a rain of missiles and never be touched'.[42] Her skill in organisation was reflected in her skills with words: the two were never entirely separable. Although image and voice were crucial to her success, she disdained matters of appearance and style. She was only interested in the practical effects of her words. She has said that she takes no satisfaction in 'people who say "You're a grand entertainer. I loved your performance"' but who do not actually consider her ideas. Those people are not really listening to her: 'they're merely somehow enthralled by the sound you're making'.[43] The purpose of her words was to build solidarity and to foster cooperation. She never assumed that these things were part and parcel of a ready-made identity: people had to be informed, educated and advised. She always attempted to reach beyond her immediate, easily accessible audiences to other working-class people in particular. To begin with, she believed that the ruling elite only needed to be informed about the real conditions of ordinary people in order to bring about change:

> I had a very moral view when I was younger. I thought everybody cared. I think it's part of a Catholic upbringing, that idea of universal solidarity. That was a journey for me ... I didn't think the government was bad. I genuinely thought they just didn't know and if I just went to London to tell them, people would say, 'Do you hear that young woman there? We need to do something about that.' But then I realised: the bastards, they do know and not only do they know, they don't see anything wrong with it.[44]

When her early, naive assumptions were proved incorrect, she concluded that although she might have looked 'pretty harmless', she could not in the end be 'disentangled from the ideas that she embodied'; so her reputation rose or fell along with 'the tide of mass movements that cannot actually be totally manipulated by the image makers'.[45]

But despite their unstudied nature, Devlin's image and rhetoric were indisputably distinctive and powerful. In some of the old black-and-white footage, with her short dresses and dark shoes, she looks like a diminutive Irish dancer at a Feis Ceoil competition. In interviews, mostly conducted in crowded public spaces, she generally has to look up at the (male) questioner. She is grave, but occasionally gives a quick gap-toothed smile, seeming to express incredulity at the line of questioning.[46] But there is a fascinating contrast between the child- or teenager-like features and the authoritative voice that issues from her. She punches out her short sentences. Here is a self-educated person determined to educate – with the long, local vowels of Tyrone (Davidson comments that in Devlin's accent, 'made poor' becomes 'mee-ad poo-er'[47]) and her pragmatic verbs (do, act, work, organise). Her eloquence is intensely local in its range of reference but syntactically without hesitation or flaw. Her cleanness of tone and diction gives her an advantage over the leaden male egoism of the traditional politician. The cadence is that of a witness, issuing an indictment of police or soldier behaviour in a particular incident, but goes up a notch when she extends the role of witness into that of analyst, describing the action as typical of oppressors against the 'people'.[48] In the opening scene of Doolan's film, Devlin is seen and heard addressing a crowd on a street. She condemns those nationalists who sing the old rebel songs but would call her an 'extremist': 'Pearse and Connolly are dead now and won't do any harm to the snug position a few people in Ireland have made for themselves out of everyone else's poverty.'[49] Her references and vocabulary are all within the confines of her audience and the crispness of her pronunciation becomes a mark of rationality. She has a rhetorical flair that can be listened to for its structure, for the pleasure it in itself provides.

Her eloquence was obviously as impressive in the House of Commons in 1969 as on the streets. Her maiden speech was described by one Tory politician as 'electrifying'.[50] In making the speech on her first day in parliament and on a controversial issue, Devlin announced that she was 'flaunt[ing] the unwritten traditions of the House', because the situation of her people 'merited the flaunting of such traditions'.

She noted that she stood in the same tradition as Markievicz, the first woman elected to that House. She joined the debate on the recent disturbances in Derry but said that 'it is impossible to consider the activity of one weekend in a city such as Derry without considering the reasons why these things happen'. She addressed herself directly to James Chichester-Clark, Unionist MP for Londonderry, who had just warned the House about the 'so-called civil rights people' and those disaffected Catholics who 'do not want to join [our] society', and to Captain Terence O'Neill, the Prime Minister of Northern Ireland, who had recently made a televised address promising some immediate changes in the province and predicting chaos if his programme of reforms was not embraced. She stated:

> I was in the Bogside on the same evening as the hon. Member for Londonderry. I assure you, Mr. Speaker – and I make no apology for the fact – that I was not strutting around with my hands behind my back examining the area and saying 'tut-tut' every time a policeman had his head scratched. I was going around building barricades because I knew that it was not safe for the police to come in ... I saw with my own eyes one thousand policemen come in military formation into an oppressed, and socially and economically depressed area – in formation of six abreast, joining up to form twelve abreast like wild Indians, screaming their heads off to terrorise the inhabitants of that area so that they could beat them off the streets and into their houses.

She spoke derisively of O'Neill's belated commitment to electoral reform:

> We come to the question of what can be done about incidents like that in Derry at the weekend. Captain O'Neill has thought of a bright idea – that tomorrow we shall be given one man, one vote. Does he think that, from 5th October until today, events have not driven it into the minds of the people that there are two ideals which are incompatible – the ideal of social justice and the ideal and existence of the Unionist Party? Both cannot exist in

the same society. This has been proved time and again throughout Northern Ireland by the actions of the Unionist Party.

A party that is, as she argued, 'based on, and survives on, discrimination' would be incapable of carrying out reform. She concluded with a warning about the consequences of sending British soldiers to Northern Ireland.[51] Her audience in the chamber and in the media professed to be deeply impressed by her. Many regarded themselves as sympathetic to the idea of reform in Northern Ireland. But Devlin was not talking about piecemeal changes. She completely rejected the existing state of affairs in the North. On that topic and at that time, dialogue was perhaps not feasible. The following year she was re-elected as an MP. But rather than making more parliamentary speeches addressing Her Majesty's government, Devlin would find herself detained in one of Her Majesty's prisons. She was convicted of inciting riots: in some circumstances, 'speechifying' was itself a crime.

Devlin's reluctance to flatter or cajole a well-disposed audience – even one already charmed by her charisma and energy – was again evident during her fund-raising political tour of the United States in late summer of 1969. As Matthew J. O'Brien comments, for older Irish-born Americans, Devlin seemed to prove that the homeland was not entirely lost in distant memory: like Cathleen Ní Houlihan (or Mother Ireland), it could shed its elderly, melancholic appearance and reveal its regenerated life and beauty.[52] He also notes that her 'popular appeal extended far beyond Devlin's ethnic base, leading to private meetings with Mayor John Lindsay [of New York] and United Nations Secretary-General U Thant, along with appearances on national television programs from *Meet the press* to Johnny Carson's *Tonight show*'.[53] However, tensions between Devlin and the Irish American community emerged as her sympathy with the Black civil rights movement became ever more apparent. This culminated in a snub to Major Richard Daley in Chicago, where she visited civil rights leader Jesse Jackson instead.[54] Devlin also later reported that most of her 'good learning' about feminism came from African American women, on this trip and later.[55] Subsequently, there was some angry debate among Irish Americans when in March of 1970 Eamonn McCann returned the honorary keys to New York, which had been received from Major Lindsay by Devlin the previous year, to a member of the Black Panthers; in his statement about this, McCann condemned Irish Americans as 'hypocrites' for their insensitivity to the politics of race in the United States.[56] Although her interest in African American issues was long-standing, clearly the direct experience of radical America had a major impact on Devlin. For one thing, she would no longer stand in the streets talking about 'Irishmen' rather than 'men and women' or just 'human beings'. This was more than a matter of 'political correctness', given the preponderance of women over men in many of the crowds. Devlin would regularly acknowledge the specific ways in which women were affected by the conflict that was to become entrenched in Northern Ireland after 1972; no remotely comparable female political voice would emerge there for decades. And the impulse to reach beyond Irish Catholics in order to build alliances with people who might be seen as 'others' by that group – Protestants, African Americans, Travellers or, most recently, migrants – has been a consistent one.

Bloody Sunday was a pivotal moment both for Devlin and for the civil rights campaign. Hours after she struck Maudling in the House of Commons, she was accosted by a crowd of reporters on the street. The surviving footage is extraordinary: it is hard to credit that this was indeed an entirely spontaneous and unscripted exchange. She was perfectly composed and spoke evenly and emphatically. She said that the Home Secretary, during his three-minute long statement, had failed even to state that he regretted the deaths of thirteen people. A journalist speaking in a languid upper-class English accent goes on to ask her if this had been a 'proper way' to make her protest: was it not 'unladylike' and 'undemocratic'? She opens her mouth to answer but then hesitates. The interview misses a beat. She looks up at him, smiles, shakes her head very slightly. She resumes. 'There was a young girl whose body was carried out of the Bogside this morning,' she says, 'shot in the back by paratroopers who did not ask if she was a *lady*.' She again insists that she should have been permitted to speak on behalf of the 20,000 marchers in Derry. Moments later, she is asked if she intends to apologise to the Home Secretary. She stares and pauses again. No smile this time. She answers slowly and deliberately: 'I'm only sorry I didn't get him by the throat.'[57] Clearly, the representatives of the media regarded Devlin's violent act as more worthy of comment than the killings perpetrated by the paratroopers.

The culpability of the civil rights protesters, in supposedly stimulating the forces of the state to violence in Northern Ireland and so 'causing' the Troubles, was extensively debated in Ireland over this period. Conor Cruise O'Brien remarked that after 1969 the 'radical orators' had nothing further to offer the Catholic population and the scene was set for the IRA and other paramilitary groups to take over in the early 1970s: 'the men who brought the guns and were able to use them would have the key to the situation in the Catholic ghettos and the initiative elsewhere'.[58] As we have seen, he dwells particularly on Devlin, the most prominent woman involved. Like Sophocles' Antigone, she comes into conflict with what O'Brien regards as the necessary force of the law, embodied in the play by Creon, the king of Thebes:

> The spirit of Antigone, which animates the bravest of the war-resisters, disdains ... pragmatic distinctions: these young people are against the war, as against racism and other forms of oppression, because it is wrong: since their struggle is right, they are not concerned with its consequence or its costs. ... [Antigone represents] an ethical and religious force ... as dangerous in her own way as Creon, whom she perpetually challenges and provokes.[59]

The protesters had not meddled merely with some local matters of discrimination and unjust provision of housing, but with the basis of the political settlement that had created Northern Ireland. For the agitators and their constituency knew 'that much more is involved than the correction of an electoral anomaly: it is a question of changing historic relations between conqueror and conquered – something not likely to happen without violence'.[60] He himself acknowledges the colonial roots and gross inequities of the situation but evidently thinks that it would have been more prudent not to challenge these directly.

Nell McCafferty has described how McAliskey acquired a reputation among women's groups in the Republic as a sympathiser with 'armed struggle' mainly for refusing to condemn the IRA in the wake of Bloody Sunday.[61] McAliskey accepted that she was seen 'in the shadow of a gunman'; but she believed that the conflict was best described as a 'war'.[62] This put her at odds with, for example, the Social and Democratic Labour Party (SDLP), which contested her Mid Ulster seat on behalf of moderate nationalist opinion in 1974. She had also lost favour with more conservative Catholics north and south of the border when she gave birth to a daughter outside marriage in 1971. McCafferty recounts how Devlin was forced to defend herself from charges that she was 'giving scandal' by proposing to care for her 'illegitimate' child herself.[63] (Two years later, Devlin married Michael McAliskey, a teacher, and went on to have two more children.) The nationalist vote in Mid Ulster was split and she lost the seat.

It would be tempting to regard 1969–72 as Devlin's 'shining moment'[64] and to take her relative obscurity since as a sign of failure. However, for her own part she has always expressed indifference to the loss of her once high-profile political career. As early as *The Price of my soul* in 1969, she lamented that being an MP had taken her away from community activism for a role to which she was not well suited.[65] The very title of her autobiography, which was published when she was only twenty-two, announces that she expects to make sacrifices, which would certainly include the sacrifice of such incidentals as media attention and fame, in order to stay true to what she regards as her core identity.[66] Her time in the spotlight was a temporary anomaly: 'The instruments for [the] conveying of images are owned by the most powerful of people who have the most powerful of interests in maintaining the system as it is. They are an integral and vital part of the control mechanism of the system and therefore they make mistakes. I was one of them.'[67] She laments only the waste and trauma of the last half-century in Northern Ireland and she is outside mainstream opinion in considering that these were wholly unresolved by the Peace Process and the Good Friday Agreement.

During the Troubles, McAliskey was associated with left-wing Republican groups, but believed that the Provisional IRA was a politically bankrupt organisation, too uncritically accepting of traditional nationalist ideology and dominated by the imperatives of maintaining an underground army. The IRA's commitment to militarism was – among other things – likely to foster secrecy, masculine ascendancy and the abuse of power. She was a founder member of the Irish Republican Socialist Party in 1974 (the first Irish political party to support abortion rights and gay rights) but left when she found herself on the losing side of a dispute about what she considered to be the necessity of keeping the paramilitary wing of the party (the INLA) under the control of the political organisation. She does not believe that 'power comes from the barrel of a gun'; she thinks it deluded of Sinn Féin and the IRA to have imagined in the 1990s that they had succeeded even in fighting their way to a stalemate with the British state or to a place at the negotiating table.[68] So she ascribes what she regards as the inadequacies of the current arrangements for government in the North, established under the Good Friday Agreement, in part to the solipsism of the republican paramilitarists: while they eventually embraced the democracy of the ballot box, they could not accept the broader, radical principles of participative democracy that she advocates.

McAliskey's vision of republican working-class communities during the conflict seems to have been to some degree moulded by the formative experience of her own family life in Cookstown. Men were respected, but not always there: her own father had worked in England and died young, while republican men were often absent because they had been interned or killed. Suffering and loss helped to create solidarity and cooperation among the women left behind. Thus, as a result of these unfortunate conditions, an image of a good society came into view. In 1994, McAliskey said:

> People may not like the war, they may not agree with the war, but the war exists. It has been a reality for me and my community. It has filled graveyards. It has filled prisons. It has created orphans. It has left women particularly, and I am not simply saying within my community, but it has left women particularly carrying a work load which does not simply entail community organizing and debate. Within the only lives that we have got, a very complex, dynamic existence of caring, welfare, holding each other's heads above water, interchanging positions

– when I am the comforter, you are the bereaved, or I am the bereaved and you are the comforter – of taking on collectively in a very unstructured way, taking on collectively the caring for each other's children, the caring for each other's families. The replacement on a day-to-day basis of gaps in the social structure by ourselves who are there.[69]

In the same year, it was Nuala O'Faolain's assertion that such women were in fact unquestioningly subservient to men that particularly angered McAliskey and others at the meeting in Derry. O'Faolain claimed that 'women who lived on tea and biscuits brought steak to their husbands in jail and the men took it without apology'.[70] McAliskey's words on this occasion were not recorded by O'Faolain. However, her own idealised image of men and women cooperating in different roles but on equal terms in the republican movement clearly came under some strain during the course of the prison protests which culminated in the hunger strikes of 1981. In addition, it was apparent that these forms of protest had quite different resonances when undertaken by women prisoners in Armagh Jail rather than in the H-Blocks at Long Kesh. Some years later, the specificities of women's experiences of incarceration were also brought home by a case involving McAliskey's daughter Róisín. Her daughter, whose partner was a republican ex-prisoner, was arrested in 1996 while three months pregnant due to an extradition warrant issued by Germany which named her as a suspect in a mortar attack on a British Army compound at Osnabrück. She was held as a high-risk Category A prisoner in Holloway prison in London, despite being in poor mental and physical health and enduring severe complications with the pregnancy, and bailed to hospital to give birth to a daughter, Loinnir.[71] The British authorities eventually released Róisín without charge after a long campaign led by her mother.

In 1976, republican and loyalist prisoners in the North had lost the right to Special Category Status and began to be treated by the state as ordinary criminals. Protests against this 'criminalisation' of prisoners escalated over several years until Bobby Sands and nine other republican prisoners starved themselves to death in 1981. It could be argued that this campaign was in a sense about the prisoners' desire to remain 'at home' while in jail. Among other demands, they sought the right to wear their own clothes, to avoid participation in prison work and to associate freely with each other. When their insistence on 'political status' – or for the expression of a collective identity – was denied, the prisoners in turn refused to preserve their human identity: they went naked and unwashed, they ceased to 'slop out' and smeared the walls of their cells with excrement. Ultimately some of them rejected even the food they were offered. The stoicism of Sands and the others in the isolation and agony of their last days was inspired by their confidence that they would be recognised as martyrs by their community within and outside the prisons. There were parallels with Patrick Pearse and the other leaders of 1916, who had been executed by firing squad in Kilmainham: the manner of their deaths aroused widespread sympathy and support among Irish people who had previously been indifferent to the rebels. So, on a smaller but nevertheless significant scale, the intransigence of the British prime minister Margaret Thatcher in 1981 outraged many in Ireland who would also have condemned the actions of the IRA and the other paramilitaries.

According to the journalist Vincent Browne, McAliskey was the person most active in trying to convert this pro-prisoner sentiment into a broad-based political campaign. This involved encouraging 'diehards' to work alongside those who were opposed to paramilitary violence and attempting to build on wider public concern about conditions in the prisons.[72] The 'Anti H-Blocks' coalition gained huge support across the Northern Catholic community and to some extent in the Republic. Sands was elected as an MP in the Fermanagh and South Tyrone constituency while on hunger strike in April 1981 and two H-Block candidates were successful in the general election in the Republic the following June. But the hunger strikes petered out as relatives intervened to allow life-saving treatment for men who were close to death and the British made no meaningful concessions. McAliskey regarded the outcome of the H-Block campaign as a major defeat. The chief political beneficiary was Sinn Féin which, encouraged by the success of the H-Block candidates, embraced mainstream electoral politics and eventually became the largest nationalist party in the North. Many of the leading left-wing organisers of the H-Block campaign were assassinated by loyalists; McAliskey and her husband were left for dead after the UDA attack in their home in January 1981.

The hunger strike had first been deployed as a form of protest in British prisons by suffragists and although claims were made for its roots in Gaelic tradition, it is somewhat unclear how it came to be adopted by Irish republicans. Irish suffragist Hanna Sheehy Skeffington was a pioneer in this regard but reported that, at first, 'Sinn Féin [she is referring to the early twentieth-century party of that name] and its allies regarded the hunger-strike as a womanish thing'.[73] Routine jail punishments such as strip searches were also potentially 'feminising', in that they emphasised the physical vulnerability of the prisoners as they tried to conceal written messages and other contraband items in their bodies. But self-starvation, strongly associated with the female anorectic, was surely a weapon wielded only by the weak. Yet all this was seemingly transformed by the self-discipline of the prisoners and their common faith in their ideological purpose into demonstrations of heroic fortitude. Sands and his comrades liked to quote Terence McSwiney, the republican Lord Mayor of Cork who died on hunger strike in Brixton Prison in 1920: 'it is not those who can inflict the most, but those who can suffer the most who will conquer'.[74] Photographs smuggled out of the prison of the long-haired, bearded protesters, naked apart from the blankets draped over their shoulders, resembled popular images of Christ.

Women prisoners at Armagh participated in a 'no wash' protest and in a hunger strike in 1980. They called off their actions the following year so as not to distract attention from the events then unfolding in the H-Blocks. The women protesters claimed parity with their male counterparts. But in some ways their situation clearly had an additional, gendered dimension; for example, they were subjected to frequent, sexualised verbal abuse and violence by male prison officers. However, the spectacle of young women inhabiting filth-encrusted cells aroused even more public disgust and/or indignation than the H-Block protests and also a good deal of concern that was heavily paternalistic in nature.[75] It was not easy for republicanism to politicise the plight of women in such conditions – maybe this was just degradation, not 'martyrdom'? Nor was it easy to encourage any broader feminist solidarity with the situation of the women prisoners.

Some tried. McCafferty wrote an article for the *Irish Times* in August 1980 with the title 'It is my belief that Armagh is a feminist issue'. The first line read: 'There is menstrual blood on the walls of Armagh prison in Northern Ireland.'[76] But was this merely to present an image of abject victimhood, regardless of whether the blame was to be laid with the British government or – as many feminists believed – with the women's own subjection to republican ideology? Or was it an inspiring image of political resistance? Were republican feminists demanding engagement from women on the grounds that they should sympathise with each other's victimhood – as they would with a woman who had experienced domestic violence or rape – or, rather, were they being asked to affirm these actions as legitimate expressions of anti-imperialist sentiment in a specifically feminist form? In any case, there does not seem to have been any notable mainstream Irish feminist reaction.[77]

McAliskey's public rhetoric is somewhat different to McCafferty's particular style of what we might call Irish feminist reportage. However, because so many pioneering feminist voices in Irish feminism were those of journalists (including Mary Holland, Mary Maher and a host of others), it is reportage, journalism with a literary inflection, that has a claim to be recognised as the key genre in which the second-wave feminist critique of Ireland emerged. These female authors did not write out of any immediate sense of their own victimhood. Rather they self-consciously lent their voices to a woman or to a group of women who had been silenced (as well as on other occasions to other marginalised groups). An unvarnished, direct style suggests that a mere statement of the facts about a situation will disclose breath-taking unfairness and hypocrisy. We might think of Susan McKay or Kitty Holland as journalists and writers currently working in this mode. (It is noteworthy that although all of these writers have dealt with key scandals or events in the Republic, several of them are from the North and also address issues arising from the conflict. This is not the case with a later wave of Irish feminist analysis produced mainly by academics based in universities in the Republic.[78]) Some of McAliskey's concerns overlap with such writing. She is certainly not given to confessional writing: in her early memoir, she stated she was interested only in how a 'phenomenon' such as herself was produced out of 'the complex of economic, social and political problems of Northern Ireland'.[79] She avoided dwelling on (say) her grief at losing her adored father as a young child and instead everywhere underlines the importance of pragmatism, discipline and resilience. Equally, in her political rhetoric, she does not linger over the suffering of those whom she understands to be oppressed, no doubt in case this could potentially inhibit analysis and action. Instead, it is interesting to consider the various other ways in which she has spoken for or sought to operate as an ally of the victimised over the course of her career.

McAliskey has suggested that the reason she, rather than her male colleagues in People's Democracy, turned out be such an appealing electoral prospect during the civil rights campaign was because 'people identified with me ... perhaps because I looked like their daughters or their granddaughters'.[80] Of course, it was perhaps more accurately a question of recognition combined with novelty. She was in appearance and background more or less one of their own yet she was prepared to confront and displace the pusillanimous older leaders of her community. And as we have noted, any female firebrand carries with her a good mythological pedigree. So, there was evidently something both startlingly incongruous and entirely appropriate about seeing this 'girl' declaiming in parliament or yelling instructions about street fighting through a megaphone in Derry. However, the semiotics of this were bound to evolve as Devlin got older and as horrifying violence continued over many years.

During the H-Block protests, McAliskey did not seek to sanctify the image of the hunger strikers as martyrs. She wanted to contribute to the pressure on the authorities to grant their demands and, above all, she sought to convert sympathy for their protest into a new republican mass movement in Ireland. However, although she had won 6 per cent of the vote in the Northern Irish European Elections in 1979 as an independent candidate on an H-Block platform, she stood aside in favour of Bobby Sands in the Fermanagh and South Tyrone by-election in 1981. While she accepted that this was the right political decision ('If we got him elected, we had a card to play'[81]), she also believed that Sinn Féin was afraid that the broader movement was a threat to their centrality.[82] If so, the organisation need not have worried. Its reluctant abandonment of abstentionism in elections paid enormous political dividends and brought many new recruits into the party. But later, McAliskey's hostile account of the behind-the-scenes negotiations that led to the Peace Process includes repeated criticism of the arrogance and secrecy of Sinn Féin; clearly, it struck her that the 'band of brothers' from the prisons, and their supporters in the broader Sinn Féin movement, had transformed themselves into professional politicians with surprising alacrity, ease and even eagerness.

In a 1994 speech, she described how she believed that her life-long struggle in 'open and non-violent movements' had been reduced to a game of dice played 'by half-a-dozen men' within 'the existing electoral mechanism of the state'. Women, she stated, were being invited to go home and iron the shirts that men would wear to stand in elections, or maybe they would even stand in elections themselves ('in this day and age you need the odd woman about'). But in her view, the basis for the negotiations provided no real recognition of the nature of the problem (presumably, sectarianism stemming from colonialism and social inequality) or any outline of a proper resolution of the conflict (which for her would have to include fundamental economic change and an effort to desegregate a divided society).[83] McAliskey regarded the new dispensation in Northern Ireland as little more than power-sharing on the basis of sectarian identity – creating a situation where, for example, Sinn Féin would work with unionists to implement Tory policies on austerity.[84] The increased visibility of women (for example, Arlene Foster of the Democratic Unionist Party became the first female First Minister of Northern Ireland in 2016) was not so important as the failure to absorb the lessons of radical feminism, as McAliskey understands them.[85] She said that she herself could not enter the new assembly, which she obviously regards as a place where bloodshed and sacrifice have been whitewashed over – although she hoped that new activists would.[86] For her, it was a grievous disappointment that Bloody Sunday and the H-Blocks had led back to Stormont: a false and repellent home. Instead, she carried on working at community level to support immigrant workers – a new 'out-group' in Northern Ireland – in Co. Tyrone.[87]

It is clear from this history that the ways in which McAliskey could be imagined as a leader, or as a person who represented a community, grew more constricted as time passed. Two groups of women featured most prominently in press coverage of the hunger strikes. First were the grieving female relatives of the dead, understood by many to have endured great loss for the sake of a noble cause. Then, as the strike took its course, several mothers allowed doctors to pull their sons back from the brink of death, even when this defied the men's own instructions. The latter made for gripping drama in its own right (as in Terry George's 1996 film, *Some mother's son*). Here, it appeared that one group was driven by a willingness to submit to the authority of their sons and the other by instinctive maternal feeling. Regardless of whether they were viewed positively or negatively, both sets of women could be understood in terms of received ideas of 'feminine' behaviour. An articulate female activist, such as McAliskey, or indeed the women protesters themselves, were less amenable to being understood in such familiar ways. Yeats had similar problems with his republican women friends, especially Gonne and Markievicz. After 1916, it was in some ways easier for him to commemorate male nationalists that he did not find at all congenial, including Pearse and Gonne's husband John McBride, who had nonetheless been transfigured by their heroic deaths, rather than to celebrate the only woman rebel leader. Markievicz, spared from execution because of her sex, was for that reason also kept out of the republican heaven where Yeats imagined that Pearse and his comrades now conversed 'bone to bone' with Edward Fitzgerald and Wolfe Tone.[88] Instead, she was confined to a prison cell as an inconvenient survivor. Yeats's poetry made a powerful contribution to the rhetoric and imagery surrounding 'extreme' Irish republican women, especially those who like Markievicz refused to support the Anglo-Irish Treaty of 1921. But he himself was chivalrous enough to prefer to think of her as a beautiful girl in the fine house on her family's estate, Lissadell, in Co. Sligo – although the 'chivalry' was of course itself an element in his patriarchal nostalgia and condescension. In the poem 'On a political prisoner', he suggests that the stillness and solitude of her cell may restore her to her former womanliness. In truth, Markievicz was extremely unwell during her time in prison and yet was to remain active in politics for the rest of her life.[89] The power of the stereotype may distort any accurate appreciation of a woman's own beliefs and political agency. In her speech describing how she was excluded from negotiations about the Peace Process, McAliskey details the criticisms of her that were advanced by fellow republicans. She was told that she was 'too long in the struggle' or lacked the 'political sophistication' to grasp the strategies of the negotiators. She claims that this boiled down to being told that she 'was rural, female, republican, too old, lost too much, too bitter, too narrow'. She mentions 'rural' first on this list. McAliskey is in fact from a small town and she shares a working-class background with most of the prominent Sinn Féin politicians. Nevertheless she asks: 'Is [it] because I was born in Tyrone? Is there something about the brown water and the moss, and the lack of exposure to the grime of this city [Belfast], which makes me too unsophisticated to understand the Downing Street Declaration?'[90] While Yeats liked to picture Markievicz as a girl in Sligo 'riding under Ben Bulben to the meet',[91] McAliskey's image of the countryside recalls her maiden speech of 1969, when she insisted that she stood for the 'peasants' (rather than the landlords) of Northern Ireland. It is a telling (and in this case ungendered) signifier of dispossession as the key vantage point from which an historical situation can be understood. Rebellions occur as a consequence of such conditions but the pain of rebellion may be such that the rebels merely end up joining a modified version of the system that produced them.

As time has passed, McAliskey has increasingly found herself in circumstances in which she has felt obliged to speak for people who are especially vulnerable or whose losses appear unlikely to be redeemed by any remotely foreseeable transformation of the existing order of things. This is not a style of rhetoric that would have come naturally to her in her youth. For example, she was perhaps inevitably the most prominent campaigner against the treatment in prison of her own daughter, which by urgent necessity had to focus primarily on the young woman's extreme frailty rather on the weakness of the case against her or other legal or political questions. Among other problems, Róisín's cramped and sometimes filthy conditions aggravated her already severe morning sickness, making it impossible for her to eat. This also served to underline the similarities between the plight of this young expectant mother and female republican prisoners who had endured hunger strikes and force-feeding. McAliskey has spoken vividly and sympathetically about some of these women as well. For example, in a speech in 2013 commemorating the forty-first anniversary of Bloody Sunday, she describes the regime of force-feeding experienced by Dolours and Marian Price in the early 1970s, which had permanently undermined their health, thus setting the trauma endured by these women prisoners alongside the fate of the hunger strikers.[92]

In this speech, delivered on a grey January day, McAliskey – an ordinary-looking, middle-aged woman bundled up against the cold – takes the commemoration as an occasion to reflect on the experiences of a range of people whose persecutors have enjoyed impunity under Irish or British state authority. She includes in this the 'half dozen soldiers' that fired on the crowd in 1972, although she is more concerned about the political establishment that initially covered up the massacre by blaming the victims. She states that 'Bloody Sunday' is 'not exclusive to the people of Derry ... not exclusive to Northern Ireland': it is a history shared, for example, by the victims of child sexual abuse in Irish institutions and of the Hillsborough football stadium disaster and of other scandals. She says that in all cases, concerted official efforts were made 'to maintain the lie – that demonizing of the innocent' and to perpetuate the 'long, long process of barricading the truth away from the people':

> People talk about how long the Saville enquiry took, how expensive the Saville enquiry was. It took a long time and it cost a lot of money because for every single inch of that journey, for every single day of that journey, the British government, who set the enquiry up, prevented the truth from being brought before it. That's why it cost a lot of money. That's why it took a lot of time.[93]

Her style is paratactic – she sounds controlled, patient, a little weary. At times, her voice nearly breaks down and she appears almost tearful. She has more now to remember and to mourn. Poise and articulacy are obviously harder won than they were forty years earlier. Yet there is no effort here to make an effect of her own distress. The victims are lost, but the 'we' who are still listening, even in the midst of a supposedly new political dispensation in Northern Ireland, are exhorted to carry on the struggle.

In a documentary film entitled *Mother Ireland* (1988), a number of Irish women discussed their views of the symbolic relationship between Ireland and women. Mairéad Farrell, commanding officer of the IRA women at Armagh, who was shot dead by British soldiers in Gibraltar just months after the interview, presumably spoke for many republican as well as other women when she said that she and her fellow female prisoners completely rejected the traditional image of Ireland as a mother: 'Mother Ireland, get off our back'. McAliskey's response was more ambivalent: 'I grew up very conscious of Mother Ireland before I was aware of a social, political and economic system that went with it. I still hold very strongly to it. For all her strengths and weaknesses and areas of reaction and all the problems she has caused me, I would still very much see myself as a child of Mother Ireland.'[94] In speeches such as the one for the Bloody Sunday commemoration, we can imagine how such an image of female authority and fortitude might appeal to her. Masculine authority is discredited and tainted by the misbehaviour of soldiers, priests, politicians and those who knowingly sheltered the guilty. The person who continues to manage and to encourage in these woeful conditions might well be understood as a mother in an everyday rather than an idealised sense. As McAliskey comments in *Mother Ireland*, being a mother in underprivileged conditions is not a passive or a romantic role. Mothers may be exalted in Irish culture but they are not credited with much capacity for analysis or for speaking on behalf of a community. So, in this case, revisiting and revising the stereotype is in itself a feminist act.

A journalist on the soundtrack to Doolan's film comments (over early footage of Devlin) in a clipped English voice: 'she is now in many ways the symbol of the nervous intelligent passion of the movement which is in such powerful antithesis to the necessary manipulations of government'.[95] The key phrase here ('necessary manipulations') demonstrates how tricky it is to find oneself at odds with Devlin's principled clarity. Her critics have to fall back on 'pragmatic' arguments about custom, established practice and the importance of maintaining stability. Her attempt to clarify what is 'wrong' in part of a system is more threatening when it insists that to right this wrong the system has to change completely. But to deride this by saying it is too simplistic is in effect either to deride clarity as a synoptic value or to defend as a system something that claims great complexity but is not in fact rational. Devlin in the 1960s was mesmerising to the television cameras and to audiences previously relatively unconcerned with the issues she raised. However, while her views might have had a certain acceptability or cachet in the early years, they appeared never to change in later decades and she is by now far more out of step with mainstream opinion in Ireland. She could never have approximated Robinson's popularity in the 1990s when the first female Uachtarán na hÉireann (President of Ireland) was so warmly embraced by the media, academics and many others as an icon of modern Irish post-nationalist liberalism (which is not to underestimate the importance of Robinson's later stances on human rights and climate change). But McAliskey's basic challenge is to universalise her mother's lesson that 'there was nobody better' than you, but 'there was nobody worse'.[96] That is perfect equality: even if not achieved (of course it has not been) or not achievable, it is surely the lodestar towards which all politics should tend.

Notes

1 From Lelia Doolan (director), *Bernadette: notes on a political journey* (Digital Quilts, 2011).
2 G. W. Target quotes many of the colourful epithets that were attached to Devlin in *Bernadette: the story of Bernadette Devlin* (London: Hodder & Stoughton, 1975), pp. 18–20.
3 Bernadette Devlin, 'Maiden speech to the House of Commons, 22 April 1969', see https://api.parliament.uk/historic-hansard/commons/1969/apr/22/northern-ireland#S5CV0782P0_19690422_HOC_27 (accessed 23 June 2018).
4 See Richard Bourke, *Peace in Ireland: the war of ideas* (London: Pimlico, 2003), p. 74.
5 Bernadette Devlin, *The price of my soul* (London: Pan Books, 1969), p. 192.
6 Stratton Mills, quoted in Target, *Bernadette*, p. 20.
7 Devlin, *The price of my soul*, pp. 59–61.
8 Eamonn McCann, *War in an Irish town* (London: Pluto Press, 1993), p. 131.
9 For example, Nancy Fraser argues that feminism's focus on the

politics of identity made it an unwitting contributor to some aspects of the ideology of contemporary neoliberal capitalism; see Nancy Fraser, *Fortunes of feminism* (London: Verso, 2013).
10 See Conor Cruise O'Brien, *States of Ireland* (Frogmore, Herts: Panther Books, 1974), pp. 175, 151–3.
11 From the *Daily Mirror*, quoted by Target, *Bernadette*, p. 353.
12 Quoted in Target, *Bernadette*, p. 18.
13 Bernadette McAliskey, from 'Speech to Clár na mBan conference' (1994), in Bourke *et al.* (eds), *The Field Day anthology*, vol. 5, p. 421.
14 O'Faolain, *Are you somebody?*, pp. 183–4.
15 Nuala O'Faolain, 'If I had my time back, I'd be somewhere other than in RTÉ before, during and after the hunger strikes', *The Sunday Tribune* (19 August 2007).
16 For example, see Mary McAuliffe and Liz Gillis, *Richmond Barracks 1916: 'We were there' – 77 women of the Easter Rising* (Dublin: Four Courts Press, 2016). The TV drama *Rebellion*, broadcast by RTÉ in 2016 to mark the centenary, focused particularly on the stories of three fictional female characters, one of them a participant in the Rising.
17 W. B. Yeats, 'On a political prisoner', *Collected Poems* (London: Macmillan, 1982), pp. 206–7.
18 Labour MP Willie Hamilton, quoted in Target, *Bernadette*, p. 18.
19 Louis J. Salome, *Violence, veils and bloodlines: reporting from war zones* (Jefferson, NC: McFarland, 2010), pp. 178–80.
20 Doolan (director), *Bernadette*.
21 Devlin, *The price of my soul*, p. 11.
22 Devlin, *The price of my soul*, p. 24.
23 Devlin, *The price of my soul*, p. 26.
24 Devlin, *The price of my soul*, p. 39. Vinegar Hill, just outside the town of Enniscorthy in Co. Wexford, was the site of the last stand of the United Irish rebels against the British forces in 1798.
25 Devlin, *The price of my soul*, p. 36.
26 Doolan (director), *Bernadette*.
27 See Devlin, *The price of my soul*, p. 69.
28 See Devlin, *The price of my soul*, p. 66.
29 Doolan (director), *Bernadette*.
30 Devlin, *The price of my soul*, p. 73.
31 Devlin, *The price of my soul*, p. 76; emphasis in original.
32 Devlin, *The price of my soul*, p. 76.
33 Devlin, *The price of my soul*, pp. 87–8; emphasis in original.
34 Devlin, *The price of my soul*, p. 119.
35 Devlin, *The price of my soul*, p. 72.
36 Devlin, *The price of my soul*, p. 97.

37 Rosita Sweetman, *On our knees* (London: Pan, 1972), p. 275.
38 Devlin, *The price of my soul*, p. 143.
39 Devlin, *The price of my soul*, p. 25.
40 Bourke, *Peace in Ireland*, p. 54.
41 Doolan (director), *Bernadette*.
42 See McCann, *War in an Irish town*, p. 116; and Sara Davidson, 'Bernadette Devlin: an Irish revolutionary in Irish America', *Harper's Magazine*, 240:1436 (January 1970), p. 82.
43 Doolan (director), *Bernadette*.
44 McAliskey interviewed by Kitty Holland, 'I am astounded I survived. I made some mad decisions', *Irish Times* (22 September 2016).
45 Doolan (director), *Bernadette*.
46 For example, see 'Britain's youngest MP, Bernadette Devlin, gives a press conference', www.youtube.com/watch?v=XWOHgVS3E8M (accessed 23 June 2018).
47 Davidson, 'Bernadette Devlin', p. 79.
48 For example, see 'Bernadette Devlin – Bogside barriers', www.youtube.com/watch?v=9n9SMYsT04g (accessed 23 June 2018).
49 Doolan (director), *Bernadette*.
50 Norman St John Stevas; see http://news.bbc.co.uk/onthisday/hi/dates/stories/april/17/newsid_2524000/2524881.stm (accessed 23 June 2018).
51 Devlin, 'Maiden speech'.
52 Matthew J. O'Brien, 'Irish America, race and Bernadette Devlin's 1969 American tour', *New Hibernia Review*, 14:2 (Summer 2010), p. 89.
53 O'Brien, 'Irish America', p. 84.
54 O'Brien, 'Irish America', p. 85.
55 Doolan (director), *Bernadette*.
56 O'Brien, 'Irish America', p. 98. He notes that the assumption that Irish Americans were generally racist or implacably hostile to the civil rights movement in the United States was resented by many Irish Americans and is not borne out by a close scrutiny of the Irish American press. For example, the editorial in the leading paper *The Irish Echo* objected to McCann's ignoring of moderate African American protest groups and caricaturing of all Irish Americans as illiberal or racist. See O'Brien, pp. 97–100.
57 See 'Bernadette Devlin interview after Home Secretary Commons attack', www.youtube.com/watch?v=KLlpVQFdjCo (accessed 23 June 2018); and 'Bernadette Devlin delivers a proletarian protest', www.youtube.com/watch?v=3EKxowOFQP8 (accessed 23 June 2018).
58 O'Brien, *States of Ireland*, p. 177.

59 O'Brien, *States of Ireland*, p. 152.
60 O'Brien, *States of Ireland*, p. 152.
61 Nell McCafferty, *Nell: a disorderly woman* (Dublin: Penguin Books, 2005), p. 293.
62 From Doolan (director), *Bernadette*; and McAliskey, 'Speech to Clár na mBan conference', p. 421.
63 McCafferty, *Nell*, p. 235.
64 Salome, *Violence, veils and bloodlines*, p. 78.
65 Devlin, *The price of my soul*, p. 159.
66 She glosses the title of the book, *The price of my soul*, as a comment on integrity. Her point was that 'to gain that which is worth having, it may be necessary to lose everything else'; *The price of my soul*, p. 9.
67 Doolan (director), *Bernadette*.
68 Doolan (director), *Bernadette*; Bernadette McAliskey, 'A terrible state of chassis', Seamus Deane honorary Field Day lecture (2016), www.youtube.com/watch?v=42yJcDQSsRQ (accessed 23 June 2018).
69 McAliskey, 'Speech to Clár na mBan conference', p. 421.
70 O'Faolain said that she later regretted this 'insensitive' remark; see *Are you somebody?*, p. 184.
71 Ros Wynne-Jones, 'It's not a crime to fall in love with an IRA man', *Independent*, 31 May 1997; see also Susan McKay, 'Interview with Róisín McAliskey', in Bourke et al. (eds), *The Field Day anthology*, vol. 5, pp. 1533–6.
72 Vincent Browne, 'The politics of H-Block', *Magill* (December 1980), see https://magill.ie/archive/politics-h-block (accessed 23 June 2018).
73 See Maud Ellmann, *The hunger artists: starving, writing, and imprisonment* (Cambridge, MA: Harvard University Press, 1993), p. 12.
74 See Ellmann, *The hunger artists*, p. 60.
75 See Laura Weinstein, 'The significance of the Armagh dirty protest', *Éire-Ireland*, 4:3 and 4 (Fall/Winter 2006), pp. 11–41. Sinn Féin did not initially approve of women's involvement in the prison protests, but supported the Armagh women once their protest was underway; not coincidentally, around this time the party also began to formulate policies on women's rights more generally. Weinstein also discusses the significance of the efforts made on behalf of the protesters by prominent Catholic clerics who (among others) articulated a case for the prisoners that was both non-feminist and non-republican. See Weinstein, 'The significance of the Armagh dirty protest', pp. 22–4, 32–4.
76 Quoted in Weinstein, 'The significance of the Armagh dirty protest', p. 27; McCafferty also wrote a book about the protest, *The Armagh women* (Dublin: Co-op Books, 1981).
77 The fifth volume of *The Field Day anthology* includes a rich selection

of material from women's organisations and activists from north and south of the border in this period; it does not include material on the Armagh dirty protest although it covers the issue of strip searching and includes an extract from an interview with Mairéad Farrell, one of the Armagh prisoners. See Bourke et al. (eds), *The Field Day anthology*, vol. 5, pp. 1505–8. On divisions and tensions within the Northern Irish women's movement, see Eileen Evason, *Against the grain: the contemporary women's movement in Northern Ireland* (Dublin: Attic Press, 1991); on McCafferty's writing about the Armagh prisoners, and on the prisoners' own self-representation, see Fiona McCann, 'Writing by and about Republican women prisoners', *Irish University Review*, 47, issue supplement (November, 2017), pp. 502–14.

78 See, for example, such works as Nell McCafferty, *A woman to blame: the Kerry babies case* (Dublin: Attic Press, 1985) and, for a selection of her journalism, *The best of Nell* (Dublin: Attic Press, 1984); her memoir, *Nell*, adopted a more confessional mode. See also Susan McKay's book about the woman at the centre of a shocking child abuse case in Kilkenny, *Sophia's story* (Dublin: Gill & Macmillan, 2004), or her work memorialising victims of the Troubles, *Bear in mind these dead* (London: Faber & Faber, 2008).

79 Devlin, *The price of my soul*, p. 9.

80 Devlin, *The price of my soul*, p. 165.

81 Quoted by F. Stuart Ross, *Smashing H-Block: the rise and fall of the popular campaign against criminalization, 1976–82* (Liverpool: Liverpool University Press, 2011), p. 126.

82 Quoted in Stuart Ross, *Smashing H-Block*, p. 180.

83 McAliskey, 'Speech to Clár na mBan conference', pp. 420–2.

84 McAliskey, 'A terrible state of chassis'.

85 Defined in the closing lines of the extract from the speech to the Clár na mBan conference as a 'whole way of thinking' about women's rights, community rights and democracy, McAliskey, 'Speech to Clár na mBan conference', p. 423.

86 Doolan (director), *Bernadette*.

87 McAliskey is a founder of the STEP organisation (South Tyrone Empowerment Programme) in Dungannon.

88 W. B. Yeats, 'Sixteen dead men'; on Pearse and MacBride, see also Yeats, 'Easter 1916'. *Collected Poems*, pp. 205, 202–5.

89 Nuala O'Faolain also had occasion to discuss Markievicz's time in Aylesbury Prison. In her biography of Longford-born 'Chicago May' Duignan, who had a colourful life of crime in America, O'Faolain draws on Duignan's memoirs of years of imprisonment in Aylesbury, where she claimed to have been friends with Markievicz. When both were punished for refusing to pray for a British victory in the war,

they were forced to spend many hours distributing gruel. Markevicz passed the time by reciting Dante in Italian. O'Faolain remarks that 'it was an unexpected kindness done to May by history that she was allowed to make common cause with a woman like Constance'; see O'Faolain, *The story of Chicago May* (New York: Riverhead Books, 2005), p. 211.
90 McAliskey, 'Speech to Clár na mBan conference', p. 420. The Downing Street Declaration, issued by the British Prime Minister and the Irish Taoiseach in December 1993, acknowledged the right of the Irish people to self-determination but also affirmed the principle of consent – that is, that unification would only occur in Ireland when and if a majority in both Northern Ireland and the Republic favoured it.
91 Yeats, 'On a political prisoner', p. 207.
92 See McAliskey, 'Address to Bloody Sunday march' (2013), http://thepensivequill.am/2013/01/end-impunity-bernadette-mcaliskey.html (accessed 23 June 2018). The Price sisters, convicted of involvement in an IRA bombing in London in 1973, were among the last prisoners to be force-fed in a British prison before the technique, first used on suffragists, was abandoned as too dangerous and degrading. None of the hunger strikers in the 1980s were force-fed.
93 McAliskey, along with some but not all of the families of victims, rejected the Saville report of 2010, which exonerated the unarmed victims of Bloody Sunday but did not find anyone criminally responsible for the events in Derry.
94 Anne Crilly (director), *Mother Ireland* (Derry Film and Video, 1988).
95 Doolan (director), *Bernadette*.
96 Doolan (director), *Bernadette*.

4
Nuala O'Faolain: an emotional episode in public life

The death of Nuala O'Faolain in May 2008 at the age of sixty-eight was headline news in Ireland. The *Guardian* and the *New York Times*, among other international papers, published tributes and obituaries. This was startling because it was only in the last decade of her life that O'Faolain became famous as a best-selling author as well as an Irish public figure of a most unusual kind, held in great affection and widely admired for revealing her belief that her own life story was part of the general exposure of a repressive society to which she herself had almost unselfconsciously belonged.

Other women discussed here, including Edna O'Brien and Sinéad O'Connor, were famous from a young age. Both combined artistic talent with remarkable physical beauty. For O'Connor in particular, romantic relationships became part of the subject matter of her own work as well as the focus of huge media attention. She became a celebrity whose life and career was dominated by that dangerous cult. However much she evolved and changed, she remained soldered to that initial image. Even in trying to escape it, she reawakened and even enhanced it.

O'Faolain's work and reputation are not captured by that pernicious kind of fame. She did not start out as a creative artist. Nor was she primarily a journalist, activist or campaigner in the style of so many influential Irish women writers of her generation. O'Faolain was a prize-winning student of literature at University College Dublin (UCD); she wrote a thesis at Oxford University and lectured in the Department of English at UCD for a time on her return to Ireland. However, she did not become a professional scholar and the often brilliantly insightful critical writing she published was in the form of short essays and reviews. She made television programmes for the Open University at the BBC in London, and later worked for the Irish state broadcaster, Raidió Teilifís Éireann (RTÉ), as a producer and presenter of documentary and arts programmes. From the mid-1980s, she wrote a weekly opinion column for the *Irish Times*. But by her own account, this career was completely unplanned. She claimed to have got through university and later to have been offered prestigious jobs in large measure thanks to the generosity of friends and mentors. She stated that she greatly relished these chances to have her 'say'[1] on cultural and political matters in Ireland. But O'Faolain went on to make her most astonishing impact on the Irish public when she was already, in her own words, 'that specially unloved thing in a misogynist society, a middle-aged woman with opinions'.[2] And she did so in forms of the spoken and printed word that would usually be reckoned among the most informal and ephemeral. While she often appeared to affect an extreme humility or naivety, she created a persona and voice that rapidly became associated with a unique blend of confessional self-revelation and cultural authority.

When she was invited by a publisher to put together a volume of her newspaper columns, O'Faolain readily agreed. As she comments, 'a book, at least, goes places'; it would be in the catalogue of the National Library in Dublin.[3] She was asked to write an introduction, but produced instead the 200-page memoir *Are you somebody?*, which went on to became a publishing sensation in 1996. The weekend before the book appeared, O'Faolain was interviewed by Gay Byrne on *The late late show* on RTÉ. His opening question was 'Well, Nuala, you've slept with a lot of men, haven't you?'[4] This was not inaccurate in one sense: the book details many affairs including several with well-known people. But there was nothing salacious in O'Faolain's account of these relationships. The stories were told vividly but in melancholy retrospect and through the perspective of a feminist consciousness that she believed she had arrived at rather belatedly. O'Faolain succeeded in changing the potentially gossipy tone of the interview mainly by gaining the sympathy of the audience. Byrne quickly realised that he had misjudged the situation and adjusted his questions.[5] She afterwards counted the twenty minutes of the interview as 'among the highlights of her life': she considered that for that brief interval, she had reached a 'rare honesty'.[6] Certainly, many of those who heard her were deeply moved and the first print runs of the book sold out as soon as they appeared.[7]

In the wake of the success of *Are you somebody?*, O'Faolain published a novel, a second instalment of memoir and a biography of 'Chicago May' Duignan; another work of fiction and a further collection of journalism appeared posthumously. When in March 2008 she was diagnosed with cancer, she was a full-time writer living comfortably between New York and rural Co. Clare. On hearing the news that the illness was incurable, she returned to Ireland. Six weeks before her death, RTÉ broadcast another astonishing interview with O'Faolain, this time on radio; the interviewer was her former colleague, Marian Finucane. Although the two women were close friends, Finucane made none of the standard attempts to comfort a gravely sick person and O'Faolain did not attempt to disguise or soften in any way her terror and despair. John Waters, a journalist who had strongly disagreed with O'Faolain about many issues, claimed that:

> No book I can think of, no painting, no movie, no speech, no television programme, no newspaper article or poem, had touched the places this interview touched. Nothing that occurred or was said in the Irish public square in the previous generation had, in one piercing moment, so comprehensively summoned up, and in a manner that allowed everyone an opportunity to examine it, the condition of human existence at a frozen moment in Irish life.[8]

Waters went on to describe his own emotional reaction on hearing about the imminent death of this colleague with whom he had quarrelled, particularly about feminism. His response included 'a certain element of curiosity, of fascination with the remorseless action of the force that creates and destroys us'; he also admitted to 'a kind of wonderment and even a perverse kind of envy that someone finding herself in this dizzying, once-in-a-lifetime situation, could attain such presence of mind in describing her feelings'.[9] O'Faolain, who stated that she had always had great difficulty with personal utterance in her private life,[10] had once again made an intensely intimate connection with the public at large. Curiously, she achieved this in traditional media forms just at the time when digital social media were coming to prominence but were still unfamiliar to most people of her age. Unlike some other well-known public figures – and women including O'Brien and O'Connor in particular – she was accorded an almost flawlessly kind reception for her work. This final interview confirmed her status as someone who had been, so to speak, taken into public ownership by her audience. Even at the end of her life, friends reported that she had taken comfort from the enormous number of responses and sympathetic messages that she received following the broadcast.

In his obituary for O'Faolain, her friend Luke Dodd considered the reasons for her popularity. Why had this particular personal story become so emblematic, in Waters's formulation, of 'the condition of human existence at a frozen moment in Irish life'? Dodd opened with an observation about O'Faolain's relationship with Irish feminism: 'The very pure strain of patriarchy that evolved in post-independence Ireland, where church and state were often indistinguishable, produced a noble tradition of female dissent. The long and illustrious list of women who challenged the status quo – and changed Irish society in the process – had no more eloquent an exponent than Nuala O'Faolain.'[11] This is an essential point in any account of O'Faolain's career. She became a skilled analyst of her own experiences and choices in relation to the ideal of women's freedom promoted by feminism. While she was not directly involved in the earlier years of the women's movement in Ireland, she was one of the most prominent voices in debates in the 1980s and afterwards about issues such as divorce, abortion and child abuse. O'Faolain herself, astonished at having become so important, pondered the reasons for her success in this role in her follow-up memoir, *Almost there*. In all her writing, she dwelt on the history that had shaped the lives of her father and mother and in turn her own life in such different ways, and on the changes that had helped to allow her to articulate her own life experience in such a remarkable style. It is evident that she would share the view of Margaret O'Callaghan, already quoted in the introduction to this book, that 'the story of Irish women is part of the complex story of partitioned Ireland's self-fashioning ... it is at the heart of that story and not an addendum to it'.[12] In the slogan of the time, the women's movement raised O'Faolain's consciousness in a very dramatic way, illuminating much of significance about her childhood, her education and adult relationships. But she reports that this unfolded only long after she had begun to understand feminism in relation to the lives of other women and society in general.[13] It became part of her retrospective understanding of a personal trauma – one that arose from a collective political movement to which her own work eventually contributed.

Dodd notes that O'Faolain's feminism chimed with a broader commitment to social justice in Ireland. This is true, but can be elaborated further. It would seem that O'Faolain's passionate concern with Irish history and culture, like her views on gender, only developed fully in maturity; indeed, as she relates in *Are you somebody?*, both were initially connected to a sense of deep personal crisis that she experienced in early middle age. She was inspired to return to the country, when she took up the position at RTÉ, as much by her realisation of how much of it was unknown to her, rather than because of its familiarity. O'Faolain stated that she could not recall much interest in questions of the nation or nationalism in the academic or bohemian culture of Dublin in her student days. Even the ostensible obsession with 'writing' in the pubs and bedsits at that time did not even involve much genuine concern about or engagement with Irish literary traditions. Her own academic interests were in English literature – although she wrote her Oxford dissertation on the reception of a novel, *Esther Waters* (1894), by the Anglo-Irish George Moore, the artist son of a landlord from Co. Mayo who pioneered the experimental naturalist novel in England. She was encouraged to attend the Merriman Summer School in Clare by her friend the broadcaster Seán Mac Réamoinn and this event, with its combination of formal classes and a distinctively Irish sociability, was a revelation to her. Although she was not an academic writer, the worldview conveyed in her journalism and other mature work was informed both by her love of 'high' literature ('I don't have any problem with the art made by dead white males'[14]) and a scholarly understanding of and sense of emotional affinity with the culture of 'ordinary' people, both in Ireland and England. The latter was deepened by her friendships with Irish scholars and intellectuals such as Mac Réamoinn and Liam de Paor, and the British labour historian Raphael Samuel and Marxist literary critic Arnold Kettle. Her awareness of class was sharpened by her own childhood experience of material want and deprivation – even though her father was a journalist who became a media personality, enjoying the best of what Dublin then had to offer of the newly emerging world of glitzy public relations. And in some ways, as a journalist herself, although in a more serious vein, O'Faolain described herself as a person who 'lived in public', like her father. She thought that she had lived a 'man's life' in Ireland, which was by far the better option compared to the lives of most Irish women.[15] She experienced Ireland as a place where conversation mattered. It was a society with a respect for eloquence in speech and where values and issues were endlessly debated with a fluency and passion she did not find elsewhere. O'Faolain was to earn a place as a participant in this national conversation, but she seems to have believed in its importance for a long time and committed herself to Ireland in large part because of it. Although she wrote exceptionally well about Irish migrants' often positive experiences of Britain and, later, of America, she was fundamentally a patriot, of a critical but also an instinctive kind. As she wrote after pondering the advice of someone who urged her to leave Ireland for good: 'It's a bit embarrassing to say so, but there is such a thing as loving Ireland. There are good reasons for sticking it out in this damp little shambles of a democracy on the edge of the Western world.'[16] In the same column, she continued: 'In the past year, on television, I've seen the faces of two men – Peadar O'Donnell and Noel Browne – who led noble lives here. For as long as Ireland can solicit such lives, it can certainly solicit mine.'[17] Of course, at moments when her 'seduction'[18] by Ireland, and her deep appreciation of its cultural distinctiveness and finer political traditions, were countered by evidence of its past and present failures, cruelty and misogyny, she experienced a sense of tremendous emotional and intellectual conflict. However, some of her best writing is produced from this sense of a collision between such different values and loyalties.

O'Faolain was the second child in a family of nine. Her father, known professionally as 'Terry O'Sullivan', was in the Irish army at the time of her birth, and later became the author of the long-running 'Dubliner's diary' social column for the *Evening Press*. She remembers that, while her mother, Katherine, struggled to manage their large brood on little money, her father was chauffeured around Dublin every night to attend all the most glamorous events. Although her parents' relationship had been affectionate and passionate at the outset, her father did not include her mother in his working life or his socialising and had several long-term affairs. Katherine declined into depression and alcoholism. As with the maternal figure in O'Brien's *The country girls* and in many other of her stories, it seems that Katherine too passed on the lesson that romantic or conjugal love was essential for women's happiness – although for O'Faolain's mother, this certainly included sex. In neither case is maternity an adequate compensation for the lack of the all-absorbing passion that evidently only a man can provide. While O'Brien's mothers cling to and suffocate their children with despairing affection, O'Faolain believed that she and her siblings suffered most acutely as a consequence of their mother's emotional absence and of her practical incapacity to look after domestic matters. Her mother tried to gain other satisfactions through alcohol and compulsive reading. Ultimately, she outlived her husband but drank herself to a humiliating death. O'Faolain attributed the premature deaths of two of her siblings, also heavy drinkers, to childhood misery and emotional neglect.

The story of O'Faolain's original family does not need to be uncovered from her work by any process of critical detective work. She returns to it again and again in her autobiographical writing. In the opening pages of *Are you somebody?*, she recounts how at a low point in London, when she had just split up with the man she had planned to marry and was drinking alone every night, a psychiatrist she had just met announced to her: 'You are going to great trouble, and flying in the face of the facts of your life, to recreate your mother's life.'[19] She wrote of her mother that she herself had 'understood long, long before I had words for it, that the real thing driving her was a loneliness and anxiety from which passion provided her only real relief. It was an existential anxiety, an experience of being unloved by anything in the universe, which I have no doubt she endured, and had no choice but to pass on.'[20]

This was in large measure a cultural condition, as well as one related to gender: O'Faolain wrote of her mother that 'she was the most motherless of women, herself'.[21] Her maternal grandmother had reared seven children destined for emigration in ostensibly respectable but impoverished conditions and enjoyed no pleasure or fulfilment in life. In marrying and having children herself, her mother was simply 'in the wrong job'.[22] But in addition, O'Faolain consistently places great emphasis on cultural dislocation, poverty and emigration in explaining the lowly status of children and the prevalence of child abuse in twentieth-century Ireland: 'only seeing children as rats who would eat the last of the grain can begin to explain why they were treated as they were'.[23]

O'Faolain was saved from early marriage and a similar fate by what she regarded as the lucky chance of never having fallen pregnant as a sexually active young woman. Instead, she had the opportunity to gain an advanced education and to take up creative and rewarding work. But she always imagined she would also work out how to live successfully with a male partner, while never critically examining this expectation in relation to the myriad difficulties encountered by the women around her in their personal lives. And when romantic passion failed her too, she always had the same alternative narcotics as her mother: drink and books. However, these things were not merely escapist. Alcohol was associated, even for O'Faolain's mother, with the pub and therefore with a space away from the confinement and labour of domesticity. Drinking was strongly linked to a sense of conviviality that for O'Faolain was in a profound sense 'Irish'. And although her father made his living from writing, literature belonged to her mother's realm. The latter read voraciously, apparently in all genres, embracing both popular romance and classic novels. She had published some book reviews when she was young that she kept among a small collection of personal treasures all her life.[24] But by her later years, reading was not a way for her to 'feed reflection' but rather to avoid it.[25] Her daughter also sometimes looked for oblivion in books, but more often she thought of literature as a way of connecting the individual self to a broader, even utopian, ideal of shared humanity. O'Faolain repeatedly discussed art as a privileged mode of human communication that was bound up with collective political aspirations. As we shall see, she eventually went on to examine her own success as a female writer in a confessional mode in Ireland in the mid-1990s in this light.

In this chapter, I will seek to analyse O'Faolain's already highly self-aware reflections on the emotional lives of Irish women and men in relation to her political and philosophical interests. Indeed, one key question about O'Faolain might be why someone so apparently well equipped for and invested in the so-called life of the mind did not remain in a university environment and never wrote extensively in supposedly more objective or analytical modes. Of course, a large part of the answer is to be found in the account of the cultural and academic world inhabited by a clever young Irish woman in the

1950s and 1960s that is provided in the pages of *Are you somebody?* Nevertheless, this seems to be something that O'Faolain ultimately regretted: in her final interview, she told Finucane, 'I just shot around. I would like it if I had been a better thinker.' However, it was O'Faolain's gift to bring 'opinion' back a step to that molten state in which it still had the warmth of personal discovery. This is how she irradiated Irish feminism and Irish writing by such a sense of wonder – of waking out of a drugged sleep to a new awareness of the world – that was so central to her vivid personal history.

In the time-honoured traditions of the Irish *Bildungsroman*, including *A Portrait of the artist as a young man* and *The country girls*, O'Faolain's memoir charts the downward social trajectory of her family through various states of domestic disorder. For most of her childhood the O'Faolains lived in isolated rented houses in the far northern coastal suburbs of Dublin. The children were sent to school hungry and in dirty clothes; there were never enough beds or blankets for everyone. No one noticed if you were ill or unhappy. Her mother drank every day and pined for her husband. It is not entirely clear from the memoir how O'Faolain's father spent his presumably quite adequate income while neglecting his family so cruelly. But like Joyce's father (and unlike Edna O'Brien's) he was charming and gregarious and a man entirely at home in the city. O'Faolain offers a complex explanation for his 'amorality'[26] which also sheds a good deal of light on her broader account of modern Ireland.

Tomás O'Faolain was not merely a grim domestic tyrant, of the kind memorialised by John McGahern in novels such as *The dark* (1965) or *Amongst women* (1990). As 'Terry O'Sullivan', he belonged not to De Valera's austere world of faith and patriotism but to the emerging Ireland of Seán Lemass. The latter was a key evangelist for economic liberalisation, first as Minister for Trade and Commerce and later as Taoiseach. O'Faolain writes that her father became 'alienated from a domestic role by the opportunity which Lemass's Ireland happened to present to him'.[27] She had no illusions about the harshness of Irish families in the past. For example, she is highly sceptical concerning her grandfather's nostalgic sketch, recorded in an old copybook, of an idyllic family scene on a rural smallholding on a typical evening in the early 1890s – all songs in Irish and firelight gleaming on the crockery on the dresser, his father reading the political news out loud from the weekly paper as his mother did her sewing and listened attentively. As O'Faolain comments, these are the reminiscences of a man who took no responsibility at all for the fact that three of his own children, including her mother, became 'ferocious alcoholics'.[28] But even the effort to adhere to traditional values inspired much better behaviour than her parents displayed: 'Whatever the people they came from had lived by just fell away in their generation. But they didn't have other values, to replace what they had lost. They were just careless.'[29] An early letter from her father to her mother, when he was stationed by the army in Donegal, strikes her as intensely poignant, with its words in the Irish language and its vision of loving cooperation between her parents. Her father was looking forward to his wife and their young children (Nuala and her older sister) joining him in the countryside, to enjoy rural life, the farm animals and good food. His daughter remarks: '"*A chroidhe dhil*", he begins. For years I could not read this letter. "Beloved heart", when they ended so badly!'[30] Eventually, her father became '"Terry O'Sullivan" through and through ... – the idealistic schoolteacher and lieutenant in the Army, Tomás O'Faolain, who had written to his "*chroidhe dhil*" with such affection and energy ... [was] overtaken by another identity.'[31] As Michael G. Cronin comments, it is thus not adherence to nationalism that creates the misery that blights O'Faolain's life and the lives of her siblings, but rather her parents' (or perhaps more specifically her father's) 'abandonment of the youthful idealism ... invested in their national culture'.[32]

In this, O'Faolain associates her father with several prominent Irish men of the time, especially Charles J. Haughey, three-time Taoiseach (prime minister) and a dominant political figure in Ireland from the late 1960s until the 1990s. Haughey was another bright boy from the north side of Dublin who had gone to the same school as her father. He also fell prey to the temptations that lay all around for these 'kings of a rainy country',[33] especially a new sexual licence. But despite their own loss of personal morality, O'Faolain believed that such men were still patriots of a certain kind. They felt privileged to have inherited the new state for which their parents' generation had struggled: 'Ireland was to be cherished as it had come to them ... it would be impertinence to seek to change it.' It was as if the willingness to innovate had been exhausted, and it was now possible to enjoy this 'marvellous new gift'.[34] The more radical aspirations of the revolutionaries could be set aside. Ireland was what it was: for example, it was passive rather than dissenting, capitalist rather than socialist, tribal rather than civic.[35] But O'Faolain nevertheless appreciates that the 'fun' that her father relished so much was real: she had doubts whether she could have resisted such lures.[36] After all, she too always delighted in pubs, chat and sexual intrigue. She considered that her father's Dublin was still Joyce's Dublin, where there was always plenty of serious talking. The city was inhabited by men who were 'scholars of the city, constantly commenting on it, and contributing to its complexity themselves'.[37] The place – for those who could escape from the petit bourgeois respectability of the new Ireland – had something in common with an older, communal social world: as she writes, 'the centre of Dublin used to be as inescapably social as a Travellers' camp'.[38] Of course, when O'Faolain herself experienced the last years of that Dublin (which lasted, she claimed, up until it was killed by the Celtic Tiger[39]), she did so in some senses as an 'honorary man'.[40] But inevitably, she also had to negotiate that world as a desiring woman who was often as reckless and appetitive as her male counterparts. She acknowledges that she failed to take account of women (like her mother) who were effectively confined to their suburban homes and marriages.[41] And her indifference to these female casualties had a lot in common with a more general Irish mindset. O'Faolain confesses that she and many others shared the bad faith of a politician such as Haughey: 'A lot of people know that our society is unjust and dishonest and double-faced. But, deep down, they think it's wonderful all the same, and that this is the most charming country in the world.'[42] This was a country (or at least a dominant class) proud of the measure of freedom and modernisation that had been achieved. People were prepared to overlook further difficult questions about fairness and equality; they had not even begun to think about the issue of gender. Valuable traces of an older identity persisted. These could be glimpsed, O'Faolain believed, in Irish people's love for the Irish language and in the distinctive form of their religious practices. But modern Ireland was not seriously committed to preserving or developing such things. Nor was it much given to political anger. At moments, she was herself disgusted by the pervasive complacency. But she was also vulnerable to the charm.

O'Faolain would eventually become an inhabitant of that same Irish public space where her father had lived like a lord. But the passions which drove her as a girl and young woman were the ones that she shared with her mother: a deep interest in literature and a yearning for romantic love. At school, her essays were always being read out while she (a 'confused and emotional exhibitionist') listened in embarrassment; English teachers valued her, and in return she adored them.[43] In some ways, reading and trying to work out her sexual or marital destiny went together. She was most interested in fiction, whether by Proust, Henry James or Judith Krantz ('I don't have to observe any hierarchy. But there is a hierarchy. There is great and less great and so on, down to trash'). Novels asked the questions she cared about: 'How do lives get lived? How is love found?'[44] But in adolescence, the desires of the body and the discipline demanded by education were at odds with each other. When at the age of thirteen she created a scandal by going home from dances with a married man, her parents arranged to send her away to a convent boarding school in Monaghan. In retrospect, she was immensely grateful for this intervention as it kept men and all the risks they represented in this era at bay for a few more crucial years.[45] When she left school, she won a scholarship to go to UCD; later, she was awarded scholarships at the universities of Hull and Oxford. But lacking any real sense of the possibility of a literary or intellectual career, she credits not (for example) vocational ambition but rather the 'strong forces of love and sex' for inspiring her to escape from the 'sinking ship' of her family home.[46] At UCD and living in Dublin – first as a student and then as a teacher – she was a citizen of an Irish Bohemia, where 'women and men were closest, in those days when the sexes were such strangers'.[47] But of course women and men were not equal even in that territory.

The young O'Faolain may not exactly have aspired to be what Beauvoir would categorise as an 'independent woman',[48] but neither was she entirely conventionally 'feminine' in her behaviour or attitudes. For example, she makes almost no reference to concerns about appearance or dress in the accounts of her romantic liaisons in *Are you somebody?* (Later on, there is an unsparing account of the physical effects of aging but no additionally oppressive sense that these should or could be 'fought' in order to stay attractive to men.) She takes it for granted that significant romantic relationships involve friendship of a particular kind: she recalls conversations, books, shared work and travel. O'Faolain does not gloss over the benighted sexual culture of Dublin, especially in her student days ('Sex was in everyone's mind, often obsessively. But no-one believed it was a healthy thing'[49]). She does not even broach the question of what conditions might have been like for gay or lesbian people. The consequences of pregnancy for young women were devastating. In one melancholy episode, she tells how an unmarried friend gave birth in secret in Belfast and O'Faolain brought the baby on the train back to Dublin to deliver him to a home – she recalls especially the complete silence of the infant on the long journey away from his mother.[50] She experienced betrayal and even violence in some of her own relationships. But despite the prevailing conditions, she felt lucky to have discovered sexual pleasure with her first important partner, Michael.[51] Indeed, the memoir is by no means a straightforward record of male perfidy and female victimhood: Michael, for example, was 'in every way a good influence' on her.[52] The only lover she actually despises, looking back, is the one who wrote her a letter – a piece of 'perfectly unqualified egotism', as she describes it – advising her that while it is all very well 'to prize highly "interesting people", brain knowledge and the world of books', all her 'man' will want is for her to look nice and for her eyes to 'heed' him.[53]

Thus, the memoir demonstrates that O'Faolain's dealings with men as a young adult involved some positive as well as some more dubious impulses. Both the gratifications and the pitfalls are perhaps bound up with what she refers to as her inclination to 'hero worship'[54] talented men: this could more accurately and sympathetically be described as her inability to separate erotic attraction from a burning curiosity about art and culture in general. But this was a society in which even young men were expected to have more knowledge, confidence and ambition than their female counterparts: thus women often sought access, through men, to things that they could not claim directly for themselves. O'Faolain recalls studying with Raphael Samuel or listening to Denis Donoghue (her Professor of English at UCD) as euphoric and formative experiences. Clearly, such moments had something in common with the excitement of falling in love with 'Rob' at Oxford (her pseudonym for art historian Tim Hilton – she describes being in his company as like enrolling in a 'one-person university'), or of the brief, intense affair she had with the critic and writer John Berger while they were working together on a documentary about the novelist Zola.[55] Indeed quite often in *Are you somebody?* it is actually unclear to what extent a particular relationship involved camaraderie, reverence or sex. Perhaps these things were not clearly distinguishable even at the time, especially as the repression of Ireland gave way to the era of 'sexual liberation' in England in the 1960s and 1970s. However, it is obvious that – even when they were themselves being unfaithful – the men she was close to generally returned her admiration and did not regard her as anything less than a valuable interlocutor.

Simone de Beauvoir is in many ways the exemplary image of the twentieth-century woman thinker. As Toril Moi argues, Beauvoir's key feminist work, *The second sex*, provides a compelling analysis of the sexual dilemmas of the female intellectual, who wants to be loved for her mind as well as physically desired: such a woman's erotic career is bound to be beset with difficulties, because she is trying to 'live the future' in what is still a sexist society.[56] Beauvoir's life-long commitment to fellow philosopher Jean-Paul Sartre was one 'solution' to this problem. They first bonded while arguing about intellectual issues together as students in Paris: Moi suggests that given Sartre's willingness to take Beauvoir's ideas seriously, it was no wonder 'that the erotico-theoretical dynamics flourished between Simone and Jean-Paul in the Luxembourg Gardens'.[57] However, over later decades their relationship would itself prove far from ideal, producing a great deal of emotional chaos: they both had many 'lesser' and in some cases rather exploitative dalliances with other people.[58]

However, it is a long way from the Left Bank to the pubs of Dublin. O'Faolain, although she excelled in her studies, did not define herself as a thinker. She was on friendly terms with some of the few woman scholars around: the critic Lorna Reynolds in UCD supported her by providing proof-reading work and invited her around for tea and cake.[59] (More improbably – and intriguingly – she reports that she once debated 'something about women' with Dame Helen Gardner, the first woman Merton Professor of English at Oxford, for the amusement of the all-male hearties of the Bullingdon Club.[60]) But she knew that women such as Reynolds and the historian Maureen Wall were not respected by the university: in her disputes with UCD, Reynolds, for example, was 'constantly embattled. And she never won'.[61] In some ways, matters might have been more straightforward for O'Faolain had she aspired to be a creative writer. It was generally allowed that women could occasionally produce distinguished literary works – albeit in an instinctive and spontaneous way. (This may help to account for Edna O'Brien's often-repeated insistence that she wrote *The country girls* almost without any conscious effort: she claims to remember 'the words tumbled out, like the oats on threshing day that tumble down the shaft, the hard pellets of oats funnelled into bags and the chaff flying everywhere'.[62]) But O'Faolain says that although lots of people in Dublin were constantly writing, she was possibly the only student of her whole generation 'who never wrote a poem or a story'.[63] She knew women writers who had been destroyed by male arrogance; she dwells especially on the brilliant Patricia Avis, none of whose works were published in her lifetime.[64] She knew also of exceptional survivors who were also warm and generous people – Mary Lavin, Maura Laverty, Leland Bardwell. These particular writers were mothers, but none had husbands: O'Faolain was not aware of 'any functioning wife or mistress who wrote'.[65] In literary Dublin, 'women had to either make no demands and be liked, or be much larger than life, and feared. It wasn't at all easy to be formidable and also desirable.'[66] You could only have a career (that is, 'express your gifts, and earn your own money') by either not having sex at all, or having it without getting pregnant.[67] Neither seemed feasible as long-term options. She assumed that notwithstanding her passion for English literature and her later professional competence as a teacher and broadcaster, the governing element in all these activities was the emotional one: she admitted that while 'there were new possibilities' in Ireland in the 1960s, 'what arrangement you came to with what sort of man was still the most important question by far for a woman'.[68] In her world, 'men had money and interesting lives and could show you things and bring you around'.[69] She had 'no sense of being at the start of a career. My aim in life was something to do with loving and being loved.'[70] Yet 'love' – eventually leading inexorably to marriage and motherhood – 'was supposed to work out differently for me than it had for any woman I actually knew'.[71]

O'Faolain describes herself, along with the people around her at this time, as living in a moral 'fog'; she includes her thoughts about, for example, John Berger's wife and children at the time of their affair in her book as an 'epitaph, almost, on unconsciousness'.[72] Even when she took part in the first big marches in London for women's liberation in the 1970s, she did not consider that she needed to interrogate her own behaviour.[73] Later, her sister expressed scepticism about her relationship with Harry Craig, a famously seductive but callous Hollywood scriptwriter: O'Faolain could understand, but not respond to, the feminist call to self-respect ('I wanted to know Harry, and the conditions of knowing him were not negotiable'[74]). She always remained doubtful that people of her generation could easily jettison the old sexist codes. At the same time, as the relationship with Rob disintegrated, she was faced with a new realisation of the degree to which she had been psychologically damaged as a child and of her deep compulsion to stay loyal to her mother's tragic fate. She later blamed the breakdown of her fifteen-year relationship with journalist and writer Nell McCafferty – the longest and 'by far the most life-giving' she had known – largely on these factors.[75] *Are you somebody?* was written during the time of near despair that followed that separation. Later again, after she had become a well-known writer and moved part-time to New York, she found that the same feelings of primal loneliness and unreasonable jealousy came between her and her final partner, John Low-Beer. She admitted that she even sometimes found it painful to witness his loving treatment of his own young daughter, as this involved him placing the child's needs above hers.[76] But she never regressed to a pre-feminist understanding of the world ('I could see sexism in operation everywhere in society: once your consciousness goes "ping" you can never again stop seeing that'[77]) and was adamant that in the sphere of sex and gender, Ireland was a 'much, much better place now than it used to be'.[78]

In this context, some readers of *Are you somebody?* note that O'Faolain's own time with McCafferty had 'marked less of a transformation than one would expect'; moreover, O'Faolain did not take the opportunity to reflect at any length on the reasons why her most enduring and supportive relationship had been with another woman.[79] Her *Late late show* interview in 1996 was remarkable in several respects, but its candour concerning a long-standing lesbian relationship between two well-known public figures was potentially hugely significant for Irish society at the time. However, McCafferty herself was shocked and upset by the way in which her former lover portrayed their life together. She observed that O'Faolain did not celebrate their intellectual and political companionship; in McCafferty's view, she also underplayed the sexual element of the relationship and had clearly been reluctant to describe herself as a lesbian.[80] McCafferty's own later memoir, *Nell*, was structured around a 'coming out' narrative mainly focused on the reactions of her mother and her community of origin in Derry's Bogside to her being a lesbian. Even given the prevailing prejudice against homosexuality in the culture at the time, was O'Faolain, to put it bluntly, simply being dishonest about her sexuality? Again, Beauvoir provides an interesting perspective. The chapter on lesbianism in *The second sex* – written, of course, in the very different circumstances of the 1940s – has proven controversial. Lesbianism is discussed there as another 'solution' to the sexuality of the 'independent woman' – in some ways, more reciprocal and nurturing than sex with men, but also potentially lacking the creative potential of encountering a radically different kind of body and psyche.[81] The sometimes disdainful tone of her treatment of female homosexuality has led to charges of bad faith against Beauvoir, given her own erotic entanglements with women. But in keeping with her broader existential philosophy, lesbianism is understood by her to be a choice rather than an element in a pre-given 'nature': it is a particular sexual option which may have positive or negative consequences depending on how it is lived out by a particular individual.[82] Living with another woman evidently did not in itself add up to a political identity for O'Faolain and nor did it solve the dilemmas she recurrently experienced in relationships. However, in one sense the fact of McCafferty's gender does seem to have been especially significant, as the latter seems to have played a rather 'maternal' role within the relationship. O'Faolain was particularly impressed by Nell's practical, domestic capabilities relative to her own: it was the first time she had enjoyed a comfortable refuge from the public world and this made her feel 'as if I had come in from being on the road almost since I was born'.[83] (This is possibly one of the reasons why she neglected to pay more attention to McCafferty's well-known public career in the book – she may have assumed that no Irish reader, at least, would have associated Nell primarily with traditional homemaking skills.) It is tempting to suggest that McCafferty acted like the mother Nuala had lacked – and indeed like her own mother in Derry, who was poorer even than Nuala's but lived at the heart of a warm and supportive community. By O'Faolain's own account, Nell was cheerful and endlessly reliable and loyal. Regardless, O'Faolain behaved too often in return like the mother *she* had actually had – dismissive, distant and indifferent.[84]

But O'Faolain is at least cautiously optimistic about the possibility of happier ways of managing relationships and families. (As we have seen, this is not a view shared by her near-contemporary Edna O'Brien, born just eight years earlier.) For example, O'Faolain regards her own parents' behaviour as shocking and anomalous: 'How did my mother and father not care more for the small children around them? How did they not pick them up, not comfort them? How did my father strap his defenseless sons with his army belt?'[85] She can only speculate that something had destroyed their instinctive responses: they were people damaged by the legacies of poverty and cultural upheaval and then further denatured by the longing for selfish pleasure that stemmed from these conditions. But she knew that others in similar or worse circumstances had nevertheless made better parents. Nor does it seem from her account that she believes that sexual relationships inevitably go awry: individuals with more self-respect, restraint and honesty – and with access to proper contraception – would surely fare better than her and so many of her contemporaries. And as we have seen, for all her complicated liaisons, she herself never quite conformed to Beauvoir's classic portrayal of the helpless *amoureuse* in *The second sex*:[86] while O'Faolain may have been subject to regular crises, she was clearly generally energetic, active and idealistic. One key reason that her own relationships became more desperate and abject, especially after the breakup with McCafferty in her fifties, was that in Ireland older women were not taken seriously as sexual beings. This was evidently not the case in the United States, where she met Low-Beer through an Internet dating site. Here we find a further example of fairly straightforward societal change – overcoming ageism – of which she thoroughly approves. However, there is more to O'Faolain's view of modern society than this heartfelt endorsement of sexual enlightenment – crucial though that may have been, especially in her native country. If that had not been the case, she would surely have been more inclined to remain in England, a country that was apparently far more hospitable than Ireland to women in its prevailing political culture and laws, especially after she became a feminist in the 1970s; she might also have been less drastically unsure and conflicted about living outside Ireland in the 1990s, at a time when she had plenty of money, a fulfilling career and a supportive partner in New York. O'Faolain talks about the 'fog' that enveloped her until her forties. This refers in part to the myths and delusions that prevented her from understanding the true situation of women. But it also refers to her alienation from Ireland: she was equally keen to overcome the latter.

One of O'Faolain's key complaints about Irish intellectual life ('if that is not too grand a word for it') in her youth was 'that it wasn't interested in the condition of Ireland. Nothing was happening. Northern Ireland was a far-off place'.[87] This was both a political and cultural malaise: the protest marches about poverty and unemployment of the 1950s had come to an end, and there was no stimulus for debate like that which had been provided by *The Bell* magazine.[88] Although the memoir includes anecdotes about the likes of Patrick Kavanagh and Flann O'Brien, O'Faolain shows no particular interest in their work or that of her other contemporaries. Indeed, among Irish writers she only talks in detail about Joyce (as a writer about Dublin) and especially Yeats (not so much for his Irish themes, but for his 'majestic tone'[89]). This does not suggest any overwhelming regard for mid-twentieth-century or later Irish literature. O'Faolain ascribes a general loss of ambition and engagement to all the time that was spent drinking in pubs by the kind of people 'who drifted around the Stephen's Green area, trading short-term pleasure for long-term strain and difficulty'.[90] Of course, she did this herself. Another sense of Irish possibility could be glimpsed only through the enthusiasms of a Seán Mac Réamoinn or a rare artistic work that made a deep impact on her and others such as Seán Ó Riada's score for the film *Mise Éire*.[51]

However, when O'Faolain decided to return to take up the job at RTÉ, she did not conceive simply of returning to this milieu. Inspired by the Merriman School, she discovered a new sense of belonging – even though in London she had never thought much about the Irish people she encountered on the streets ('My countrymen, my countrywomen, reeling and nodding, their faces swollen purple with alcohol and rough living'[92]) or even noticed 'the curtain going up on Northern Ireland'.[93] The move was inspired by a feeling for geography as well as curiosity about the past: she discovered that she had an 'intemperate love for the fabric of Ireland',[94] as well as for a few streets in the middle of Dublin. Finding out about Ireland helped her to find better ways to understand and possibly to heal her own wounds. This brought the comfort of an alternative, more capacious sense of home – she now identified with a broader community, beyond the confines of the family.

Taura S. Napier suggests that for female autobiographers in Ireland 'the concept of nation tends to limit severely, rather than complete, their apprehension of a full identity'.[95] However, both of O'Faolain's novels, *My dream of you* (2001) and *Best love, Rosie* (2009), feature central characters who are middle-aged women emigrants whose return to Ireland is ultimately redemptive – although the second novel also tells the story of an elderly woman who moves to America in pursuit of the personal freedoms that she never enjoyed in Ireland.[96] (The first-person narrator in *My dream of you*, in many ways an obvious autobiographical counterpart to O'Faolain herself, is named Kathleen – surely a nod to Cathleen Ní Houlihan, to her own mother and to *The country girls?*) Napier's conclusion is also belied, for instance, by two key passages (among others) from this pivotal section of O'Faolain's memoir:

> I flew to Shannon one August day and got myself across the country to the grey stone market-village of Scariff, in a mild, turquoise landscape of wooded hills and water-meadows and lakes and broad reaches of the River Shannon. I had never been

in rural Clare before. I could number on my fingers the days I had spent anywhere in rural Ireland. It was so beautiful, after the grey streets and dirty tube stations I walked through in London every day. The voices of the people were so expressive. At that School, I fell completely in love with an Ireland which turned out not to exist. Yet this visionary Ireland gave me the impetus to break my links with England. And it pointed me in the direction of the real Ireland I am getting to know now. If I hadn't encountered modern Ireland late in life, and if I hadn't – because of my ignorance and because of being away – thought it was magically interesting, I wouldn't have been so eager to learn about it. And learning about it has meant more and more to me with every passing year. A new concept of 'home' came into my life when I realised that Ireland, in all its aspects, present and past, was mine. That I belong to Ireland, just because I am Irish.[97]

An aspect of being vulnerable is that you are very open. I used to lie on the bed and look at the sky as it very, very slowly got dark on summer evenings. There was a kind of perfection of melancholy ... I thought nothing was happening, then. But my head was filling with riches. The mosaic of the country was being assembled inside it. The mysterious valleys between Leitrim and the sea with their oily black rivers full of fat trout. The stretch of plain – deepest, silkiest green – out beyond Lissadell with its abrupt end at the fierce beaches, as indifferently beautiful as when the little curled ships of the Armada foundered on their rocks. The Shannon welling up silently into its round pot, and then changing character, discovering youth, prancing out towards Dowra to begin its long slide down the country. Down through the silver-greys of the water-meadows, down past what were stone hotels, corn mills, old canal buildings, past the swans waiting beside half-submerged alder trees. In winter, when you get the train that crosses the Shannon river, it seems to go across the surface of a huge water into low country. In the wintry light, the train goes into the water and the water is steel, and carries the train. But Ireland isn't just landscape, but history, and present society. There was famine and brutality and emptiness in the country. And the damaged underclass I was part of in the afternoon pubs was as much a part of Ireland as its beauty.[98]

At such moments, the reconstitution of the self after a terrible defeat – as in the crucial scene at the strategically chosen Waterloo Station in the third volume of O'Brien's *The country girls* – is worked out as a kind of cartography. O'Brien's and O'Faolain's respective visions of the country are not entirely the same. Unlike the former, O'Faolain does not sponsor the idea of Ireland's 'femininity' in any explicit way, nor does she believe that a state of 'exile' is her personal destiny. She portrays ordinary social life and literary culture as thoroughly sexist but nevertheless she sees Ireland as considerably less segregated by gender than O'Brien does. In O'Faolain's experience, Irish women and men participate in cultural and religious rituals in shared spaces. One gets the impression from O'Brien of a marginalised or submerged world of Irish rural women, in particular – a realm of fearful whispering about sex or childbirth and implausible fantasies about glamour and escape. O'Faolain does not seem to have been exposed to or absorbed the romantic ideology of Mother Ireland when she was a child; by the time she became a writer, she was self-consciously in the business of questioning, rather than merely reproducing, the ideals of heterosexual romance. As a columnist and commentator working within the country, O'Faolain is obviously far more engaged with the local political scene – even when she can see no clear alternative to the present state of Ireland. But they certainly have an intense topophilia in common. They share a particular attachment to Co. Clare – O'Brien as a native of the county and O'Faolain as someone who chose to live there. But this phenomenon is not limited to that region. The adult Kate in *The country girls* can see again the faded map of Ireland on the classroom wall as the litany of ordinary place names she once recited in geography lessons becomes suddenly meaningful and even enchanting.[99] So too, O'Faolain recalls her first few years working in Irish television: 'RTÉ crews stayed in every second-class hotel in every town in Ireland. Bailieborough. Youghal. Birr. Dungarvan. Loughrea. Listowel. Cavan. Each of these names – every name in the country – evokes a whole complex of memoires and impressions, has a distinct taste, calls up an atmosphere as definite as a colour.'[100]

So, what specificity, pleasure or meaning does O'Faolain find in her vision of this 'imagined community'?[101] Slavoj Žižek suggests that the community of the nation is formed around a collective sense of a national 'Thing':

> If we are asked how we can recognize the presence of this Thing, the only consistent answer is that the Thing is present in that elusive entity called 'our way of life.' All we can do is enumerate disconnected fragments of the way our community organizes its feasts, its rituals of mating, its initiation ceremonies, in short, all the details by which is made visible the unique way in which a community *organizes its enjoyment.*[102]

For example, one important dimension of this community was the pub itself. As O'Faolain writes:

> There is hardly a spot in the country that doesn't have, near enough to hand, a nice, quiet, dim bar with the glasses all shiny and a peaceful barman. In those numinous spaces love-affairs are begun and ended, family crises are faced, criminals conspire, deals are done. I don't know how they manage such things in Iran, or Turkey, or Outer Mongolia. I don't know how anyone who doesn't use pubs can enjoy living here, or even be said to live here at all.[103]

She is keenly aware of the immense harm caused by some of Ireland's ways of doing things, but she is nevertheless intimately familiar with these mentalities and habits. For example, she is also an admirer of the Irish Catholic funeral. She wrote a column (pithily entitled 'Death') after attending the funeral in Dublin of an elderly woman related to her by marriage. Even after the shocking revelations about clerical sexual abuse and the protection of abusers by the Church, she comments that 'scandals are only part of the whole'. She points out that the hymns sung at Mrs Devitt's funeral ('Oh Mary we crown you with blossoms today, Queen of the Angels and Queen of the

May'. '*Ag Críost an Síol*'. 'Ave, Ave'.) were 'cornerstones of popular culture': 'If half the priests in the country were scandalous and the other half were covering up for them, this funeral would still have been a product of Irish Catholicism.'[104] She is not the same kind of person as Mrs Devitt and could not have such a funeral: she has not led a traditional, family-oriented life and she is an agnostic. But she recognises what feels 'right and natural' (such as the mourners gathering in a warm pub after the burial) – despite the well-deserved decline in the credibility of the clergy.[105] Most poignantly, O'Faolain elsewhere tells us that words from the Catholic prayer for the dead – 'may perpetual light shine upon them' – are a comfort to her when she thinks of her own little god-daughter, who died when she was only eight: she imagines her 'held somewhere in some golden radiance'.[106]

This is not to say that O'Faolain necessarily feels fully enclosed in this culture: 'I don't know that I can get very close to belonging, myself.'[107] Indeed, the placement of the final word in this sentence is a good example of her characteristic syntax, which softens rather than emphasises the authoritative first-person pronoun. Even to say 'I myself' would have weakened the communal cadence of a sentence that is apparently saying that she doubted her stake in communal feeling. She has enough distance to achieve analytic clarity, but a community – most conveniently defined in national terms – provides, for most of her career, both her subject matter and her audience. Fintan O'Toole notes her brilliant fashioning of a 'public "I"', through her characteristic blending of intimacy and reportage: for example, he points to the opening lines of so many columns, such as 'Imagine wanting to die', 'Laois had always seemed to me to be one of the flatter counties' or even 'Well ... I don't know...'.[108] These are the idioms of 'us'.

O'Faolain regarded high art, a category in which she had an absolute faith, as the realm in which the highest, universal ideals of love and community were expressed. Other kinds of work – local history, archaeology, journalism, documentary television, her own writing – arose out of and were limited in their impact to narrower horizons. But at their best, even scholars or programme-makers dedicated themselves to recovering and explaining how people had tried to make sense of their fates; this too represented a sincere if imperfect effort to broaden human understanding, using whatever media came to hand.

Art was special – and ultimately political. As a young woman, O'Faolain had been gripped by a 'Messianic belief' in 'the capacity of the academic study of English literature to change a person, utterly'.[109] She believed that 'the student was meant to learn to hold on to the self while going out of the self to enter into the literature that someone else had made – to find a poise between subjectivity and objectivity. This poise could then be rehearsed and made more stable with each access of understanding of a piece of art.'[110] She venerated not just artists, but those critics that could shed new light on particular works of art (or 'show' them to others, as she often puts it – she describes Donoghue 'showing' American poetry to the class in UCD or herself as attempting 'to show the texts properly' to exhausted night students[111]). She recalls seeing Beethoven's *Fidelio* in Covent Garden with Arnold Kettle, who taught English at the Open University. She asked him: 'Why is ensemble singing so beautiful? What makes it move us so much?' He said: 'People would be like that all the time, if they could.'[112] For O'Faolain, Kettle's comment, true to his socialism, was 'full of meaning'. As she puts it: 'Music prefigures whatever there can be of human and social perfection. There is an ideal, perfect, shape behind the appearance of things. There is the possibility of perfect communication, and to try to establish social justice is a way of moving towards it.'[113]

However, these political ideals were elusive; Ireland, for example, had become a 'neo-American, small-capitalist nation, whatever the rhetoric of our founding events'.[114] O'Faolain argued that Ireland's modernist literary achievement ('the single imaginative construct we might admire – what Irish men did with words') had not helped Irish women, in so far as these writers had so completely 'transcended the literal'.[115] In search perhaps of a new 'realism',[116] she turned instead to the new possibilities of documentary radio and television, including the educational experiment of the Open University. At RTÉ, she worked on pioneering programmes that featured ordinary women from all over Ireland speaking with each other or directly to camera, including *Women talking*, *The women's programme* and *Plain tales*.[117] Having insisted that 'every woman's condition is profoundly a shared one',

O'Faolain had once lamented that no one apart from Edna O'Brien had captured the specificity of Irish women's experience: no woman writer was willing to 'accomplish a description of us'.[118] Although it is unlikely that she consciously set out to address this lacuna (that is, the lack in Irish literature of what she called any 'startling, womanly statement'[119]) in her own work, she did in this one regard eventually acknowledge her own achievement. She had, she judged, in fact succeeded in being 'more candid than any Irish woman had yet been, outside the less direct forms of novels or poems'.[120]

O'Faolain did not regret her decision to live in Ireland 'where I know the politicians and where the woman beside me on a bus was at school with my aunt and where people take the trouble to try to talk well and where I can hear my own language, my own music, jokes I understand'.[121] She was prepared to defend some of its supposedly regressive features. She approved of the persistence of religious and other traditions because 'although, on a public level, one would like Ireland to be run in a reasonable, pluralist, modern way, there is more to living here than being a citizen'.[122] Unusually for a committed feminist, she was not simply horrified by the protracted debates about abortion in the 1980s: 'I'm not sorry that the fundamental mystery of life itself was examined at length by this society, even if it was so often done at the expense of the loving empathy that grown women deserve quite as much as the unborn do.'[123] In one column, she was particularly scathing about the demands that were heard every few years for RTÉ to stop broadcasting the Angelus call to prayer. She did not accept that evidence of popular devotions really constituted the problem faced, for example, by Irish Protestants.[124] After all, this was a country where you can 'hardly walk a hundred yards ... without coming across something – a cross scratched on a rock, maybe – which reminds you that the culture of the Irish people is a Christian one'.[125] She concluded: 'The human voice is not adequate to everything humans have to say. That's why there are bells. Reason is not always the appropriate discourse. That's why there are prayers.'[126]

However, O'Faolain also registered some of the exceptionally dark aspects of the society that she had described as 'floating on a sea of grief': she used this phrase at the very beginning of a wave of revelations about child abuse, correctly predicting that many terrible stories were still to come.[127] She too shared in this condition of sadness. But she knew it could produce a sense of helplessness and even of guilty complicity. She also felt this keenly in relation to Northern Ireland. 'The fact is,' she wrote, 'that Northern Ireland has been the most important thing about Ireland in my lifetime.'[128] At the outset of the Troubles, she had made some documentaries for British television that she later found laughably inadequate, especially in the way they exoticised the place: 'I had no option but to make the most noncommittal of films. They looked terrific. Tanks reared through the heat-distorted air behind burning gorse ...'[129] She could always hear, in Dublin, how 'at ease everyone is with remarks about the North full of a contempt and revulsion';[130] as we have seen, she was horrified by the regime of censorship at RTÉ.[131] But although she avoids disclosing outright disagreement, she was clearly uncomfortable with aspects of McCafferty's republican politics.[132] And so, while joking that she had 'taken on board decades of scathing reproach about us pleasure-loving, bourgeois-collaborationist Free Staters' from Northerners, she felt guilty when she forgot about Northern Ireland, but also uncomfortably aware 'that bearing it in mind never did me or it any good'.[133] She welcomed the Good Friday Agreement as a new start – 'a structure within which difference could possibly be managed' – one that would be accepted by weary people 'who have had so much of suffering that they've given up asking what it is for'.[134] O'Faolain celebrated the (in her view miraculous) fact that most people in Northern Ireland, 'in the face of a history designed to make them hate each other', did not in fact hate each other and believed that hatred was wrong.[135] Of course – as she knows – this could all seem like so much well-meaning hand-wringing. But at least it could be said that O'Faolain had made considerable efforts seriously to engage with Northern Irish society as a writer, including moving there for some months in the late 1990s. Problems even closer to hand – such as homeless people begging on the streets of Dublin – were surely evident to all her fellow citizens apart from the most wilfully complacent. But even without sponsoring any definite or coherent political programme that might promise an alternative to such injustices, her work searchingly analyses the connections between trauma, demoralisation and confusion on both a personal and a societal level. And she never suggests that it is possible just to accept things as they are. For example, she always refused the nostrums of Celtic Tiger Ireland, disdaining the shopping malls and consumerist pleasures of the economic boom time.[136]

O'Faolain once asserted that she did not know how 'we all got into a position of simultaneously feeling responsible for Ireland and being unable to do anything about it'.[137] It could be argued that such statements simply generalise her own sensibility. They certainly indicate that she accepts that she conforms to a national (and perhaps implicitly gendered) stereotype. She is to some degree disabled rather than motivated by empathy. The Jewish American art critic Clement Greenberg, with whom she had a desultory affair, complained to her that all Irish people were 'losers', 'soft and melancholy and depressed instead of out there in the bright, hard world, fighting for success'.[138] She remains loyal to this characterisation both of herself and of the whole society. Decades later, after she had in fact herself experienced so many unexpected triumphs, she felt torn between Ireland and America. She concedes that New York is a much more positive place for a childless, unmarried, agnostic, older woman such as herself. But she doesn't want to live 'somewhere that's good for you' – where she only really 'belongs' in one half of her lover's bed.[139]

Indeed, O'Faolain regularly associates such varying conceptions of the self with the experience of inhabiting different cultures or countries, especially England and America. She relates this ultimately to the Irish historical experience of emigration. The Great Famine was the historical catastrophe that uprooted and destroyed rural Irish-speaking communities on a devastating scale. Robert Scally's book, *The end of hidden Ireland: rebellion, famine and emigration* (1995), a study of the post-Famine clearance of the peasant population from one Co. Roscommon estate, was one key source for the passages on Irish history in *My dream of you*. In her review of the same book, she notes that the ordinary people had belonged 'to the intimately familiar spaces and shapes of their everyday surroundings, more than [to] any abstract idea of Ireland as a nation'.[140] But in flight from disease and hunger, they were forced into a new understanding of themselves. O'Faolain quotes Scally's description of how the Famine Irish, passing the southern coast of Ireland on the perilous voyage from Liverpool to New York, gathered at the sterns of the ships for their final glimpse of what they now understood was 'the country of their birth': 'that backward glance at the incongruous palms and gaily painted houses along the shore at Skibbereen was not only their last sight of Ireland but their first sight of themselves'.[141] Her own voyage back to Ireland, to the new discoveries of the west and of the adult lives and new families of her siblings, was self-consciously a reverse of this melancholy journey. Similarly, forsaking London is what also helps her protagonist in *My dream of you* to escape from the pursuit of futile love affairs; she takes sustenance instead from natural beauty, female friendships and other kinds of relationship. (O'Brien's heroines also try out such alternatives but even in old age 'passion' is missed.) O'Faolain's plots represent both a repudiation of the false promises of romance – one fully informed by a modern individualist feminism – and an affirmation of an older common life. Indeed, Clair Wills has commented that the frailty of the idea of the private self and the bourgeois family in twentieth-century Ireland 'allowed for the persistence of certain inherited patterns – such as identification with the community as much as the family, and a recourse to collective memory and shared symbolic forms of orientation, as much as to individual experience'.[142]

One way in which O'Faolain signals this sense of intimacy with Ireland is by refusing to write in a formal or abstract register. To declare, for example, that 'most people don't know anything about economics'[143] is also a way of announcing an identification with 'most' people: we do not anticipate that a lesson about banking or financial systems will follow such a statement. She does not aim to expose, satirise or transcend what she takes to be the language of 'ordinary' people or to distinguish herself through tone or vocabulary from popular wisdom. Faced with gross inequality in Ireland, the prevalent response may well be bafflement. But this is not the same as indifference: 'Ordinary people don't know why things are the way they are. They don't know how it comes about that some are fortunate and some are not. They feel themselves to be individually compassionate – they would make things better for other people if they could. But they see no route from themselves to the general good.'[144] Nor, of course, are such injustices confined to Ireland:

What's so great about pornography being the most popular industry on the internet? About walking through cities at night and seeing fellow human beings asleep in doorways? About watching the toil and privation men and women endure in order just to subsist – in mines in South America, in brothels, on their knees on peasant farms – while the likes of Paris Hilton and Stephanie of Monaco and Mike Tyson are worshipped? ... The fact has to be acknowledged that human beings have failed in the project of living together, and they've failed everywhere'.[145]

And the essential human values are also more general – muted, exploited but still real and widely shared. For example, O'Faolain wrote an indignant review of a performance of the musical *Les misérables* in Dublin in 1993. She argued that this production ripped off the 'human capacity to feel real pity':

The desire for justice is not just another plotline, another random narrative. Indeed, the authors turned to Hugo's book not just because it was out of copyright but because we can still respond emotionally to it. We can be relied upon to be thrilled by the idea of the poor finding peace and love and hope. We come out of the theatre under the impression that it was the articulation of that idea that was thrilling. But it's all a slick illusion: the poor are where they always were, outside the door of the theatre, and the authors of *Les misérables* are multimillionaires, thanks to the power of the rhetoric the show deploys.[146]

The concept of revolution, she asserts, is still powerfully affecting. While communism might be dead in Eastern Europe and everywhere else, 'what socialism stood for is not dead in ordinary life'.[147] For example, in literature, 'heroines aren't noted for greed and selfishness', and while it is uncomfortable to see ideals of freedom and equality served up as light entertainment for well-heeled theatregoers, somehow 'even a bourgeois audience recognises that there is a possible social goodness greater than anything they know.'[148]

But failing to see a clear 'route to the general good', the Irish produced stories and songs instead. Reflecting on the proclivity of her siblings, as well as herself, for near-compulsive writing, she asked if this was a pattern of response shared by her family, her sex and the country:

> Can a whole family be predisposed to deploy the written word, the way another family might play tennis? Or a whole gender – isn't it women, mostly who use journals to assert the fact of their existence? Or a whole nation? Didn't Ireland form itself around the experience of looking back so as to escape the experience of being unvalued by its colonial masters?[149]

However, the relationship between self-expression and trauma is complicated. O'Faolain's memoir transfixed readers just at the time when Ireland and the wider world were beginning to wake up to the horrifying prevalence of child abuse. Her own approach to the issue was clearly influenced by her unhappy memories of childhood – although she stressed that there was nothing comparably tragic about her personal fate.[150] She mentions in particular her shock at the revelations concerning the crimes of Marc Dutroux in Belgium (who tortured and murdered several young girls) and the case of Brendan O'Donnell in Co. Clare.[151] She wrote that the story of O'Donnell's early deprivation and suffering and of his brutal murders of a young mother, her son and a priest 'dislodged' something in her and was connected with the impulse to write her memoir.[152] (O'Donnell's killings also inspired Edna O'Brien's novel *In the forest*.) O'Faolain suggested in 1996 that

> until our times and the spread of the mass media, all this was hidden. Now, the depth and extent of the ordinary, everyday, endemic evil done to children is coming out. This is not a holocaust, but it is like the Holocaust in at least one way. It changes everything. The state of knowing and fully acknowledging the reality of child abuse is a state utterly different from not knowing it.[153]

Such revelations come at a psychic cost. The insights of feminism too – when O'Faolain realised how deeply she had absorbed prevailing attitudes, and how profoundly destructive these had been for her, her mother, Irish women and women in general – were destructive as well as emancipatory. But sorrow and rage at the violation of children were even more difficult to process and politicise. For example, after the sentence of the man who raped and impregnated a child in the 1994 so-called 'X' case was reduced to a mere four years, O'Faolain wrote of her 'despair' at living in a society 'streaked with rottenness': the problem was not just male violence but the mentality of those men in power, including judges, who were not themselves violent, but who 'forgive male violence and belittle its effects'.[154] She compared the effect of the judgment on her – and on Irish women – to how she had felt 'bowed' and 'lashed' as an Irish person as she stood in the Old Bailey in London listening as the Lord Chief Justice contemptuously threw out the appeal of the Birmingham Six.[155]

In O'Faolain's autobiographical writing, which has itself been described as 'one of the defining cultural events of *fin-de-siècle* Ireland',[156] there is no straightforward relationship between writing about such abysmal moments and achieving transformation at either the individual or collective level. However, this is belied to some extent by the way in which *Are you somebody?* was received by an international audience, especially in America. For the American edition, the subtitle 'The life and times of Nuala O'Faolain' – with its assumption of an audience already familiar with her name – was dropped in favour of 'The accidental memoir of a Dublin woman' and her opinion columns were not reprinted. This seems to suggest that the emphasis was placed here firmly on the 'life' rather than the 'times'. In any event, the book reached the top of the *New York Times* bestseller list. In the preface to the new edition O'Faolain tried to explain how her book had become 'an emotional episode, somehow, in public life, in Ireland'.[157] This produced a much more generic account of her identity than in the memoir itself – she was born, as she recalls it, one among nine children, among the 'teeming, penniless, anonymous Irish of the day', facing the oppressiveness of 'a conservative Catholic country'.[158] Transformation had initially come from without ('The world changed around Ireland, and even Ireland changed'[159]); she had both benefited from these changes and contributed to them. In the later memoir, she suggested that her timing was 'perfect' because some of the worst stories of life in Irish institutions and families had at that point been told and could no longer be 'managed by denial'.[160]

There is no question that *Are you somebody?* depended for a large part of its impact on its power as a confessional female narrative in a culture that had not produced many significant works in this mode, despite its centrality to the recent development of feminism.[161] Rita Felski defines the feminist confessional narrative as one in which 'the *representative* aspects of experience, rather than those that mark the protagonist/narrator as unique ... [are] emphasized in relation to the notion of a communal female identity'.[162] O'Faolain memorably articulates the reasons that readers – and especially, perhaps, women – might be attracted to such works: 'My life burned inside me. Even such as it was, it was the only record of me, and it was my only creation, and something inside me would not accept that it was insignificant ... I've never done anything remarkable; neither have most people. Yet most people, like me, feel remarkable.'[163] She did not set out with any therapeutic purpose in mind, either in relation to herself or other people. However, when thousands of O'Faolain's readers (male and female) wrote confiding letters to her about their own experiences, she evidently felt a strong desire to advise or help them.[164] Such people were obviously responding to what Felski describes as the 'longing for, and belief in, the value of intimacy'[165] typically expressed in confessional stories. It is also clear that she cites what Liam Harte calls a 'narrative of patriarchal nationess' as an inhibition that she eventually managed to overcome (albeit that there is a much heavier stress on the patriarchy than on the nation throughout O'Faolain's writing).[166] But there are also ambiguities in her achievement.

To begin with, O'Faolain was dubious about the capacity of even the most accomplished storytelling to 'heal' either the narrator or the reader.[167] For example, she never felt that she was 'over' her grief for her mother. She said, semi-jokingly, that while she did not expect any further sympathy for her obsession with a 'pitiably selfish Irish housewife with a drink problem', nevertheless the truth was that, 'if anything, I restrain myself about her'.[168] Her memoir left many people feeling misrepresented and hurt, including 'Rob', McCafferty and her brothers and sisters.[169] Of course, there was the large and unresolvable problem that while modernisation led to more awareness of sexism and of sexual exploitation, it also facilitated such horrors as sex tourism for paedophiles.[170] In addition, there was a paradox involved in any reader taking O'Faolain's story, which was so unusual for a woman of her generation, as typical of women's conditions in Ireland. *Are you somebody?* was the record of an exceptional person – a high-profile, BBC-trained, Oxford graduate with an unusually interesting private life. In this regard, the book more closely resembles an example of 'female literary autobiography', along the lines of works by Mary McCarthy or Nathalie Sarraute, than it does some other prominent examples of confessional feminist narrative.[171] In one sense, O'Faolain need not have worried that she had concentrated so much on personal and sexual relationships in her life at the expense of activities that might have demanded more sustained self-belief or discipline – as it turned out, reflecting on those various collaborative projects and romantic liaisons turned out itself to *be* her most memorable work. However, when she tries to give counsel to other unhappy women (or men), she does not dwell particularly on the importance of trying to achieve more enlightened relationships or on the value of self-realisation through work of the kind she had engaged in; instead she concentrates on sources of comfort and meaning that she hopes are more democratically available – friends, animals, music, the natural world. She is aware that these are the remedies that 'every magazine article peddles'.[172] Nevertheless, aside from an elusive all-satisfying passion, these are 'all there is': 'I don't believe that life offers us many consolations of the same size and weight as it offers us hurts. But we can patch things over with what life does offer.'[173]

In this way, O'Faolain struggles to offer a balanced account of the life of the independent woman. This resembles the life that has been lived by Edna O'Brien in a pioneering and courageous fashion, although rarely celebrated by her. These are both exemplary, if contradictory, feminist lives – perhaps exemplary *because* contradictory. But O'Faolain tended to be perceived, especially in the eyes of her American readers, as an image of the traditional, downtrodden, voiceless Irish woman (such as her mother), albeit one who had made an abrupt transition to a more joyful world of opportunity – in a kind of feminist version of Frank McCourt's *Angela's ashes*.[174] This is to overlook the fact that the modern, autonomous Irish woman's choices and dilemmas, as explored by O'Faolain, were new and complicated. And although Ireland as it was presented in the first memoir was certainly gloomy, she was aware that it could at the same time quite readily be sentimentalised or stereotyped as the exotically primitive backdrop to her lucky 'escape'. She and her book were embraced by America – or more specifically Irish America. It was the era of the Peace Process and the first phase of the Celtic Tiger; the apparent uplift of the times was difficult to resist. She first promoted her book alongside McCourt on a St Patrick's Day edition of the television show *Good morning America*, drinking green soup and singing 'When Irish eyes are smiling' for a nation-wide breakfast-time audience. They were asked about politics; or rather they were asked, 'How come you beautiful, beautiful Irish people fight with each other?' But she comments: 'The kitsch was a liberation: it was like coming out of an Ireland leached of its malice and into a bright place where identity is a matter for lighthearted celebration, not bitter division.'[175] But despite the appeal of all this, she had 'something thicker than blood, more intimate than love with Ireland, the actual place, and Ireland the concatenation of past, present and personal experience',[176] and she did not choose either to leave it altogether or to contemplate it from a simplifying distance. In its very brokenness and discontinuity, the country resembles a record of her own experience. Thinking of a Christmas Day walk, alone with her dog, looking out on the Atlantic above Fanore in Co. Clare, she ends her memoir by reflecting:

> Behind me, up in the Burren, nothing knitted together. There's a pre-historic burial site. There's a village abandoned in the Famine. There's a tiny twelfth-century church. There's a holy well. There's a mound of shells near a cooking-pit. Each thing is itself, discrete. Near each other, and made from the same material, but never flowing into each other. That's how the life I have described here has been. There has been no steady accumulation: it has all been in moments.[177]

In these images, the representative life of a modern Irish woman finds a counterpart in the ruins and revivals legible in the landscape.

However, O'Faolain realises that in attempting to respect the history of a people – or of communities anywhere – it is easy to turn the authentically 'popular' (in the sense of 'of the people') into the merely 'popular' (in the sense of light, commercial or mass produced). Even after she becomes an author of books, rather than a journalist or a programme-maker, she has no notion of herself producing Great Art. She is not remotely anxious about the issue. She is happy to be more democratic and ordinary, one might even say 'feminine' – indeed, she is astounded and pleased to be received so sympathetically by so many grateful readers. But there is a tension between her own sensibility and the advice-giving persona she felt compelled to adopt after so many people turned to her for comfort and guidance. This is comically dramatised in O'Faolain's second novel: when the Irish narrator decides to try out some 'self-help' writing in a 'Celtic' mode for American readers, her publisher has to plead with her to lay off the quotes from Rilke and all the 'European gloom'.[178] O'Faolain wants to be accessible but to avoid mere cliché. Sometimes, she seeks to explain the grandeur of literature or classical music in everyday language; elsewhere, she looks for the wisdom in the supposed banalities of popular art. However, O'Faolain ultimately explained the impact of her own life-writing by comparing it to the popular, collective form of the ballad – even though this very form could so often lend itself to schmaltz (as in her American television experience of singing 'When Irish eyes are smiling'). O'Faolain considered that when readers responded to her in her confessional work, they were not looking for practical help, or to become writers themselves: they just wanted to join in, and be heard. She suggested that:

> It's not what you have but what you have lost that links the reader and writer. The longing to repair loss is in the rhythm and tone of the written piece, not in its words. The rhythm is where the reader senses the writer's truthfulness, as unerringly, I think, as the infant senses whether the person who is holding it loves it. The writer and the reader are always singing along together, both confident of the tune, but the writer more certain of the words than the reader.[179]

It is a modest gesture for a writer to compare herself to a singer of ballads, but it does emphasise the shared and sociable elements of her art.

But such a sense of hard-won togetherness, based on an appreciation of individual tragedy and the difficulty of maintaining love or collective feeling, was fragile. When O'Faolain received her fatal diagnosis in 2008, she told Finucane that it was as if 'the world had turned its back on her'.[180] She concluded the interview with a request that the broadcast end with a particular song:

> And yet I want to mention one thing that you might play at the end, particularly for dying people, but I picked up little bits here and there about Ireland, largely at the Merriman Summer School, which is one of the great things in my life, a song I heard a few years ago 'Thois i lar an glanna' – a kind of modern song sung by Albert Fry and other Donegal singers. And the last two lines are two things, asking God up there in the heavens, even though you don't believe in him, to send you back last night even though you know it can't happen. Those two things sum up where I am now [she weeps].[181]

The final lines of the song are:

> A rún mo chléibh nár mhilis
> Ár súgradh croí 's nár ghairid
> Ó 's a Rí na glóire gile
> Tabhair ar ais an oíche aréir.

And in English:

> Love of my heart, wasn't our
> heart playing sweet and short?
> Oh King of the bright glory
> Bring back last night.[182]

She knows this as a song sung by a male singer to a woman, but it could be the other way around (or any way around). But such songs, although addressed to God or to one other person, are meant for communal performance. Because of this, missing 'oíche aréir' (last night) suggests the longing for chat and good company as well as the afterglow of passion. As O'Faolain had written, the audience senses the sincerity of a writer or a singer in the way that 'the infant senses the person who is holding it loves it'. Such an image of care and trust avoids the gendered and (for her) troubled idea of maternal love. There is another kind of love, apart from the sexual and the familial: here, in her last public words, she remembers learning about its joys and its ultimate transience, through Irish, in Co. Clare.

Notes

1 Nuala O'Faolain, *Are you somebody?: the life and times of Nuala O'Faolain* (Dublin: New Island Books, 1996), p. 9.
2 Nuala O'Faolain, *Almost there: the onward journey of a Dublin woman* (London: Penguin, 2003), p. 16.
3 O'Faolain, *Are you somebody?*, p. 9.
4 O'Faolain, *Almost there*, p. 55.
5 O'Faolain, *Almost there*, p. 55.
6 O'Faolain, *Almost there*, pp. 56–7.
7 O'Faolain, *Almost there*, p. 59.
8 John Waters, *Beyond consolation* (London: Continuum, 2010), p. 1. A podcast of O'Faolain's interview with Finucane is available at https://soundcloud.com/keessentials/nuala-ofaolains-interview-on (accessed 25 June 2018).
9 Waters' own answer was that O'Faolain's anguish arose from the secular mentality that she herself had sought to promote in Ireland; as we will see here, this somewhat misrepresents O'Faolain's views on religion. See Waters, *Beyond consolation*, pp. 9–10. Bridget English also discusses the interview as casting significant light on evolving contemporary attitudes to death and dying in her *Laying out the bones: death and dying in the modern Irish novel* (Syracuse, NY: Syracuse University Press, 2017), pp. 1–5; English describes this as a 'visceral moment in Irish culture', p. 4.
10 O'Faolain, *Are you somebody?*, p. 10.
11 Luke Dodd, 'Nuala O'Faolain: obituary', *Guardian* (12 May 2008).
12 Margaret O'Callaghan, 'Women and politics in independent Ireland, 1921–68', in Bourke *et al.* (eds), *The Field Day anthology*, vol. 5, p. 134.
13 O'Faolain, *Are you somebody?*, p. 140.
14 O'Faolain, *Are you somebody?*, p. 34.
15 O'Faolain, *Almost there*, p. 236.
16 O'Faolain, *Are you somebody?*, p. 208.

17 O'Faolain, *Are you somebody?*, p. 211.
18 O'Faolain, *Are you somebody?*, p. 211.
19 O'Faolain, *Are you somebody?*, p. 11.
20 O'Faolain, *Almost there*, p. 84.
21 O'Faolain, *Are you somebody?*, pp. 13–14.
22 O'Faolain, *Are you somebody?*, p. 14.
23 Nuala O'Faolain, *A more complex truth: selected writing* (Dublin: New Island Books, 2010), p. 279.
24 O'Faolain, *Are you somebody?*, p. 17.
25 O'Faolain, *Are you somebody?*, p. 12.
26 O'Faolain, *A more complex truth*, p. 246.
27 O'Faolain, *Are you somebody?*, p. 47.
28 O'Faolain, *Are you somebody?*, pp. 13–14.
29 O'Faolain, *Are you somebody?*, p. 21.
30 O'Faolain, *Are you somebody?*, p. 16.
31 O'Faolain, *Are you somebody?*, p. 47.
32 Cronin, *Impure thoughts*, p. 215.
33 O'Faolain, *A more complex truth*, p. 246.
34 O'Faolain, *Are you somebody?*, p. 251.
35 O'Faolain, *Are you somebody?*, p. 252.
36 O'Faolain, *A more complex truth*, p. 246.
37 O'Faolain, *A more complex truth*, p. 138.
38 O'Faolain, *A more complex truth*, p. 136.
39 O'Faolain, *A more complex truth*, p. 138.
40 O'Faolain, *Almost there*, p. 22.
41 O'Faolain, *Are you somebody?*, p. 91.
42 O'Faolain, *Are you somebody?*, p. 251.
43 O'Faolain, *Are you somebody?*, p. 31.
44 O'Faolain, *Are you somebody?*, pp. 34–5.
45 O'Faolain, *Are you somebody?*, p. 42.
46 O'Faolain, *Are you somebody?*, p. 53.
47 O'Faolain, *Are you somebody?*, p. 68.
48 See Beauvoir, *The second sex*, pp. 689–724.
49 O'Faolain, *Are you somebody?*, p. 87.
50 O'Faolain, *Are you somebody?*, p. 58.
51 O'Faolain, *Are you somebody?*, p. 69.
52 O'Faolain, *Are you somebody?*, p. 69.
53 O'Faolain, *Are you somebody?*, p. 60.
54 O'Faolain, *Are you somebody?*, p. 93.
55 See O'Faolain, *Are you somebody?*, pp. 54, 100, 101, 75–6.
56 Toril Moi, *Simone de Beauvoir: the making of an intellectual woman* (Oxford: Blackwell, 1994), p. 198.
57 Moi, *Beauvoir*, p. 253.

58 See Moi on feminists' impatience with Beauvoir's inexhaustible loyalty to Sartre; Moi, *Beauvoir*, pp. 253–5.
59 O'Faolain, *Are you somebody?*, p. 90.
60 O'Faolain, *Are you somebody?*, p. 97.
61 O'Faolain, *Are you somebody?*, p. 90.
62 O'Brien, *Country girl: a memoir*, p. 128.
63 O'Faolain, *Are you somebody?*, p. 65.
64 O'Faolain, *Are you somebody?*, pp. 76–7.
65 O'Faolain, *Are you somebody?*, p. 77.
66 O'Faolain, *Are you somebody?*, p. 8.
67 O'Faolain, *Are you somebody?*, p. 90.
68 O'Faolain, *Are you somebody?*, p. 88.
69 O'Faolain, *Are you somebody?*, p. 89.
70 O'Faolain, *Are you somebody?*, p. 105.
71 O'Faolain, *Are you somebody?*, p. 86.
72 O'Faolain, *Are you somebody?*, pp. 92, 76.
73 O'Faolain, *Are you somebody?*, p. 140.
74 O'Faolain, *Are you somebody?*, p. 143.
75 O'Faolain, *Are you somebody?*, p. 175.
76 See O'Faolain, *Almost there*, p. 251.
77 O'Faolain, *Are you somebody?*, p. 140.
78 O'Faolain, *Are you somebody?*, p. 28.
79 Cronin, *Impure thoughts*, p. 214.
80 See McCafferty, *Nell*, pp. 402–6.
81 See Beauvoir, *The second sex*, pp. 436–7.
82 Beauvoir, *The second sex*, p. 444.
83 O'Faolain, *Are you somebody?*, p. 178.
84 O'Faolain, *Are you somebody?*, p. 176.
85 O'Faolain, *Are you somebody?*, p. 197.
86 See Beauvoir, *The second sex*, pp. 652–79.
87 O'Faolain, *Are you somebody?*, p. 64.
88 O'Faolain, *Are you somebody?*, pp. 63, 64.
89 O'Faolain, *Are you somebody?*, p. 33.
90 O'Faolain, *Are you somebody?*, p. 108.
91 O'Faolain, *Are you somebody?*, p. 65.
92 O'Faolain, *Are you somebody?*, p. 125.
93 O'Faolain, *Are you somebody?*, p. 124.
94 O'Faolain, *Are you somebody?*, pp. 198–9.
95 Taura S. Napier, 'Pilgrimage to the self: autobiographies of twentieth-century Irish women', in Liam Harte (ed.), *Modern Irish autobiography: self, nation and society* (London: Palgrave Macmillan, 2007), p. 85.
96 See Jill Franks's exploration of the theme of the return to Ireland

and the rediscovery of 'Irish communal values' in O'Faolain's autobiographical works and her fiction: *British and Irish women writers and the women's movement*, especially p. 185.
97 O'Faolain, *Are you somebody?*, p. 152.
98 O'Faolain, *Are you somebody?*, pp. 161–2.
99 O'Brien, *The country girls trilogy*, p. 456.
100 O'Faolain, *Are you somebody?*, p. 156.
101 This famous definition of modern nationality is taken from Benedict Anderson's *Imagined communities: reflections on the origin and spread of nationalism*, revised edition (London: Verso, 1991).
102 Slavoj Žižek, *Tarrying with the negative* (Durham, NC: Duke University Press, 1993), p. 201.
103 O'Faolain, *Are you somebody?*, pp. 209–10.
104 O'Faolain, *Are you somebody?*, pp. 346–7.
105 O'Faolain, *Are you somebody?*, pp. 347.
106 O'Faolain, *Are you somebody?*, p. 188.
107 O'Faolain, *Are you somebody?*, p. 345.
108 Fintan O'Toole, 'Foreword', in O'Faolain, *A more complex truth*, p. xiii.
109 O'Faolain, *Are you somebody?*, p. 106.
110 O'Faolain, *Are you somebody?*, p. 106.
111 O'Faolain, *Are you somebody?*, pp. 54, 107.
112 O'Faolain, *Are you somebody?*, p. 128.
113 O'Faolain, *Are you somebody?*, p. 128.
114 O'Faolain, 'Irish women and writing in modern Ireland', p. 1601.
115 O'Faolain, 'Irish women and writing in modern Ireland', p. 1603.
116 O'Faolain, 'Irish women and writing in modern Ireland', pp. 1603–4.
117 O'Faolain, *Are you somebody?*, pp. 161–2.
118 O'Faolain, 'Irish women and writing in modern Ireland', pp. 1604–5. In later years, however, O'Faolain was one of the first commentators to condemn the under-representation of Irish women writers and the neglect of feminist concerns in the first three volumes of *Field Day anthology of Irish writing*, edited by her former UCD colleague, Seamus Deane, in 1991. For a comprehensive account of the controversy and of O'Faolain's contribution to the feminist critique of the anthology (which led eventually to the production of a further two substantial volumes on 'Women's writing and traditions' in 2002, edited by a team of women scholars), see Catriona Crowe, 'Testimony to a flowering', *The Dublin Review*, 10 (Spring 2003), https://thedublinreview.com/article/testimony-to-a-flowering (accessed 25 June 2018).
119 O'Faolain, 'Irish women and writing in modern Ireland', p. 1602.

120 O'Faolain, *Almost there*, p. 59.
121 O'Faolain, *Almost there*, p. 235.
122 O'Faolain, *Are you somebody?*, p. 351.
123 O'Faolain, *Are you somebody?*, p. 323.
124 O'Faolain, *Are you somebody?*, p. 339.
125 O'Faolain, *Are you somebody?*, p. 336.
126 O'Faolain, *Are you somebody?*, p. 339.
127 She is commenting on the mistreatment of children in the industrial school at Goldenbridge run by the Sisters of Mercy which came to light in the late 1990s; she observes that the incarceration of women who had children outside marriage was among the many issues yet to be addressed by Irish society. O'Faolain, *Are you somebody?*, p. 283.
128 O'Faolain, *A more complex truth*, p. 167.
129 O'Faolain, *Are you somebody?*, p. 135.
130 O'Faolain, *A more complex truth*, p. 164.
131 See O'Faolain, 'If I had my time back'.
132 O'Faolain, *Are you somebody?*, p. 184.
133 O'Faolain, *A more complex truth*, p. 267.
134 O'Faolain, *A more complex truth*, pp. 112–13.
135 O'Faolain, *A more complex truth*, p. 163.
136 See her account of new Dublin shopping centres during the boom as 'temples to trade'; O'Faolain, *A more complex truth*, pp. 105–9.
137 O'Faolain, *Are you somebody?*, p. 137.
138 O'Faolain, *Are you somebody?*, p. 146.
139 O'Faolain, *Almost there*, pp. 235–6.
140 O'Faolain, *A more complex truth*, p. 132.
141 Robert Scally, quoted by O'Faolain, *A more complex truth*, p. 134.
142 Wills, 'Women, domesticity and the family', p. 37.
143 O'Faolain, *Are you somebody?*, p. 289.
144 O'Faolain, *Are you somebody?*, p. 288.
145 O'Faolain, *A more complex truth*, p. 258.
146 O'Faolain, *A more complex truth*, pp. 57–8.
147 O'Faolain, *A more complex truth*, p. 58.
148 O'Faolain, *A more complex truth*, p. 59.
149 O'Faolain, *Almost there*, p. 182.
150 For example, see O'Faolain, *Are you somebody?*, p. 188.
151 See O'Faolain, *A more complex truth*, p. 102; *Are you somebody?*, p. 187.
152 O'Faolain, *Are you somebody?*, p. 187.
153 O'Faolain, *A more complex truth*, p. 102.
154 O'Faolain, *Are you somebody?*, p. 317.
155 O'Faolain, *Are you somebody?*, pp. 319–20.

156 Cronin, *Impure thoughts*, p. 214.
157 Nuala O'Faolain, *Are you somebody?: the accidental memoir of a Dublin woman* [revised US edition of *Are you somebody?: the life and times of Nuala O'Faolain*] (New York: Henry Holt, 1998), p. 189.
158 O'Faolain, *Are you somebody?* [US edition], p. 3.
159 O'Faolain, *Are you somebody?* [US edition], p. 3.
160 O'Faolain, *Almost there*, p. 59.
161 As O'Faolain had complained a decade earlier, when she stated that no Irish feminist used 'imaginative modes' in a way that exhibited 'philosophical range'; see 'Irish women and writing in modern Ireland', p. 1602. Some Irish feminists produced memoirs of the Irish women's movement and of their own lives – see, for example, June Levine's *Sisters: the personal story of an Irish feminist* (Dublin: Ward River Press, 1982) – but no other work rivals the popularity of O'Faolain's autobiography.
162 Rita Felski, 'On confession', in Sidonie Smith and Julia Watson (eds), *Women, autobiography, theory: a reader* (Madison: University of Wisconsin Press, 1998), p. 85; emphasis in original.
163 O'Faolain, *Are you somebody?* [US edition], pp. 4–5.
164 In the American edition of *Are you somebody*, O'Faolain records her delight at the warm responses of readers ('I never imagined awakening something a bit like love', p. 189). However, in the later memoir, it is obvious that hearing about so much distress, and feeling obliged to respond to it in some useful way, took a considerable emotional toll on her (see *Almost there*, pp. 129–42).
165 Felski, 'On confession', p. 91.
166 See Liam Harte, 'Introduction', in Liam Harte (ed.), *Modern Irish autobiography: self, nation and society* (London: Palgrave Macmillan, 2007), p. 8.
167 O'Faolain, *Almost there*, p. 36.
168 O'Faolain, *Almost there*, p. 186.
169 As O'Faolain records in the chapter entitled 'Germination' in *Almost there*.
170 See, for example, the narrator's horror at the sexualised behaviour of a young girl who is living with two other children on the edge of a highway in Manila, in *My dream of you*, pp. 11, 499. This disturbing scene lingers in the memory of the central woman character in the novel in the same way that discoveries about child abuse unsettled and haunted O'Faolain in the 1990s.
171 I am drawing here on Felski's distinction between this more stylised literary genre and feminist confession; see 'On confession', p. 83.
172 O'Faolain, *Almost there*, p. 152.

173 O'Faolain, *Almost there*, p. 152.
174 *Are you somebody?* appeared in the same year as Frank McCourt's immensely successful memoir of a (comically exaggerated) miserable Irish childhood in Limerick and of his subsequent migration to America, the best-selling *Angela's ashes*; McCourt became a champion of O'Faolain's book and wrote a cover recommendation for the US edition.
175 O'Faolain, *Almost there*, pp. 62–4.
176 O'Faolain, *Almost there*, p. 236.
177 O'Faolain, *Are you somebody?*, p. 200.
178 Nuala O'Faolain, *Best love, Rosie* (Dublin: New Island Books, 2009), pp. 169, 77.
179 O'Faolain, *Almost there*, pp. 140–1.
180 See O'Faolain, interview with Finucane.
181 See O'Faolain, interview with Finucane.
182 For lyrics and translation of 'Tráthnóna beag aréir' (an alternative title of the song), see www.celticlyricscorner.net/clannad/trathnona.htm (accessed 25 June 2018).

5
Anne Enright: taking the Green Road

Anne Enright, one of Ireland's most celebrated writers, the first Irish female winner of the Man Booker prize (in 2007) for her novel *The Gathering*, and from 2015 to 2018 the inaugural Laureate for Irish Fiction sponsored by the Arts Council, cannot be usefully addressed or described as a confessional artist in the style of Edna O'Brien or Sinéad O'Connor. However, she has discussed aspects of her own life in interviews, reviews and essays, including numerous contributions to the *Guardian*, the Diary column of the *London Review of Books* and in a memoir of early motherhood, *Making babies* (2004). Unlike other women I discuss here, Enright does not profess a passionate attachment to Ireland. Nor does she use the language of trauma in relation to herself or her own family to any great extent: for example, she often writes affectionately about her supportive parents and husband. To begin with at least, the country was not in its own right an object of investigation in her fiction ('I don't write about Ireland so much as from Ireland.'[1]). Although she was born in 1962, four years earlier than Sinéad O'Connor, in some regards Enright seems the most 'contemporary' of the figures considered in this book – the one least likely to suggest that she is, personally, a casualty of Irish history.

At an early stage of her career, her fellow novelist Colm Tóibín pointed to Enright's work as an example of the 'waning of national themes in Irish writing',[2] a condition that some Irish commentators at that time and since had come to identify with a new 'maturity'. He stated that she wrote about a Dublin that was 'post-feminist and, of course ... post-nationalist'.[3] Tóibín implies that the settlement, or at least the soothing, of old historical disputes emancipated the Irish writer to engage with other concerns. Enright's public persona is ironic, smart and mischievous. She has declared that there is no place for 'anger' or for 'ideology' in her art.[4] From the outset, journalists constantly asked her about Ireland and about gender. She took the line that the politics of identity, even in relation to identities taken to be oppositional, was limiting and reductive: 'I can't be Irish all day long; it's too much of an effort. I can't be a woman all day long; the work of it is far too strenuous ... It needs constant attention; I can't be bothered.'[5] Her earlier novels were predominantly set against the backdrop of the suburban Dublin of her childhood in the 1970s and 1980s; this was broadly understood as a rapidly modernising society locked in a struggle with traditional Catholic mores. But in what might fairly be described as her mature fiction so far – *The gathering* (2007), *The forgotten waltz* (2011) and *The Green Road* (2015) – she deals with the transformation of that Irish middle-class world by the Celtic Tiger boom, as well as with topics more familiar from earlier traditions in twentieth-century Irish fiction, including the dysfunctional Irish family, child sexual and institutional abuse, emigration, rural Ireland and historical memory. During the last few years, she has also lectured and written about Edna O'Brien and other Irish women writers, about scandals involving women and children (in particular, the discovery of hundreds of infant remains at a former Mother and Baby Home at Tuam, Co. Galway) and about abortion. To paraphrase her own words of refusal, it looks increasingly as though being an 'Irish' writer is in fact a job that she has 'applied for'.[6] Or we could perhaps say that the more she wrote – regardless of her conscious intentions, perhaps – the more she became an Irish (and a more accomplished) writer. The 'Ireland' of fiction, at first held at arm's length, became real; or at least it was no longer the excluded fiction of 'Ireland'.

Enright grew up in a fairly comfortable area of south Dublin. Her parents were civil servants; her mother was from the (less affluent) north side of the city and her father had arrived in the city as a young man from a small farm in Clare (the county in which much of *The Green Road* is set). Comparing the intense focus on social class in the English realist novel to its Irish equivalent, Enright noted that this new Irish bourgeoisie did not cultivate much of a snobbish sense of privilege: 'We were reared not to judge people by their things or class ... The project when I was growing up was the accomplishment of the nation-state, so we were separate, we were Irish. Poor Irish and rich Irish were part of the same project.'[7] (It could be argued that a sense of pride in the attainment of independence also tended to blind those who had fared modestly well in the new state to the persistence of deep social divisions.) Enright has never engaged in her fiction with the issue of Northern Ireland; she suggests that 'my generation is sloppy about the North. It's gone on too long, too boring, too horrible'.[8] So she laid imaginative claim primarily to the terrain of suburban

Dublin – although in modes that were dominated by fantasy and the surreal. Tóibín reached for comparisons with Laurence Sterne or Flann O'Brien as earlier exponents of an absurdist Irish fiction.[9] She herself invokes Joyce as, for her, an enabling rather than inhibiting presence. She suggests that male Irish writers fret about Joyce because they believe that they cannot compete with him; by contrast, she states that she feels no sense of Oedipal rivalry with her male national precursors and therefore no deep anxiety about their achievements ('I like Joyce ... He was a wonderful writer. He makes me free'[10]). She asserts that Joyce is in fact the 'first Irish woman writer' and that 'she [sic] writes domestic and introspective books, not the slightest bit socially aware'.[11] While this claim about the range and significance of his work is provocatively one-sided and inaccurate, Enright is pointing to the 'feminine' dimensions of Joyce's treatment of sexuality and consciousness. For instance, she argues that he has no 'disgust' in relation to sexual desire or the female body.[12] However, this strategic reduction of Joyce has perhaps unintended limiting consequences for what the 'feminine' in art might include.

Enright has on a number of occasions analysed her own creative development in the context of her experience of Ireland. In particular, she recalls two episodes of depression that she suffered as a young woman. After graduating from Trinity College in Dublin, she enrolled on the Master's programme in Creative Writing at the University of East Anglia. However, this proved to be an unhappy spell during which she was unable to write and at one point she took an overdose. Some years later, settled back in Dublin and working as a producer at RTÉ, she was hospitalised after a breakdown. Both periods of difficulty for Enright ultimately helped her to define her artistic vocation as an Irish woman in the final decades of the twentieth century. These episodes were successfully resolved. In each case, she charts her emotional and creative recovery in relation to other women: in England, to the novelist Angela Carter, who was Enright's tutor and mentor on the MA course; and in Dublin, to 'Connie', a fellow patient in the psychiatric hospital, whom she came to see was a much more damaged person than she herself.

In *Making babies*, Enright recalls the creative blockage she experienced at university in East Anglia. Although she struggled every night for many months, she could not produce fiction.[13] The Ireland she had left was an 'incoherent country'; when she did find a way to tell stories again, her books were 'slightly surreal, because Ireland was unreal'.[14] In a column remembering Carter, she stresses other aspects of the experience. There, Enright invites but does not fully embrace the notion of her own sense of 'incoherence' as something that had been determined by Ireland – either as a country that had stymied her development, or one that she missed as a migrant. She certainly does not seek for any illumination of her plight in relation to colonialism or its legacies: indeed, she abhorred the clichéd 'business' of being an Irish person in England which seemed 'old-fashioned and, in tiny ways, ghastly'. She is more inclined to explain her writing block by reference to broader human dilemmas about dependence and autonomy, complicated by the question of gender. Enright had known emotional distress before, but had managed to turn this to creative advantage. But now, she felt that she had 'no idea how to live in the world, let alone write about it; and the self who was supposed to produce some narrative by the end of the year seemed increasingly fugitive and fragmented'. She compares herself to an abandoned child ('the infant who cannot invent, who cannot make things up, is, in the absence of the mother, bereft').[15] Carter was kind and insightful; her work encouraged play and experiment. However, Enright states that in some ways she envied the feminist writers of the 1960s and 1970s (presumably including her teacher, whom she describes as 'a socialist and a materialist') for their 'iconclastic clarity'. They protested against the reduction of women to silent passivity; Enright summarises their project as: 'The object speaks back.' But Enright considered that she needed be faithful in her own writing to the more ambiguous and confused dimensions of selfhood and embodiment. As she puts it, her own work is 'mired' in issues to do with 'not the body as object or image, but the seeing, desiring, penetrated, pregnant, mortal and happy body: also the fragmented body, the body that contains the eye'.[16] Enright's version of *her* body – less solid, less dogmatic, less 'ideological', less authoritative – is also, for all her distaste for national stereotypes, a recognisable version of the opposition between the anarchic, imaginative Celt and a more utilitarian Englishness. When she tells Carter she is going back to Ireland at the end of the course, the English woman asks 'Why?', by which she meant something more emphatic, according to Enright: 'Whatever for?' Enright answers that she is returning 'for a man' – and Carter intuits that this is about a particular man, rather than one who is 'merely Irish'. As a young reader, and later as an apprentice writer, Enright had looked to such literary traditions as the Japanese novel, hoping that these might show her 'ways to be foreign' in Ireland of the 1970s. But just as in this essay Enright suggests that a little 'falling apart ... a tincture of four in the morning' is necessary to create fiction, so too what we might call a 'tincture' of Irishness was also involved in the process for her.

An anecdote in *Making babies* about the second crisis is the Carter story in obverse. Enright was working in television at the time; she had still not properly found her vocation as a writer. She was admitted to a hospital where she remained for several months. It was a 'middle-class home for the tearful' and not the sort of place where you might expect to encounter people who had experienced the worst of Irish society's treatment of women or the mentally ill. Nevertheless, Enright's roommate Connie, a woman of fifty or sixty, highly conscious of respectability and with 'a little tea-and-sandwiches'[17] face, clutching the blankets up to her chin and whispering to the doctor like a frightened child, is certainly a gender and national victim of a kind. No one comes to see Connie. She seems to have led a sexless, lonely life: 'Of course she was single and her parents were dead.'[18] (Indeed, she would have been born around the time when Ireland had the highest proportion of unmarried and therefore presumably celibate people of any country where records have been kept.[19]) Enright, suicidally unwell but young and talented, was visited every day by her concerned parents and boyfriend. She feels little sense of identification with this woman: 'From the way she talked to the doctor (Yes, Daddy. No, Daddy) I would guess that whatever did for Connie happened when she was very small. We were opposites, in a way. The place where she was damaged was the place where I was happiest. It was time I took my good fortune seriously, and went home.'[20] She left the hospital and then 'gave up the job and married the man and wrote some books'.[21] This is Enright's way of getting rid of history and psychodrama and assuming a bluff asperity. No rhetoric about 'art' here: she wrote 'some books'. Trauma is the fate of others – although in this case, as victims of a history of which the writer could claim some considerable knowledge.

'Old' Ireland is consistently taken by Enright to be the Catholic-dominated, independent state that fiercely resisted greater freedom for women especially in relation to contraception, divorce and abortion. These issues, deeply embroiled in the sexual obsessions of the Church, defender of the traditional against the modern, also became integral to the quarrel between Dublin and a more conservative rural Ireland. At times, Enright presents these intensifying disputes as forces that altered and indeed formed her sensibility. She recalls that a series of divisive referenda were held around the time that she was reaching adulthood; the 'real religious wars', she comments, 'are fought over the bodies of women'.[22] Thus she was herself just 'establishing a sexual identity' as the broader society was rancorously debating issues of sexual morality – it was, she notes, 'not the best environment' for a young woman.[23] She briefly became a born-again Christian as a teenager, which added to her sense of disorientation: 'For a woman of my generation, the break between the old and the new Ireland happened in my head; it was a confusing and disturbing time.'[24] At other times, she suggests that her own parents were not especially repressive or authoritarian, although there was 'a gap between a very easygoing family life and a kind of Catholic thing overlaid on it'.[25] But then again, she describes the key moment of the referendum on the 'Pro-life' amendment to the constitution in 1983 (according equal status to the life of the pregnant mother and the 'unborn child') as 'a moral civil war that was fought out in people's homes – including my own – with unfathomable bitterness'.[26] The careful use of such terms as the *real* religious war, the *moral* civil war, makes it clear that these, for Enright, are the defining and crucial confrontations in modern Irish history – to be distinguished from (say) the conflict between Ireland and Britain, pro-Treaty and republican sides in the early 1920s, or Protestants and Catholics in the North.

Enright describes her first books as dealing with 'purity' (because 'the chastity of Irish women was one of the founding myths of the Nation State (well that was my excuse)') and as full of 'corpses'. In her account, the latter seem to represent the body in general, dead or alive: speaking bodies, sexual bodies, her own body and the Catholic idea of a body ('Christ, the dead body on a stick'). And the fate of the body also dramatises 'the past that lies down but will not shut up, the elephant in the national living-room'.[27] Irish sexual repression, the weight of national history, the legacy of Catholicism: this reads like a widely recognisable agenda of the key preoccupations of the modern Irish novel. Well before the establishment of the independent state, Irish novelists had pioneered the fictional critique of what they saw as the pathologies of Catholic nationalist Ireland.[28] Enright would not claim to have endured the kind of treatment which would have been the likely lot of the woman in the next bed to hers in the hospital – indeed, she is in many ways self-consciously the 'opposite' of such a person. Nor – unlike Edna O'Brien, Nuala O'Faolain or other key writers such as Joyce or John McGahern – does she understand her own mother's life to have been ruined by Irish conditions. She produces an interesting variant of the Irish novel of dissent, one initially less informed by the political urge to 'expose' cruel but occluded realities and in many other regards tonally at odds with earlier writing in this line (signalled above by the aside: 'well that was my excuse'). What we see here is the formation of Enright as narrator, the goodbye-to-all-that survivor who can't afford to talk about trauma. But that *is* a way of dealing with it – she mentions it, assigns it to other times and other people. The past is another country and ordinary, suburban people are those who have survived by concentrating on the here-and-now and by not being moulded by killing influences or memories. That doubled purposiveness, to fully inhabit the present and to escape the past, reveals a determination to be unashamedly hedonistic and aggressively opposed to historical influences that would always be understood as petrifying, as having the effect of stereotyping the individual experience.

Enright describes fictional narrative as having two axes: 'Modernism is often concerned with a kind of ever-expanding present, a moment. Realism ... is about continuity, about cause and effect, about change, about growth, all these.'[29] She has demonstrated greater interest in the second axis – in personal and collective history – as her work has advanced. But she remains compelled by the 'pleasure' of exploring the 'now' and is sceptical about any 'linear self that is connected moment by moment through a life'.[30] In her treatment of motherhood, Enright was primarily concerned with capturing 'the anxiety of reproduction, the oddness of it'; we might say something similar of her depictions of sex (her novel *The pleasure of Eliza Lynch* (2002) begins with the sentence 'Francisco Solana López put his penis inside Eliza Lynch on a lovely Spring day in Paris, in 1854' – the next ten pages mainly recount Eliza's thoughts during the twenty thrusts that follow).[31] One key insight of psychoanalysis – in which Enright is consistently interested – would surely be that love, sex or intense parental feeling tend to bring us closer again to our unsocialised infant selves and to the uncanny realm of the unconscious.[32] These unsettling effects are not going to be entirely subdued by any particular social arrangements. For Enright, neither Irish nor any other specifiable national conditions are in themselves to blame for the sheer oddness of much human experience – although they may contribute to further upsetting our sense of stable identity, even though such a sense is itself, as she has indicated, challenged by the modern and/or contemporary novel.

Reading an early Enright novel, such as *What are you like?* (2000), we can appreciate that people from Ireland may be more likely than some others to suffer the negative consequences of – for instance – the mistreatment of pregnant women, secrecy about adoption, or emigration. However, given that she does not in any case have much faith in the notion of stable, unified individuality, Ireland might be regarded as a place, for Enright, fortuitously good at producing the kind of psychic volatility that interests her so much. By contrast, most Irish feminist critique focuses on historical investigation, and especially on explanations of how and why so many Irish women (among other groups) fared so poorly in independent Ireland. Feminists are also committed to the rights of women to autonomy, to reproductive choice and so on – all that might go with being a 'linear self'. (This is why O'Faolain, for example, called for a new Irish realism – as distinct from the brilliant experimental tradition dominated historically by male writers – that would address the 'shared condition' of Irish women.[33]) Attention to the 'historic axis' on the part of other Irish women writers such as O'Brien and O'Faolain also tends to produce a much more sympathetic view of aspects of the 'traditional' and of anti-colonial and nationalist political currents in Irish culture than we uncover in Enright's fiction. However, her work has been taken up most strongly within Ireland by feminist critics working with psychoanalytic theory who would suggest that her real cultural importance lies in her non-realist accounts of the liminal states experienced, for example, by lovers or by what she calls that other 'peculiar, mutant, double self – motherandchild'.[34] Hence, Anne Mulhall, for example, hails Enright's 'significant rearticulation of the feminine and the maternal' as an element in a feminist aesthetic radically at odds with what Mulhall argues is 'the nervous verisimilitude' (by which she means a defensive, conservative realism) that dominates mainstream Irish fiction.[35] However, she does not identify any specific 'realists' with whom Enright might be contrasted and the relationship between Irish writers' resistance to realism and any longer historical view of Irish conditions is not considered.[36]

Enright certainly casts a comic and estranging eye on what might be described as 'women's' concerns in fiction. Take for example the following enraptured description of a newborn baby in the first paragraph of *What are you like?* (2000), with its arresting images of cannibalism and violence:

> She saw everything, she ate it with her eyes, she made women's breasts ache and men rattle their keys. Naked, she brought tears to your eyes. You felt this baby was all skin, holding the soft little parcel of her insides: her fresh little kidneys, the squiggle of her guts, her quail's bones. You could eat her, that's all, her bladder like a sweet little onion and her softly sprouting brain. You could bend down and kiss her on the tummy: she was so neatly packed, like the gift she was. So perfect, they said, you could almost take her home with you. And they handed her on from arm to arm, with the dip that people make when they give away a baby – letting her body go and guiding her head, as though it might not be attached. Nothing worse than being left holding the baby, they seemed to say, except being left with the baby's head.[37]

Elsewhere, Enright frequently writes about the transformation of Ireland by new media technologies including television. In this passage from *The wig my father wore* (1995), she depicts a television signal bouncing around the country. The roll-call of place names is redolent of the conclusion of Joyce's 'The Dead' (and indeed of similar passages from other Irish women writers that we have discussed):

> It shot along the link to Cairn Hill, to Truskmore and Maghera, snaked up the tip and was hurled into the wide blue. It was caught in Achill and Kilkeaveragh, on Mount Gabriel and Holywell Hill, patted on the head and thrown further on … and the televisions in Kiltemagh and Gowra, in Newry and Inch glowed red and green and blue just like the cameras did, just the same. Because it spun over rivers and graveyards, over chippers and cowsheds, over children running in the dusk and old men forgetting where they were. It spilled westward over the sea from Malin Head to Slyne Head to Valencia over sleeping fish and ghost nets still catching the waves. It dropped without a sigh into a sitting room in Granard, where a woman was bathing a baby, into a front parlour in Carrigaholt where a man left his dishes out in the rain, into a lounge in Abbeyleix where it was still too early for a drink.[38]

But while the technology is a marvel, the place names seem somewhat arbitrary and carry no loud historical echoes – the liturgy of the weather forecast is briefly there, but this actually enhances the randomness of the catalogue. The most salient divide on the island, in Enright's imagination, is perhaps not the partition between Northern Ireland (some places in the North are included here) and the Republic, but that between Dublin and the country. This is handled humorously at one point in *The wig my father wore*, when the main character Grace and her college friend Marcus debate the key question of when people in Dublin got access to British television (so enabling their children to watch BBC programmes like *Top of the pops* or *Doctor Who* and therefore to feel entirely at home with British popular culture). Grace is from Dublin where – as she puts it – Marcus imagines that 'we sat around forgetting who we really were and trying to speak proper'; he is from Leitrim where 'everyone went to Mass and lived in a cow's arse and fucked their uncle on a Saturday night'. For Marcus, watching

British children's programmes instead of the RTÉ favourite *Wanderly wagon* was tantamount to pretending to be a Protestant. He also points out that, contrary to what she remembers, it was in fact 1971 before 'suburban Dublin, that centre and flower of modern civilization, went multi-channel'.[39] This is an amusing conversation about the importance of what might seem to an outsider to be minor shades of cultural difference. But later Grace expresses relief that while she could have had 'Marcus's father, coming up the stairs in his long-johns, with the soft rain streaming down and the mastitis on the heifer in the haggart', she is grateful that – allowing for his eccentricities – she instead had a 'suburban father, an ordinary man', working for the electricity company to extend light and power to the countryside, 'who bought his new house for his new children and built a better life'.[40]

The changes in style of her novels after *The pleasure of Eliza Lynch* evidently are a result, at least in part, to Enright's wish to play a bigger part in mainstream literary culture: 'I am moving in my own head more from the periphery toward the centre. I used to think that subversion and refusal and tricks and all kinds of play were the ways to slither around the male establishment, but I want to occupy the middle ground as I get older.'[41] Enright declares that she 'didn't necessarily *want* those earlier books to be so fragmented',[42] and so she deliberately reoriented herself towards more conventional approaches. The later books are concerned with family narratives, encompassing a range of stories about marital, sibling and parental relationships, told in more realist modes. Could this be seen as reflecting as a retreat to more standard expectations of the Irish novel? Enright has indicated that she wants to participate in discussion rooted in a specific society:

> You can complain about Ireland being small, but it also can be quite livable. In most good writing, there is an argument taking place, and to keep the argument going, it's good to be in fairly close contact ... But as I say, it's a conversation; as I go along, I am doing less and less overt making up of things. I am making it closer to the credible.[43]

As Helena Wulff comments, Enright is also currently the only Irish female writer who is frequently invited to report on Irish issues to global readerships in publications such as the *London Review of Books*; according to Wulff, when dealing with storylines that can readily be identified as 'Irish', including emigration, the influence of the Church, or the Celtic Tiger, the Irish writer becomes more recognisable as a public intellectual in an international literary marketplace.[44] Enright has also used her own prominent position to call for more attention to other women writers as well and for women's perspectives in general to be regarded as at least equally valuable as those of men.[45]

The gathering is set in 1998, around the time that the Celtic Tiger took its famous leap; it was published in 2007, just as the beast was beginning its headlong descent into the rubble of the Irish economic crash. The novel explores the present situation and childhood memories of the central character, Veronica Hegarty, as she prepares for the wake and funeral of her brother Liam, who has committed suicide in England. She and Liam had come from a family of twelve children. They had been dispatched to live in their grandmother's house in another part of Dublin during a time when their mother was unable to cope with the strain of her enormous brood. At the time of her brother's death, Veronica is in her late thirties, a former lifestyle journalist and now a full-time mother of two young girls; she is married to a man who is doing well in corporate finance. They live in a new five-bedroomed house – in marked contrast to the claustrophobic domestic spaces of her childhood – and her children are 'not obliged to fight over who is wearing the other one's knickers in the morning before they go to school'.[46] In the aftermath of Liam's death, Veronica comes to believe that he was sexually abused, at the age of nine, by a man called Lambert Nugent, who was a constant presence in her grandmother's house. She wonders if Nugent may have abused her also.

To some extent, Enright embraces the idea of writing an allegory of Irish social history over the period of the existence of the state – the narrator speculates that her grandmother Ada must have first met Nugent in the 1920s, and Enright includes a lot of amusing and brilliantly observed material about the Celtic Tiger era. Child sexual abuse is of course a widespread phenomenon. But in modern Ireland, the exposure of children to the unfettered authority of priests, brothers, nuns and teachers in Catholic-run institutions and schools – and the history of Church and state indifference and cover-up – is widely seen as key to understanding what Liam Harte describes as 'the unacknowledged trauma endured by generations of unknown Irish bodies made abject by postcolonial nationalism'.[47] The narrator of *The gathering* makes informed reference to the exposure of child abuse from the 1990s onwards; this promises to shed new light on both the fictional Hegartys and on Ireland. Veronica declares (in a perhaps incongruous idiom) that 'this is the anatomy and mechanism of a family – a whole fucking country – drowning in shame'.[48] She thinks that she may have been able to recover a distorted visual memory of her brother being abused thanks to the courageous disclosures of other Irish people on the radio and in the newspapers.[49] But in this novel, stereotypes of the dysfunctional Irish family are also subjected to irony. Veronica talks to a man who comes to clean her carpets; he is the youngest child in a family of twenty-one. 'All big families are the same', she observes: 'There is always a drunk. There is always someone who has been interfered with, as a child. There is always a colossal success, with several houses in various countries ... There is a mysterious sister ... We pity our mothers, what they had to put it up with in bed or in the kitchen, and we hate them or we worship them, but we always cry for them – at least I do.'[50] This could be a comment too on big families in Irish *novels*, including this one; an indication – as one reviewer puts it – that in her recent work, Enright is 'unafraid' of being exaggeratedly or 'provocatively' Irish.[51] But the tone is at odds with other statements Veronica makes elsewhere about the dark secret of abuse (and about the irresponsibility and culpability of her mother).

Both Liam and his uncle Brendan (Ada's son, a long-term resident of a psychiatric institution) are understood as national victims in the novel. But the contexts of Irish religious culture or family structures is given little attention – even in the sections where Veronica imagines her grandparents' lives in the 1920s, virtually no reference is made to the background of conflict or the emergence of the new state. While the gas-lit period atmosphere of these passages owes something to *Dubliners*, there is no counterpart here to Joyce's diagnoses of the historical origins of Irish pathologies of fearfulness or moral paralysis.

Brendan is the more 'typical' victim, abandoned after death to an unmarked grave in the hospital's mass-burial grounds. Although we know almost nothing of the circumstances of his incarceration, his reappearance to Veronica as a child-ghost at Liam's wake makes clear that Brendan is representative not just of the revenants of her own childhood but of 'the souls of the forgotten' in Ireland.[52] There is more equivocation in relation to the abuse of Liam – or perhaps that of Veronica herself too. The novel gives a lot of attention to a possible back story involving Nugent as a disappointed suitor of Ada's and to a scene in which Veronica apparently remembers seeing Liam kneeling in front of Nugent in his grandmother's sitting room and touching the man's genitals. But these are totally revised or withdrawn later in the book – after Liam's death, Veronica discovers that Nugent was in fact their grandmother's landlord, and she decides that the abuse must have happened in the garage of the home. It remains the case that Veronica ultimately believes that Liam 'was probably sexually abused by Lambert Nugent'.[53] The recovery of traumatic memory is of course a fraught process. Yet Veronica remains strikingly preoccupied with the epistemological puzzle of what 'really' happened in her grandmother's house. In this, *The gathering* seems at times out of kilter with a good deal of other writing about the topic in the same period (for example, we might recall Nuala O'Faolain's declaration that 'the state of knowing and fully acknowledging the reality of child abuse is a state utterly different from not knowing it'[54]). Veronica believes that if she had been abused, it might 'explain some things', but when she adds the event into her brother's life, 'it is the place where all cause meets all effect, the crux of the X': yet, 'in a way, it explains too much'.[55] Gerardine Meaney argues that the self-reflexive uncertainty of Enright's narrator represents a challenge to the way in which traumatic memory has become a 'fetish' in contemporary Irish culture – involving the implicit promise that the recovery of painful memories will be therapeutic and liberating, while also assuming that the worst forms of abuse now belong to history.[56] Meaney is surely right that Enright is not given to sponsoring easy resolutions of difficult experience (although the idea of a cathartic disclosure is deferred rather than abandoned in the novel; Veronica cannot yet tell her siblings about Liam and Nugent, but she plans to do this). But it seems more problematic to link this with a critical politics of the present in *The gathering* in any more general sense.

Veronica seems inclined to think of her brother as someone – presumably because of his abuse – who got stuck in the world of their childhood. She thinks sadly of his humble job, his few possessions and his life as an Irish emigrant in Britain. The latter somehow makes him into an archaic figure – 'a bit of a throwback, a hick'.[57] She weeps in Brown Thomas department store for this man who consumed so pitifully little – as she contemplates buying nine Brabantia storage jars for the polenta and the other newly fashionable foods that she and her family never actually get round to eating.[58] This is ostensibly a satirical take on irrational shopping habits. But there is also real grief expressed here for those, like Liam, 'left behind' in the 'Irish seventies'.[59] Veronica is in one sense annoyed that her father, who was so enraged by the evidence of his daughter's sex life when she was a student, never had to deal with seeing condoms openly on sale in Irish shops. But at the same time, as he died in 1986, he would never have eaten a mango: she feels she must 'console him for the distance we have moved from the place where he stopped'.[60] A certain hard-headedness has enabled Veronica to emerge from the darkness that has reclaimed her brother. Now she can at least spend her sleepless nights wandering around her enormously spacious house or driving her Saab. When they were students in the 1980s, Veronica dragged herself away from the chaotic house in London where she and Liam shared a room, because 'I wanted a shower ... I wanted a 2:1 in my arts degree'; somehow, Liam misses this exit route.[61] *The gathering* is concerned with banishing the Gothic Irish past of flimsy extensions, shared beds and stuffy parlours. Veronica speculates that her original family home could now only be sold as a site ('Level it and start again.'[62]). Her husband thinks she should buy a house on her grandmother's street – and she imagines herself one day buying the very house itself, pulling down the wallpaper and 'talking to some nice architect about gutting the place'; eventually, she would sell it for twice the price.[63] While the novel has fun with boom time excess, it is not interested in critically scrutinising the apparent social transformation that Ireland was then undergoing: money is a welcome emancipation at an individual level. At the end of the novel,

Veronica contemplates a sexual reconciliation with her husband and the possibility of conceiving a third and final child. Her children will have plenty of everything; the dilemmas of contemporary parenting include such issues as deciding exactly how many Barbie dolls should be enough for a little girl to own.[64] Veronica's plan to recommit herself to her own family may be entirely positive for a woman currently haunted by memories of her doomed brother, but it is a matter entirely of the private sphere. It is the spectre of others who are 'drowning in shame' that makes it possible to be so affirmative of domestic normality and a heroine fluent in brand names.

The narrator of *The forgotten waltz* (2011), Gina Moynihan, has an affair with a married man; they both leave their spouses and start over together. Gina does not feel guilty but she does ruminate about how and why it all happened. In effect, she is asking herself about the enigmatic nature of gratification – or, as Enright puts it elsewhere, 'what is it that you get, when you get what you want?'[65] Her main failing being lust rather than greed, Gina is entertainingly scathing about the mindless acquisitiveness of other people – especially women – during these demented final days of Ireland's belle époque. Indeed, she suspects that the women she knows would much rather spend money than have sex. For example, she would like to tell her morally disapproving sister – whose stable marriage Gina does not envy – to 'fuck off back to her muppet of a husband, who rolls on to her after his bottle of Friday-night wine, and then rolls off again. If she calls that love. Wondering has he come yet, and how much it would cost to have a horse in livery like the woman down the road.'[66] Contentedly childless herself, Gina is also a sharp but rather more forgiving observer of the over-fed, over-dressed little girls of the Celtic Tiger. These include her niece, Megan, and Megan's friend Evie, who also happens to be the daughter of Gina's lover Seán:

> The girls Megan had invited over were ridiculously large and hard to fathom. They wore over-sized party dresses, or funky tops; two at least were in tracksuit bottoms – you couldn't even tell who they thought they were. These people had, besides, no interest in us, they had each other to love; the way they looked at each other was so passionate and shy.[67]

These children have been terribly indulged but are idealistic all the same (or at least 'anti-designer label, anti-bullying'[68]). When Evie is a little older, Gina thinks that 'the world might be better if it was run by girls who were nearly twelve, the ability they have to be fully moral and fully venal at the same time. Capitalism would certainly thrive.'[69]

Gina to begin with finds Seán's devotion to his daughter both surprising and inconvenient. In the wake of the break-ups (when they 'pulled all the houses down around us; the townhouse and the cottage and the semi-d. All those mortgages'[70]) and the property crash, Gina finds herself living back in her old family home in Terenure in south Dublin (her widowed mother has recently died). She looks after Evie occasionally when the girl visits. The novel ends in the aftermath of the snowstorms of February 2009 – Enright constructs the timeline carefully, though she makes little reference to politics rather than to economics (for example, that month also saw huge mass protests on the streets of Dublin against the government's handling of the bank crisis and other issues). Gina walks into the city to pick up Evie as Seán is away in Budapest. Dublin is hushed in the unfamiliar snow. Gina's journey on foot is through well-known territory: Rathmines, St Stephen's Green. She takes Evie to try on make-up in a department store in Grafton Street (presumably Brown Thomas again) and to buy take-away hot chocolate. The girl is sweetly loyal to her mother but chatty all the same. She slides along the icy streets in her Ugg boots.

The final chapter reminds us of the limits to overweening individual desire. Even though she is not a biological parent, Gina realises that she will inevitably grow attached to Evie and mourn her childhood when she grows up. It is perhaps a new experience for her to feel part of an aging generation – to share in a sense of what we might call parentality. The scene unfolds in a city that is temporarily paralysed and fearful. Gina does not at all dread her own future. But prospects generally are not what they used to be. When the Irish economy was booming, Seán had been exhilarated by visiting Shanghai: 'He said you got on those empty roads, those eight-lane highways, completely empty, and you understood something about the future – that you could do it. Certainly, it was scary. But the future was also *normal*.'[71] His was a vision of how the Irish could continue to move with the times – here, he imagines adapting to China's new power in the world

– and maintain their recent, miraculous position as global winners. But not any longer. Familial and national horizons re-emerge in *The forgotten waltz*. In contrast to *The gathering*, the Irish past is not particularly Gothic in this story and in any case Gina doesn't think about anything much earlier than her own childhood. Alone in her parents' old house during Christmas 2008, she recalls their modest, suburban contentment (although her father drank too much and died prematurely). Staring out of the window at night, she wants to keep them company among the street lamps and traffic lights: 'my father and mother, dispersed as they are along the sweet, bright arc of the dead'.[72]

The only past available to Gina may be that of the Moynihans: the history of a family. But it would seem that in *The Green Road* Enright aimed to write a broader kind of story about a family in history. As in 'The Dead' (to which Enright surely alludes at the end of *The forgotten waltz*), this involves a journey westward towards the Atlantic coast. A series of episodes in *The Green Road* deal with the experiences of both male and female characters – some of them living far away from Ireland, in North America and Africa – over two generations from rural Clare. They grow up by the Burren, which Enright has described as 'an iconic landscape of the Irish national revival'.[73] The novel includes an especially detailed account of the mother, who is named Rosaleen and explicitly associated with an allegorical version of Ireland ('Dark Rosaleen') in various ways. Her husband is called Pat – the name of Ireland's national saint – and, curiously, all of their four children (Dan, Emmet, Constance and Hanna), bear the names of notable heroic Irish political figures.[74]

Enright wrote two essays in the same year in which *The Green Road* was published which shed light on the novel. Based on her first lecture as Laureate for Irish Fiction, 'Antigone in Galway' appeared in the *London Review of Books*; a piece in the *Guardian*, 'A return to the western shore', was about living for a time in Co. Clare with her husband and children. In the first essay, Enright explores the burial and commemoration of the dead in Ireland in relation to such issues as the centenary of 1916 and the treatment of those who died in Irish carceral institutions. The latter include the young children who perished in such places as the Mother and Baby Home in Tuam in

Co. Galway and the Magdalene women laid to rest anonymously near the laundries where some had spent nearly their entire lives as unpaid workers. Enright's inaugural lecture in her new public role therefore was sceptical about the government-sponsored 1916 commemorations and critical of the way in which the state had to date responded to revelations about conditions in Catholic-controlled institutions. The second piece is concerned with more personal reflections and with her own work. In the essay, Enright expresses surprise to find herself so happy and successful: she is now that thing she hoped to become – a writer. She is staying by the Atlantic Ocean in Clare, in a place familiar to her from summer holidays as a child. She discusses Clare and the west generally in modern Irish literature: this is a tradition which she now regards through the eyes of a mature contributor rather than those of a subversive newcomer.

'Antigone in Galway' contrasts the dead of 1916 and the Tuam mothers and babies (and the Magdelenes) – the treatment of each showing the attitude of the state to nationalist martyrs and to the anonymous victims of its sexual attitudes respectively. The oration of the then Taoiseach, Enda Kenny, on the occasion of the reinterment of the body of Thomas Kent, executed in Cork in 1916 and buried in a prison yard, is thus an act of commemoration evidently utterly unlike the patient research of local historian, Catherine Corless, in Tuam. At her own expense, Corless retrieved hundreds of death certificates for children who died in the Mother and Baby Home for whom no burial records existed. She deduced that their bodies may have been laid in an area on the grounds of the home marked on old maps as once having housed a large septic tank. Unsurprisingly, when news of her discoveries spread, shocking stories about 'nuns throwing dead babies into a septic tank' were widely reported internationally; as Enright details, these were countered by accusations from some quarters that Corless had herself sensationalised the evidence.[75] But in her battle on behalf of these 'dishonoured dead', Corless – rather than, say, Thomas Kent's nieces, to whom the Taoiseach paid tribute for 'tending the flame of his memory'[76] – is here, it seems, the likely candidate for the role of the defiant Antigone of Enright's title. This is despite the fact that Kent, like Antigone's brother, was a rebel against state authority. His female relatives are not named nor presented by

Enright as acting out of any especially commendable motives. Rather she suggests that the exhumation of the remains was inspired by some notion that the site of the former prison yard still somehow held the 'taint of Britishness'.[77]

We have here previously seen Antigone invoked in Irish political discourse by Conor Cruise O'Brien: the person he offered as her modern equivalent was Bernadette Devlin. In that instance, we were asked to believe that young Catholics in the North were given to excessively emotional behaviour, altogether too dangerous in an explosive political situation where it might lead inexorably into civil war. In effect, the young protesters were wrong to protest against the civil order – even though their complaints were, he concedes, well founded. O'Brien suggests that they would nevertheless have been better advised to model themselves after Ismene, Antigone's sister, who was prepared to submit to the law of the land and to resist the realm of ritual and the Gods.[78] But with 'Antigone in Galway', the classical tragedy is less clearly in view. Instead, we have an amalgam of contemporary horrors: the discovery of a mass grave and the exposure of yet more cruel and/or criminal treatment by the Irish Catholic church of its laity. Catholics, in this case, are now in the polar opposite condition to that in which O'Brien had placed them in the Northern conflict. They are now remarkably callous and hypocritical, because they celebrate the 1916 dead while dumping the remains of the 'illegitimate' children of the mothers in its care (if it can be so called). For example, in a concluding paragraph, Enright notes the presence of the Bishop of Cork at the Thomas Kent ceremony shortly after he had called for the exhumation of a famously pious four-year-old girl, Nellie Organ, who had died in the orphanage at Sunday's Well in Cork in 1908: it is as if singling out either the 1916 rebel or the saintly little Nellie for special posthumous treatment might both proceed from some species of religious fanaticism. What Enright has done is to use the famous heroine's name, always associated with proper burial, religious piety, ideals of universal rather than local justice, as an occasion for a critique of the official commemorations.

Corless herself thus has little enough to do with Antigone's tale of familial conflict, rebellion and self-destruction. But the figure of the classical heroine nevertheless invokes associations with the notion of tribal pieties and the Gods. Her function here is to operate as a reminder that fate is never exclusively individual: it is always communal and familial. If Enright were merely describing a conflict between Catholic nationalism and enlightened, liberal feminism this would scarcely be relevant to her. Sophocles' play is taken by Conor Cruise O'Brien and others to be concerned with the divide between the secular/political world of civil order and the metaphysical/spiritual world of religion – but this division is not available to Enright because nationalism itself claims sacrality as its defining dimension and she is here imaginatively caught within its magnetic field, involving both the 'pure' and its opposite: sex, soil, dirt, corpses. (Enright has elsewhere described Irish feminists of the 1970s as engaged in an 'urgent and very moral national enterprise'; in what she here identifies as their relative indifference to money or individual careers, 'they didn't make just me, or they didn't just make my life easier ... – they made Ireland, or they unmade it'.[79] So there as well, nationalism and feminism are something other than merely antagonistic ideologies.) Enright implicitly sets the atrocious burial place in Tuam against the 'cillíní' – traditional Irish burial places for unbaptised children, suicides, criminals or strangers to the community. According to Enright, while the latter were of course the scenes of lonely burials of babies by night – and by their male relatives rather than in ceremonies presided over by priests – they nevertheless feel like holy places. These unofficial graveyards are often positioned next to water or in ancient sacred sites: in this way, traditional culture created a kind of home, in beautiful surroundings, for the infants whose souls were understood to be banished to limbo. The cillíní conjure up an idea of the community that is older and kinder than the twentieth-century state. Enright is certainly cautious about any idealisation of 'Irish' ways or of suggesting that post-Famine Catholic mores are not necessarily 'native' to the people. But at this same point in her career, she also goes on to a new exploration of what in the national past might now prove to be usable for her as a novelist – and on what terms.

In her essay in the *Guardian*, Enright describes a mild mid-life crisis – she is fundamentally quite content and fulfilled, although this condition itself feels quite unexpected and strange to her. As she walks by the Atlantic, she takes in the wildness of Clare. She stresses that she is not in this part of the west because of her father, or because of its centrality to Irish literature: she is there to write a book. But mainly through a series of demurrals, she sets out the terms on which she now 'allows' herself to write about the west in the novel which became *The Green Road*. Despite the short distance between the two places, Enright is not wrong to suggest that it is in fact a significant departure for a writer from Dublin to set a story mainly in Clare. The countryside in general seemed backward and strange to a suburban Irish child of the 1970s (as we see in some of Enright's early fiction). In addition, the literary image of the west of Ireland in English was created by folklorists, dramatists, poets – nationalists in a cultural and often a political sense too. They understood this to be a sublime and otherworldly place. Most later novelists – Edna O'Brien being an exception – were from less spectacularly beautiful parts of the country and they were in any case suspicious of such romantic views of Irish landscape or Irish people. Enright has some concerns about affiliating herself with an earlier line of Irish authors writing about the west. (She makes no mention of any anxiety about finding new ways to write about the place; indeed, both the article and the later novel offer wonderful descriptions of the stony fields, the expansive ocean, the constantly shifting light, and so on.) She does not want 'Irishness' or 'Ireland' to get in the way of more 'universal' questions about human fate that we inevitably encounter when taking in the views of rocks, cliffs and sky on Ireland's western shore. She wishes to avoid stereotyping the inhabitants (any that are left); after all, as she points out, her own father is an individual and not some kind of specimen. She is worried too about the way the landscape has been gendered. A history of starvation, defeat and exile – all of these can evoke ideas of sorrowful, mourning motherhood. 'Female suffering', as she puts it, 'was highly valued in the Catholic Ireland of my youth, but I was never all that keen. I did not see what was in for me.'[80]

For all its loveliness and grandeur, Enright is concerned to assert that the place does not overwhelm her. She is happy to observe it while 'waiting for the story that is out there'.[81] (We might compare this to Edna O'Brien's descriptions of being spiritually possessed by her native landscape: 'County Clare inhabits my thoughts and my writing wherever I happen to be. Ireland is always speaking a story and I have to search for it.'[82]) For Enright, the time in Clare works as therapy; it 'fixes' her. She also makes the idea of writing about the west (that essential way of being an 'Irish writer') more manageable by associating the terrain with various images of maternity. While 'Mother Ireland' is ultimately portrayed as an abandoning and angry mother in the piece, the country evidently provides maternal consolation and imaginative sustenance to one, at least, among her many needy offspring – the author herself.

Enright walks the Green Road: an unpaved track across the Burren affording magnificent views across Galway Bay to the Aran Islands. This is obviously the central action in the essay (as in the later novel) – geographic and symbolic in equal measure. But she asserts that while the scenes are stunning, they are on an 'Irish' scale and 'therefore a little less than vast'. This may be her father's part of the world, yet the terrain is somehow for her 'always maternal'. She remembers it from childhood; it comforts her and allows her a sense of homecoming. It corresponds then to the mother Enright appears to have had and to be: this kind of mother appears in the novel only in the second generation with Rosaleen's more 'modern' daughters, especially Constance. The landscape of Clare delights and sustains the author – but most of her characters are impelled to leave mainly by their much more bitter experience of their own mother, who is in many senses 'Mother Ireland' for them. The primal relationship with their actual mother is endlessly complicated and unhappy – but this individual woman, with her many failings, stands here in the place of any more comprehensive examination of the historical or political influences that have moulded Irish society over the period embraced by the novel.

Enright's trip to Clare opens up a specific literary perspective on the figure of the nation as mother. When she tells her father where they plan to stay, he recites a poem he learnt there as a young boy: 'Oh, little Corca Baiscinn, the wild, the bleak the fair! / Oh, little stony pastures whose flowers are sweet, if rare!'[83] The lines are from a poem by Emily Lawless, published in 1902, about the 'Wild Geese' – exiled Irish nobles who left for Europe with their commander Sir Patrick Sarsfield after the Treaty of Limerick in 1691. The poem continues: 'The whole night long we dream of thee, and waking think we are there, / Vain dream, and foolish waking, we never shall see

Clare.'[84] Some of Lawless's poetry was extremely popular in Ireland and Enright's father, now in his eighties, remembered these lines all his life. But in her own time Lawless was in many ways an outsider to the culture of the Irish Literary Revival – she was a female Protestant unionist, doubtful of the capacity of those she saw as the degenerate Irish Catholics of her own day to manage self-government. There are several allusions to the poem ('Fontenoy') that Enright's father knew so well in *The Green Road* (along with quotations from other poets who could more readily be classified as romantic nationalists, such as Yeats and James Clarence Mangan). In the essay – though not in the novel – Enright also quotes from another well-known poem by Lawless, 'After Aughrim'. The title refers to the decisive battle which the Irish Catholic armies loyal to King James II lost to the forces of King William of Orange a few months before the Treaty of Limerick – one of the last stands of the old Gaelic order. This poem is notable and unusual for its representation of Mother Ireland as a cruel parent who has wilfully cast her children away 'like rubbish'. The Wild Geese in exile won repute as brave soldiers in other European armies. At the Battle of Fontenoy in 1745 the Irish brigade, fighting for France, won a famous victory over the English. But in Lawless's version both their success ('not mine that fame') and their longing for their homeland surprise and even disgust their mother:

> God know they owe me nought,
> I tossed them to the foaming sea,
> I tossed them to the howling waste,
> Yet still their love comes home to me.[85]

In the climactic scene of Enright's novel, it is the mother, Rosaleen Madigan, who walks the Green Road and she – like Lawless's Mother Ireland here – is to some degree a harsh and ambiguous figure. In her essay, Enright suggests that the west coast of Ireland contains 'longing the way a bog contains rain'. Both Rosaleen and her unfulfilled children share this condition of hopeless desire to different degrees. Enright was 'fixed' on the Green Road. Rosaleen is an old woman who broods on past joys. She cannot be fixed – although she is inspired to pay more attention to the present. But in essential ways, Rosaleen's children (again with the significant exception of Constance) may or may not be fixable. They are – in general – disappointed, confused, isolated from her, from each other and from the people who love them in their adult lives. Their mother is not a standard Irish mother: she is certainly anything but a self-sacrificing martyr or saint. Enright is equally anxious to avoid (or at least to be self-conscious about) standard images of 'Ireland'. But in turning away so decisively from received social or political explanations of the Irish condition, she confines herself in this novel to an internalised account of the familial and psychological stresses that explain the unhappiness experienced by Rosaleen's children. This is a novel which offers a survey of a swathe of twentieth-century Irish social history in poignant and sometimes hilarious detail, but which in a central way ends up blaming a Lawless-style mother for the condition of a subsequent generation. If Enright was not so wary of political critique (other than distaste for romantic nationalism), other accounts might perhaps have been found here of – for example – the depopulation and melancholy of the west of Ireland. The very history of the place is confined to individual (and archaic) rather than collective memory by the end of the novel. The younger characters can only carry their 'longing' away with them as aspects of their most private and incommunicable selves. For example, for Dan the landscape was 'a secret he had carried inside him; a map of things he had known and lost, these half-glimpsed houses and stone walls, the fields of solid green'.[86] As Matthew Ryan suggests of some of Enright's earlier stories, 'the trajectory away from the exhausted idea of the nation is not necessarily an escape into a generous global space'.[87]

Rosaleen is aware that she shares a name with Ireland and is delighted when her granddaughter plays the song 'Oh my dark Rosaleen' for her on the tin whistle, during what will be the last Christmas celebration in their old family house in 2005.[88] But she doesn't think about the allegory: she doesn't think about much apart from her own resentments. Rosaleen is of small-town middle-class stock (her father was a pharmacist), but her late husband was a true son of the soil, born in a small cottage by the sea. The local middle class, as represented by Constance (the only Madigan child left in Clare), seems to be thriving – her husband is a property developer and she drives a Lexus. Enright gives an entertaining account of how Constance spends €410 in the supermarket on a frenzied Christmas Eve morning ('She thought she should keep the receipt for posterity') – and that is before she returns for a few forgotten items (such as big foil for the turkey, coleslaw, smoked salmon, kitchen roll, extra toilet paper, fresh flowers).[89] She is already on the road home when she realises that she has forgotten to buy potatoes – she considers pulling over and digging a few out of a field.[90] The scene is very funny. (Never mind that Enright also mentions that the countryside is still scattered with the abandoned dwellings of Famine victims and the scores of local people who were forced to emigrate.) Constance's siblings have all left Clare. Hanna lives in Dublin with her husband and baby; she is an unsuccessful actor and an alcoholic ('She wondered what it was she had wanted, before she wanted a drink'[91]). The boys get further away. Dan is gay: as he contemplates his childhood bedroom, remembering the confusion of his youth is a mainly a sad experience ('all that withering and wasted time'[92]). Emmet is an idealist. His sister Hanna remembers him as a child, 'interested in facts and none of those facts were small and stupid, they were all about Ireland, and people getting shot'.[93] However, both men in fact seem to have been seriously damaged by things that unfolded in places other than Ireland: Dan as a witness to the AIDS epidemic in the New York gay community in the early 1990s, and Emmet as an aid worker tending to the sick and starving in Cambodia, Sudan and Mali. But they are survivors. In our last glimpse of Dan, we see him sending a message to an old acquaintance he spots on social media who, like himself, came through the disaster of AIDS physically unscathed and is now living in what looks like a Mediterranean paradise on Mallorca: '*Anyway, this is Irish Dan. I am still alive. I see that you are still alive. Enjoy the lemon groves. Enjoy. Enjoy.*'[94]

The peevish Rosaleen fails to conform to an image of a mother as a victim (an Irish 'Mammy'); she also fails as a modern 'Mum' who might nurture her children through intimacy and affection. It is interesting that her adult children don't even know what to call her. When they grew out of 'Mama', she thinks, 'they had failed to grow into anything else'.[95] 'Mum', 'Mammy', or calling your mother by her first name: these all carry different class and cultural connotations in Ireland. The children all take different options in this regard, as if Rosaleen is difficult to 'place' in some fundamental way.[96] But at the end of the final Christmas Day for the Madigans in their old house, Enright introduces an alternative, mythicised parent figure: their late father, Pat. Although we encountered him in the 1980 section of the text, and he has been recalled by his wife and children in other chapters, Pat features here, in Rosaleen's consciousness, much more pointedly as an embodiment of the spirit and memory of the place. As Rosaleen wanders the Green Road, lost in the darkness, she recalls the summertime of their courtship and how he

> pointed to the place where the three townlands met, Oughtdarra, Ballynahown and Crumlin, a gap in the cliff that belonged to none of them called Leaba na hAon Bhó, the Bed of the One Cow. There was a story, he said, about that cow and the end of the world ... And that is the way he saw the land, with no difference between the different kinds of yesterday. No difference between a man and his ghost, between a real heifer and a cow that was waiting for the end of the world. It was the rise and fall in the telling, a rounding out before the finish. A flourish. A shiver. And it was for her. He had saved every detail up for her alone, as though every rock and tree awaited her coming for its explication.[97]

Rosaleen (like an earlier heroine of an Irish novel, Molly Bloom) thinks a great deal about love and sex and not at all about God; Enright would perhaps have had more difficulty with these passages of enraptured memory if Rosaleen's religious worldview were more typical of an Irishwoman of her generation. If anything, it seems that motherhood was sidelined for Rosaleen because of her passionate marriage; again, this is quite unlike the stereotypical image of the Irish mother. Rosaleen's memories of her own romance provide a strong counter to other images of rural desolation she encounters along the Green Road: the abandoned birthplace of Pat Madigan (which her daughter Hanna later searches, poignantly recalling the dead grandmother so vividly described at the opening of the novel), or the abandoned Famine cottage with the 'hungry grass' growing at its threshold where Rosaleen eventually finds shelter.[98]

Rosaleen's children cannot follow their parents along this vision of the Green Road. Theirs is a story of discontinuity and scattering. Such ruptures are not explicitly related to the history or politics of Ireland in the novel although all this is perhaps inescapably present in the poetry about the Wild Geese and in the stories of the lonely houses that still hold the empty beds of children who grew up and went away. The current generation is occasionally nostalgic but disconnected. Dan stumbles over his blessing in Irish at Christmas dinner – although it is poignant to note that his recitation of Yeats (when he was evidently playing 'at being "Irish"') is remembered by his New York friend so many years later on his social media page.[99] Constance's daughter cannot recite the words of the Lawless poem that Enright's father remembered for so long.[100] Rosaleen's children don't even have the romantic or sexual closeness their parents shared in their own lives (although Constance and her wealthy, enterprising husband at least do seem happy and the others have not given up yet). After she is rescued from the Green Road, Rosaleen herself leaves her memories behind as she tries – belatedly – to concentrate more on her children; for example, she dotes on Hanna's baby and in the last paragraphs of the novel she even tries to embrace urban multicultural Ireland, chatting with Emmet's Kenyan housemate in Dublin. The 'west' is available to the author – and to the central character – as something that can usefully be revisited and then set aside. However, it apparently cannot be accessed by those among Enright's characters who represent later Irish generations.

Enright is concerned to get away from what she regards as false stories about a people or a nation and concentrates on individual consciousness instead. But Rosaleen's children are cut off from the past even in the form of local and familial tradition, in anything like the plenitude and intimacy in which it was available to their father and – largely through him – their mother. Her sons leave partly in search of alternative communities. Dan starts off as a priest and later lives on the fringes of a tightly knit community at the time of its devastation by illness (the chapter about his time in New York is narrated not from his perspective but from that of a nameless 'insider'). He becomes a connoisseur of art and beautiful things but he cannot find it in himself to care profoundly about anything, including his future husband.[101]

Emmet goes off to save the world, but is shattered by what he sees: on a trip home from Africa, he is completely overcome by revulsion at the consumerist excesses of the duty-free shop in Geneva airport.[102] They both in fact discover communities that are suffering – extreme versions of historical Ireland. Rather than finding new homes, ways of belonging or political solidarities, they are both in consequence further disabled primarily in their capacity for intimate relationships. Constance stays at home. A big consumer but a kind woman, she fares best, although she eats too much and is not healthy (at the end of the novel she is facing treatment for breast cancer). But she loves her husband and her own offspring. Her children in turn may at least enjoy a greater measure of the amnesiac middle-class ease that seems to be the best of all possible worlds in Enright's fiction.

In her concentration on the present (set against a lost communal past), Enright enacts a generational shift that had finally established itself in the neoliberal economic and cultural worlds of Ireland during the Celtic Tiger world of late capitalism, where shopping becomes a possibly irrational but 'liberal' action. A spectacular transformation – sexual, economic, cultural – has taken place. But – as was arguably always true of the novel – a central value abides, that of the primacy and emancipation of the individual consciousness. The here-and-now has its powerful attractions ('*Enjoy. Enjoy*'). Yet continuity (what literary 'realism', according to Enright, can also provide) is realised, if at all, in a family history that itself survives only in the absence of the collective and the historical. The ensuing sense of liberation is both intense and empty.

Notes

1 Anne Enright, quoted by Liam Harte in *Reading the contemporary Irish novel* (Chichester: Wiley, 2014), p. 14.
2 Colm Tóibín, 'Introduction', *The Penguin book of Irish fiction* (London: Viking, 1999), p. xxxiii.
3 Tóibín, 'Introduction', p. xxxiii.
4 See Anne Enright, interview with Catriona Maloney, in Catriona Maloney and Helen Thompson (eds), *Irish women writers speak out: voices from the field* (Syracuse, NY: University of Syracuse Press, 2003), p. 56. See also interview with Clare Bracken and

Susan Cahill, in Clare Bracken and Susan Cahill (eds), *Anne Enright* (Dublin: Irish Academic Press, 2011), p. 17: 'Personally, I am a feminist, I have always been a feminist, but I am not a deliberately feminist writer. I've never been an ideologue ... Ideology is a very tertiary way of describing the world.'

5 Enright, interviewed by Maloney, in Maloney and Thompson (eds), *Irish women writers speak out*, p. 63.

6 'Sometimes being Irish feels like a job you never applied for. I don't mind being Irish, but I am not a big fan of nationalism'; Enright, quoted in '"Marriage was a licence for sex": Ireland and women in 100 quotes', *Irish Times* (30 March 2017), www.irishtimes.com/life-and-style/people/marriage-was-a-licence-for-sex-ireland-and-wo men-in-100-quotes-1.3029750 (accessed 30 June 2018).

7 Enright, interviewed by Maloney, p. 62.

8 Enright, interviewed by Maloney, p. 61.

9 Tóibín, 'Introduction', p. xxxiii.

10 Enright, interviewed by Maloney, p. 57.

11 See Enright, interviewed by Bracken and Cahill, in Bracken and Cahill (eds), *Anne Enright* p. 24; and 'What Women Want: Anne Enright', interviewed by Susanna Rustin, *Guardian* (15 March 2008).

12 See Enright, interviewed by Bracken and Cahill, p. 24.

13 Anne Enright, *Making babies: stumbling into motherhood* (London: Vintage, 2005), p. 187.

14 Enright, *Making babies*, p. 194.

15 Anne Enright, 'Diary', *London Review of Books*, 33:4 (February 2011).

16 Enright, 'Diary', *London Review of Books*, 33:4.

17 Enright, *Making babies*, p. 192.

18 Enright, *Making babies*, p. 190.

19 See Terence Brown, *Ireland: a social and cultural history* (London: Harper Perennial, 2004), pp. 9–11. Brown and others explain this extraordinary statistic by reference to the economic realities of Irish life after the demographic upheaval of the Famine.

20 Enright, *Making babies*, p. 193.

21 Enright, *Making babies*, p. 193.

22 Anne Enright, 'Diary', *London Review of Books*, 29:9 (May 2007).

23 Enright, *Making babies*, p. 187.

24 Enright, interviewed by Maloney, p. 53.

25 Enright, interviewed by Maloney, p. 60.

26 Enright, *Making babies*, p. 187. The Eighth Amendment was passed by a large majority in the referendum of September 1983. For analysis of the question of abortion in Irish politics and culture, see Ailbhe

Smyth (ed.), *The abortion papers*, vol. 1 (Cork: Cork University Press, 2015), and Catherine Conlon, Sinéad Kennedy and Aideen Quilty (eds), *The abortion papers*, vol. 2 (Cork: Cork University Press, 2015). On the campaign to repeal the Eighth Amendment, see Una Mullally (ed.), *Repeal the 8th* (London: Unbound, 2018), which includes Enright's contribution, 'The question of consent', pp. 27–32, and Sinéad Kennedy, 'Ireland's fight for choice', in *Jacobin* (March 2018), www.jacobinmag.com/2018/03/irelands-fight-for-choice (accessed 30 June 2018). In May 2018, the Irish electorate voted to repeal the amendment by a two-thirds majority; this was almost a direct reversal of the referendum result thirty-five years earlier.
27 Enright, *Making babies*, p. 194.
28 I trace the emergence and development of this novelistic tradition in Nolan, *Catholic emancipations*; see especially 'Preface', pp. ix–xx.
29 Enright, interviewed by Bracken and Cahill, p. 30.
30 Enright, interviewed by Bracken and Cahill, p. 30.
31 Enright, *Making babies*, p. 3; see Anne Enright, *The pleasure of Eliza Lynch* [2002] (London: Vintage, 2003), pp. 1–11. Eliza Lynch (1833–86), from Co. Cork, became the lover of Francisco Solano López, the president of Paraguay; Enright's book, a fictionalised account of Lynch's life, is her only historical novel to date and the only one set mainly outside Ireland.
32 She notes her interest as a student in Freud and in others in the psychoanalytic tradition such as Melanie Klein in the interview with Bracken and Cahill, p. 30.
33 O'Faolain, 'Irish women and writing in modern Ireland', p. 1604.
34 Enright, *Making babies*, p. 20.
35 Anne Mulhall, 'The spectral feminine in the work of Anne Enright', in Bracken and Cahill, *Anne Enright*, pp. 77, 68. See also Bracken and Cahill's summary of the feminist critical literature on Enright; 'Introduction', *Anne Enright*, p. 9.
36 See, for example, Terry Eagleton, *Heathcliff and the great hunger* (London: Verso, 1995), chapter 5.
37 Anne Enright, *What are you like?* [2000] (London: Vintage, 2001), p. 3.
38 Anne Enright, *The wig my father wore* [1995] (London: Minerva, 1996), pp. 208–9.
39 Enright, *The wig*, pp. 34–5.
40 Enright, *The wig*, pp. 69–70.
41 Enright, interviewed by Maloney, p. 62.
42 Enright, interviewed by Bracken and Cahill, p. 16; emphasis added.

43 Enright, interviewed by Maloney, p. 55.
44 See Helena Wulff, *Rhythms of writing: an anthropology of Irish literature* (London: Bloomsbury, 2017), pp. xix, 34, 38–9.
45 See Anne Enright, 'Diary', *London Review of Books*, 39:18 (September 2017). No doubt some among an emerging generation of younger Irish women writers, including Eimear McBride and Sally Rooney, will soon attain equivalent status to Enright.
46 Anne Enright, *The gathering* [2007] (London: Vintage, 2008), p. 10.
47 Harte, *Reading the contemporary Irish novel*, p. 234.
48 Enright, *The gathering*, p. 168.
49 Enright, *The gathering*, pp. 172–3.
50 Enright, *The gathering*, pp. 184–5.
51 Belinda McKeown, 'Review of Anne Enright, *The Green Road*: so Irish it's almost provocative', *Irish Times* (2 May 2015).
52 Enright, *The gathering*, p. 216.
53 Enright, *The gathering*, p. 224.
54 O'Faolain, *A more complex truth*, p. 102.
55 Enright, *The gathering*, p. 224.
56 Gerardine Meaney, 'Waking the dead: Antigone, Ismene and Anne Enright's narrators in mourning', in Bracken and Cahill (eds), *Anne Enright*, pp. 158–9. Meaney argues that Veronica combines aspects of both Antigone and her sister Ismene – being committed to truth and to family obligations, but also to pragmatic compromise and her own survival, p. 157.
57 Enright, *The gathering*, p. 191.
58 Enright, *The gathering*, pp. 189–90.
59 Enright, *The gathering*, p. 191.
60 Enright, *The gathering*, p. 97.
61 Enright, *The gathering*, p. 123.
62 Enright, *The gathering*, p. 5.
63 Enright, *The gathering*, p. 238.
64 Enright, *The gathering*, p. 190.
65 Anne Enright, 'A return to the western shore: Anne Enright on yielding to the Irish tradition', *Guardian* (9 May 2015).
66 Anne Enright, *The forgotten waltz* (London: Jonathan Cape, 2011), pp. 142–3.
67 Enright, *The forgotten waltz*, p. 40.
68 Enright, *The forgotten waltz*, p. 221.
69 Enright, *The forgotten waltz*, p. 221.
70 Enright, *The forgotten waltz*, p. 23.
71 Enright, *The forgotten waltz*, p. 67.
72 Enright, *The forgotten waltz*, p. 175.
73 Enright, 'A return to the western shore'.

74 Daniel O'Connell, Robert Emmet, Constance Markievicz and Hanna Sheehy-Skeffington.
75 As Enright details in her essay; see 'Antigone in Galway: Anne Enright on the dishonoured dead', *London Review of Books*, 37:24 (December 2015). Since the appearance of Enright's essay, Corless's conclusions have been strongly supported by the results of excavations carried out by the Commission on Mother and Baby Homes at the site; see Elaine Edwards, 'Tuam babies: "significant" quantities of human remains found at former home', *Irish Times* (3 March 2017). For a compelling recent account of the evolution of independent Ireland's carceral system against the backdrop of the failures and compromises of the 1920s and 1930s, see Sarah-Anne Buckley, 'The Catholic cure for poverty', *Jacobin* (May 2016), www.jacobinmag.com/2016/05/catholic-church-ireland-magdalene-laundries-mother-baby-homes (accessed 30 June 2018).
76 See Enright, 'Antigone in Galway'.
77 Enright, 'Antigone in Galway'.
78 See O'Brien, *States of Ireland*, pp. 151–75; I discuss these passages from Conor Cruise O'Brien in Chapter 3.
79 Enright, from a lecture to the Merriman School in Co. Clare in 2007, quoted by Wulff, *Rhythms of writing*, p. 39.
80 Enright, 'A return to the western shore'.
81 Enright, 'A return to the western shore'.
82 Edna O'Brien, interview with Helen Thompson, in Maloney and Thompson (eds), *Irish women writers speak out*, p. 205.
83 Enright, 'A return to the western shore'.
84 Lawless, quoted by Enright, 'A return to the western shore'.
85 Lawless, quoted by Enright, 'A return to the western shore'.
86 Anne Enright, *The Green Road* (London: Jonathan Cape, 2015), p. 203.
87 Matthew Ryan, 'What am I like: writing the body and the self', in Bracken and Cahill, *Anne Enright*, 166.
88 Enright, *The Green Road*, p. 244.
89 Enright, *The Green Road*, p. 231.
90 Enright, *The Green Road*, p. 232.
91 Enright, *The Green Road*, p. 300.
92 Enright, *The Green Road*, p. 247.
93 Enright, *The Green Road*, p. 23.
94 Enright, *The Green Road*, p. 295; emphasis in original.
95 Enright, *The Green Road*, p. 156.
96 As in the scene when they all call out to their mother when she is lost in the countryside; Enright, *The Green Road*, pp. 283–4.
97 Enright, *The Green Road*, pp. 262–3.

98 As Enright explains, in Ireland 'hungry grass' was said to grow on a neglected grave or at the entrance to a house that had fallen into ruin when all its inhabitants died of hunger; anyone who stepped over this grass would be hungry for ever. See *The Green Road*, p. 278.
99 Enright, *The Green Road*, pp. 245, 294.
100 Enright, *The Green Road*, p. 243.
101 Enright, *The Green Road*, p. 180.
102 Enright, *The Green Road*, p. 123.

Afterword

A few months after the publication of her memoir, *Are you somebody?*, Nuala O'Faolain wandered around the city centre of Dublin feeling uneasy. Her book had inspired gratitude and affection; many people had written to her, many now congratulated her in the street. She had never anticipated such a warm response. It seemed that she had awakened 'something a bit like love'.[1] But it was not love of the kind that she thought she needed ('someone knowing me, but loving me completely').[2] Because it was Good Friday, the pubs were all closed.[3] So she went into a church. The tabernacle stood empty and open. 'God was absent', she reflected, 'In occlusion. Down in the underworld. But tomorrow He would rise again and irradiate the creation with His love. I tried to imagine it.'[4] The Church encourages the faithful to dwell on Christ's passion during Easter week. All around her, O'Faolain saw familiar religious images of comfort and suffering: 'Our Lady of Perpetual Succour opened her embracing arms in love; Christ was contorted on His cross in pain.'[5] But thinking about her own loneliness and that of so many of the people who contacted her, she protested: 'Look at how much ordinary men and women know about being crucified! No wonder we strain ourselves to believe that there is a God who loves us.'[6]

Those familiar with O'Faolain's work will not be surprised that she here reaches for an idea of divine love that she imagines modelled on the intimacy she looked for mainly through romantic love. For her, the biggest problem with Catholicism was in the end not its teachings on sexuality (although she had 'suffered from Rome herself.

Girls and women do'[7]) but rather the fact that she could not herself believe in the existence of a benevolent creator. But religion could not be replaced by a fantasy of finding complete fulfilment with a lover. This was the delusion that had damaged O'Faolain's mother's life and in turn those of her children: 'It wasn't marriage that did her in. She wanted him. It was motherhood. It was us.'[8] The consequence of parental failure was the creation of people like her: 'a secret society, the society of those who have truly suffered'.[9] She was especially moved by a poem by Adrienne Rich that a woman had sent to her in response to the memoir. It underlined that what she and her readers had in common was the experience of having been unhappy children. As Rich puts it in 'In the wake of home': 'what if I tell you, you are not different / it's the family albums that lie'.[10]

Other women discussed in this book also explore the legacies of Catholicism, especially in relation to the treatment of women and children in independent Ireland. They allude quite frequently to Catholic rituals and imagery. For McAliskey, the failure of the Church to support the political struggle of its Irish flock was its Original Sin and all its later failures unfold in that context. While she is the most unambiguously secular figure considered here, only one among them – Sinéad O'Connor – professes strong religious belief. As we have discussed, in a recent song ('Take off your shoes' from the album *How about I be me (and you be you)?*), she repeatedly 'pleads the blood of Jesus' over priestly offenders and their misdeeds. Christ's passion here supplies a potent image of suffering and of the sacred. O'Faolain uses a double image of Christ and Virgin to symbolise the emotional appeal of the images on display in the church she visits – the son in physical agony, the mother offering loving consolation. However, Edna O'Brien underlines the androgynous nature of the exposed and wounded male body: as one of her characters reflects, it was 'as if Christ was woman and woman was Christ in the bloodied ventricles of herself. Man in woman and woman in man.'[11] In her autobiographical writings, O'Brien associates her early loss of religious faith with sexual awakening and as she gets older she apparently does not dwell on any philosophical regrets about not being a conventional Catholic. But it is clear that what she describes, despite scandals involving the Church, as people's continuing 'need for God and salvation' is in her work to some degree transposed into the realms of sex and nation; even literature, for her, was once associated in Ireland with a 'fervour', an intensity of feeling the waning of which she now regrets.[12] As she recalls in *Mother Ireland*, such emotion was first awoken for her by religion and the stories of patriot heroes. Anne Enright, who 'hate[s] Catholicism', confesses to not being fully secular:

> I still believe in God, in some reluctant, furtive part of me. I'm not proud of it. I understand atheists, who are averse to religious people as they might be averse to fat people, as being actually quite dangerous in their weakness. So I am weak (and slightly fat, indeed) and a bit too ethnic, if it comes down to it. I just won't shape up and become a proper person who believes in nothing at all.[13]

This is cleverly written and completely without O'Faolain's sense of anguish. In the same column, Enright suggests that 'reason' does not simply triumph over belief with the forward march of history – even if this is a founding belief of modern Western societies. She hints that her own vestigial faith may stem from her peasant forbears who got their 'Renaissance' from – as she puts it with some mild sarcasm – the 'rational British'.

Several of the women considered here would, like O'Faolain, probably agree that they have been obliged to live 'in the wake of home' or at odds with conventional marriages and families. In this regard, Enright is the sole exception. In some cases, memories or artistic representations of childhood are dominated by an overwhelming impression of the unhappiness of Irish mothers; this in turn is one of the key factors that affects their daughters' own experiences of relationships and motherhood. For McAliskey, the difficulties faced by her mother and her father, as well as the isolation and stigma imposed on her family when she was a child, were clearly to be blamed on oppressive forces in their society (the 'rational British', perhaps, central to which was the sectarian and class complex). These forces were strongly resisted rather than reflected within the home itself (although both parents had hard lives and died young). But this sense of being a member of a precious but vulnerable family was reawakened in no uncertain terms during her adult life by her being shot in her own house by loyalist assassins abetted by the 'security forces' and, later, by the imprisonment of her pregnant daughter. In McAliskey's case, the domestic realm is so exposed to state violence that its affective power needs to be mobilised as a key element in the political struggle for communal justice.

In the poem that O'Faolain quotes, Rich contemplates the question of where refugees and exiles from the domestic world should look for comfort. She points them to America, 'this continent of the homeless', and beyond that to a 'planet of warworn children'.[14] This bears out the observation of Maria Dibattista and Deborah Epstein Nord that the rejection of conventional homes in the work of women writers often involves an embrace of 'public engagement rather than domestic entanglement', in a search for 'some ideal place of settlement'.[15] This is, in a curious way, a more straightforward quest for McAliskey, the only woman from the still-contested territory of Northern Ireland discussed in this book, than for the others. She believed that her most urgent political task was to struggle against a state that was understood by most of her community to be imperialist and sectarian. The historical memory and cultural resources of the Irish poor – those McAliskey calls the 'peasants' and the 'have-nots' – are in her view of enormous value. The failures of the southern Irish state underline the necessity for a radical republican project in the future. The legacies of James Connolly or Constance Markievicz remain entirely relevant. 'Ireland' is still potentially a promised land. For O'Connor, O'Faolain and O'Brien, the unhappy home is in many respects a microcosmic version of the independent Irish state. For many in the south, anti-partitionist republicanism had been discredited during the Northern Irish conflict; while these particular women take a somewhat different view, theirs is often a fraught and complicated affiliation. At the same time, they are deeply imprinted by sometimes masochistic stories of women's suffering, including those told by Catholicism, which are both a source of solace and in some ways an impediment to emancipation. And while prison protest was crucial to the development of Northern Irish republican politics, it seems that southern feminists and liberals sometimes imagined the whole state as a kind of prison camp. For example, during the 'X' case controversy of 1992, when a teenage rape victim was prevented from leaving the country for an abortion by a High Court injunction, the *Irish Times* published a cartoon by Martyn Turner. This featured a map of Ireland on which the border of the Republic was marked out by a barbed wire fence. The small figure of a pregnant girl holding a teddy bear looked out the east. The caption read: 'The introduction of internment in Ireland ... for 14 year old girls'. Both the visual imagery and the wording directly recall Northern Ireland in the 1970s, although political internment was not so unequivocally condemned by the southern media at that time.

Given these circumstances, some of these women look to an alternative in an older version of Ireland in which the Irish language, traditional music, Gaelic poetry and the ballad tradition assume a new prominence. (Only McAliskey speaks Irish well but, for example, O'Brien reports that she is glad to know a little of the language, as its rhythm is so 'rich and intoxicating ... I remember all the poems I learned in Irish and so on'.[16]) Several write about their deep attachment to an Irish rural landscape that testifies to the struggles of earlier generations in its ruined monuments or in the almost erased dwelling places even of comparatively recent times. These are all storehouses of melancholy beauty that have survived the fetishisation of a certain version of tradition in the Ireland presided over by Eamon de Valera. Feminism provides an indispensable perspective on what needs to be changed in contemporary Ireland. At the most obvious level, for example, any woman – like some of those discussed here – who wishes to rediscover even the Irish past needs the freedom to read or travel. The sexual politics of the recent past and of the present moment give rise to anger, but the question of gender does not loom as large in these women's exploration of historical traditions. In relation to Ireland – as Toril Moi puts in a more general context – such women explore solidarities that reach beyond 'the realm of sexual differences'.[17] They do not in the main regard religion or nationalism merely as hangovers from darker times: at the least, these are often associated with forms of community less claustrophobic than the patriarchal family and less isolating than the addictive pleasures of romantic love. And in their fascination with the habitus of Irish people, the writers of prose here – O'Faolain, O'Brien and Enright – are all compelled by the example of Joyce. O'Faolain alone offers a strong gender-based critique of

Joyce, regarding him as a chronicler of the male-dominated Irish public sphere, where she nevertheless unthinkingly felt at home as a young woman. Just as Jesus is androgynous for O'Brien, so too is Joyce – although she believes he in some regards cruelly exploited his family, especially the women, for the sake of his art. She states that he possessed the sensibility of both a man and a woman and that 'language is the hero and the heroine of his works'.[18] She professes to have 'served' him.[19] For Enright, as we have seen, Joyce is also an enabling presence – but only when he is construed as an apolitical domestic writer.

All of these careers can usefully be analysed in relation to feminism in Ireland. Even when they were reclaiming aspects of tradition, these women broke with conventional expectations of their sex when they demanded to be taken seriously as representative and significant voices. They were part of a movement of newly independent women who appeared to be offering to introduce Ireland to sexual liberation, counter-cultural rebelliousness and the power of the mass media as well as to the idea of equality between women and men. This is not to say that they necessarily felt compelled or supported by a feminist community.[20] Only O'Faolain specifically discusses – for example – the enormous satisfaction she felt when making television programmes about Irish women with talented female colleagues at RTÉ. But even she was more often conscious of solitude. Several were exposed to the special opprobrium then reserved for women who were sexually active outside marriage – especially in the 1960s and early 1970s when O'Brien, a notorious 'divorcée', was censored as a pornographic writer and McAliskey scandalised some previously loyal Catholic voters by giving birth to a child outside marriage. The attention they received – and audiences were at times fascinated, horrified and admiring – did not necessarily go hand in hand with feminist advances in Ireland. Progress on women's rights was mainly due to the struggles of generations of campaigners and journalists. But several of these women were glamorous icons of a feminised modernity in Ireland – fluent in a new language of feeling, at home in a world of new pleasures.

In many ways, it is inaccurate to regard these women as cheerleaders for a more affluent or consumerist Ireland. Edna O'Brien now expresses mixed feelings about the changes brought about by 'television, advertising, magazines, and tourism' and concerning the sovereignty of the 'image' in Ireland and elsewhere.[21] But arguably, for many in Ireland, her own work played a distinctive role in heralding the cultural shifts she summarises. Sinéad O'Connor, the most prominent female contributor to Irish rock music – which itself revamped the signifiers of 'Irishness' in the 1980s – nowadays denounces fashion and celebrity culture as mere vanity ('There'll be no makeup and there'll be no film crews / No Vuitton bags and no Manola shoes / When He's presiding over you / Asking you, did you love only you? / Or did you stand for something else / Besides the hankering for fame and fame itself?', 'V.I.P', from *How about I be me (and you be you)?*). For a later generation and a more high-cultural audience, Enright captured the nuances of Celtic Tiger food, clothing, conversation and interior decoration. But while hers was not a celebratory view, neither was it a clearly satirical one that depended on any secure sense that there are other, better values by which to live. Enright is not exactly given to invocations of past nationalist struggles nor to the familiar Irish refrain of 'Was it for this the men of 1916 died?' However, based on recent Irish experience, she seems at least in part to regret that in a globalised economic system the concept of the nation itself has lost, or seems to have lost, its governing influence. In the wake of the crisis (when Ireland was, as she puts it, still 'stuck on the poisoned tit of the Frankfurt banks'), she articulates a certain scepticism about what separation from the United Kingdom might mean for Scotland: in contemporary circumstances, it seems that 'independence' can deliver no more than a national 'entity' that controls everything except the money.[22] McAliskey believes that the revolutionary movement associated with 1916 may have failed but that its lost history contains 'the understanding of the battles of the future'.[23] Writing in the wake of the 2007 election in the south – which returned Fianna Fáil's Bertie Ahern to power as Taoiseach – Nuala O'Faolain commented rather despairingly on the condition of the Republic (she did not live to witness the crash of autumn 2008). Wondering why the southern establishment, especially in the media, had been so concerned with the threat of Irish people being converted to republicanism during the Troubles, she commented that 'the bullying and backbiting and fake righteous anger used against individuals suspected of sympathy with northern nationalism in RTÉ was unnecessary'. This was because she feared that 'soon there will be an all-island Ireland, united by utter, unashamed, consumer capitalism. There'll be 32 green fields full of shopping centres'.[24]

Whatever the complexities of their individual life stories, all of these women had in common the experience of having – for good and ill – themselves *become* the 'story' in the Irish media and beyond. Even Enright, who achieved literary canonisation, rather than celebrity, nearly fifty years after the appearance of O'Brien's *The country girls*, expresses some frustration with the subsequent interest in her as a person, rather than in her work.[25] This story was about the emergence of what Beauvoir refers to as the independent woman – one who is emancipated from men and who pursues her own desires and creative projects. In these particular cases, Irish women also look beyond individualistic solutions to the difficulties of their situations and look for new solidarities 'in the wake of home'. They do so with an awareness of themselves having been (or even of still being) 'other' and that, as such, they are therefore especially alert to some of the repressive effects of community. For most, Ireland remains the sublime object of affection, of ideologies of commitment and/or repudiation; only in Enright is its gravitational pull greatly weakened. In their highly self-aware and often brilliantly expressed explorations of these issues, they bear out Beauvoir's central point that such a woman may become more authentic and 'acutely human'[26] than those that pursue lives either of unchallenged subordination or of unexamined privilege. Collectively, they testify to what Jacqueline Rose calls 'the knowledge of women': not just the well-worn claim that 'the personal is political', but the realisation that once you open the door to the realm of the intimate, 'you never know what you are going to find', including some of the 'most painful, outrageous aspects of the human heart'.[27]

Irish society has changed; for example, the prospect of a vastly more sexually liberal country and of much greater gender equality has come into view. Such social reform – never to be taken for granted – owes its achievements primarily to the broader women's movement, as well as in some measure to pioneers like the individuals discussed here. They were all profoundly disillusioned by the Vatican-sponsored image of 'Holy Ireland'. This was decisively and finally rejected in the referenda on marriage equality in 2015 and on the repeal of the Eighth Amendment three years later. (In the aftermath of the vote in favour of repeal in 2018, it is interesting to note that several campaigners described the change as heralding not a repudiation but a better version of Ireland: for example, Una Mullally stated that 'what is happening now is who we are'; Colm O'Gorman declared that 'Ireland is becoming the country we've always quietly been.'[28]) But in general for the women considered here, such an emancipation would not in itself be enough. For these reasons, among many others, we can still benefit from hearing all the reverberations of their work. The repressiveness of independent Ireland has distorted our understanding of the past and of shared tradition; the project of overcoming it must also involve a collective recognition of many other – even more intractable – political and social questions. Our conceptions of traditional and modern Ireland have by now changed, but here we can see how this change came about and how the shifting valences of the traditional and the modern nevertheless continue ceaselessly to operate.

Notes

1 O'Faolain, *Are you somebody?* [US edition], p. 191.
2 O'Faolain, *Are you somebody?* [US edition], p. 191.
3 The alcohol licensing laws have now changed and pubs in Ireland were permitted to stay open on Good Friday for the first time in 2018. One can only wonder if O'Faolain would have approved.
4 O'Faolain, *Are you somebody?* [US edition], p. 191.
5 O'Faolain, *Are you somebody?* [US edition], p. 205.
6 O'Faolain, *Are you somebody?* [US edition], p. 198.
7 O'Faolain, *Are you somebody?*, p. 337.
8 O'Faolain, *Are you somebody?* [US edition], p. 213.
9 O'Faolain, *Almost there*, p. 136.
10 Adrienne Rich, quoted by O'Faolain, *Are you somebody?* [US edition], p. 205.
11 Edna O'Brien, *The high road* (London: Weidenfeld & Nicolson, 1988), p. 158.
12 O'Brien, interviewed by Helen Thompson, in Maloney and Thompson (eds), *Irish women writers speak out*, p. 204.

13 Enright, 'Diary', *London Review of Books*, 29:9.
14 Rich, quoted by O'Faolain, *Are you somebody?* [US edition], p. 205.
15 See Maria Dibattista and Deborah Epstein Nord, *At home in the world: women writers and public life, from Austen to the present* (Princeton, NJ: Princeton University Press, 2017), pp. 2, x.
16 O'Brien, interviewed by Thompson, pp. 198–9.
17 Moi, *What is a woman?*, p. 8.
18 Edna O'Brien, *James Joyce* (London: Weidenfeld & Nicolson, 1999), p. 97. See Amanda Greenwood's extensive discussion of O'Brien's comments on Joyce and feminism, in *Edna O'Brien*, chapter 8.
19 O'Brien, quoted by Greenwood, *Edna O'Brien*, p. 94.
20 On the tension between individual self-expression and the imperatives of collaborative politics in Irish feminism and in Irish women's writing, see for example Innes, *Woman and nation in Irish literature and society*, pp. 169, 179 and Franks, *British and Irish women writers and the women's movement*, p. 127.
21 O'Brien, interviewed by Thompson, p. 204.
22 Anne Enright on the idea of Scottish independence, in 'Reflections on the Independence referendum', *London Review of Books*, 36:17 (September 2014).
23 Bernadette McAliskey, 'Speech on the centenary of the Easter Rising', www.youtube.com/watch?v=J9QCArSU3-g (accessed 29 June 2018).
24 See O'Faolain, 'If I had my time back'.
25 See Enright, interview with Irene Gilsenan Nordin at Dalarna University (2013), www.youtube.com/watch?v=okr9xdfJ5e4 (accessed 29 June 2018).
26 I quote from Moi's account of Beauvoir's argument, in *Beauvoir*, p. 199.
27 Rose, *Women in dark times*, pp. ix–x.
28 See Una Mullally, 'Referendum shows us there is no Middle Ireland, just Ireland', *Irish Times* (26 May 2018); Colm O'Gorman quoted in '"Yes" campaigners react to abortion referendum win', *The Irish Independent* (26 May 2018).

Bibliography

Anderson, Benedict, *Imagined communities: reflections on the origin and spread of nationalism*, revised edition (London: Verso, 1991).
Barthes, Roland, *Image – music – text*, trans. Stephen Heath (London: Flamingo, 1977).
Beauvoir, Simone de, *The second sex*, trans. H. M. Parshley (London: Vintage, 1997).
Benjamin, Walter, *The arcades project*, trans. Howard Eiland and Kevin McLaughlin (Cambridge, MA: Harvard University Press, 1999).
Boehmer, Elleke, *Stories of women: gender and narrative in the postcolonial nation* (Manchester: Manchester University Press, 2005).
Boland, Eavan, *Object lessons: the life of the woman and the poet in our time* (London: Vintage, 1996).
Bourke, Angela et al. (eds), *The Field Day anthology of Irish writing: Irish women's writing and traditions*, vols 4 and 5 (Cork: Cork University Press, 2002).
Bourke, Richard, *Peace in Ireland: the war of ideas* (London: Pimlico, 2003).
Bracken, Clare and Susan Cahill (eds), *Anne Enright* (Dublin: Irish Academic Press, 2011).
Bracken, Clare and Susan Cahill, 'Introduction', in Bracken and Cahill (eds), *Anne Enright*, pp. 1–11.
Brown, Terence, *Ireland: a social and cultural history* (London: Harper Perennial, 2004).
Browne, Vincent, 'The politics of H-block', *Magill* (December 1980), https://magill.ie/archive/politics-h-block (accessed 23 June 2018).
Buckley, Sarah-Anne, 'The catholic cure for poverty', *Jacobin* (May 2016), www.jacobinmag.com/2016/05/catholic-church-ireland-magdalene-laundries-mother-baby-homes (accessed 30 June 2018).
Butler, Eoin, 'Isn't Sinéad O'Connor overdue a massive grovelling apology from absolutely everybody?', *Tripping along the ledge*, blogpost, www.

eoinbutler.com/home/isnt-sinead-oconnor-overdue-a-massive-grovelling-apology-from-absolutely-everybody (accessed 29 June 2018).
Butler, Judith, 'Gender is burning: questions of appropriation and subversion', in Susan Thornham (ed.), *Feminist film theory: a reader* (New York: New York University Press, 1999), pp. 381–95.
Caruth, Cathy, *Unclaimed experience: trauma, narrative, and history* (Baltimore, MD: Johns Hopkins University Press, 1996).
Cleary, Joe, *Outrageous fortune: capital and culture in modern Ireland* (Dublin: Field Day, 2007).
Cleary, Joe, '"Horseman pass by!": the neoliberal world system and the crisis in Irish literature', *Boundary 2*, 45:1 (February 2018), pp. 135–79.
Colletta, Lisa and Maureen O'Connor (eds), *Wild colonial girl: essays on Edna O'Brien* (Madison: University of Wisconsin Press, 2006).
Condron, Neil, 'Upon small shoulders', https://condron.ie/upon-small-shoulders (accessed 29 June 2018).
Conlon, Catherine, Sinéad Kennedy and Aideen Quilty (eds), *The abortion papers*, vol. 2 (Cork: Cork University Press, 2015).
Connolly, Linda, *The Irish women's movement* (London: Palgrave Macmillan, 2002).
Coughlan, Patricia, 'Killing the bats: O'Brien, abjection, and the question of agency', in Laing et al. (eds), *Edna O'Brien*, pp. 171–95.
Crilly, Anne (director), *Mother Ireland* (Derry Film and Video, 1988).
Cronin, Michael G., *Impure thoughts: sexuality, Catholicism and literature in twentieth-century Ireland* (Manchester: Manchester University Press, 2012).
Crowe, Catriona, 'Testimony to a flowering' (review of *The Field Day anthology of Irish writing*, vols 4 and 5), *The Dublin Review*, 10 (Spring 2003), https://thedublinreview.com/article/testimony-to-a-flowering (accessed 25 June 2018).
Cullingford, Elizabeth, *Ireland's others: gender and ethnicity in Irish literature and popular culture* (Cork: Cork University Press, 2001).
Davidson, Sara, 'Bernadette Devlin: an Irish revolutionary in Irish America', *Harper's Magazine*, 240:1436 (January 1970), pp. 78–87.
Devlin, Bernadette *see* McAliskey, Bernadette
Dibattista, Maria and Deborah Epstein Nord, *At home in the world: women writers and public life, from Austen to the present* (Princeton, NJ: Princeton University Press, 2017).
Dodd, Luke, 'Nuala O'Faolain: obituary', *Guardian* (12 May 2008).
Doolan, Lelia (director), *Bernadette: notes on a political journey* (Digital Quilts, 2011).
Duncan, Pamela, 'Imogen Stuart, Edna O'Brien and William Trevor elected saoithe', *Irish Times* (16 September 2015).
Eagleton, Terry, *Heathcliff and the great hunger* (London: Verso, 1995).
Edwards, Elaine, 'Tuam babies: "significant" quantities of human remains found at former home', *Irish Times* (3 March 2017).

Ellmann, Maud, *The hunger artists: starving, writing, and imprisonment* (Cambridge, MA: Harvard University Press, 1993).
English, Bridget, *Laying out the bones: death and dying in the modern Irish novel* (Syracuse, NY: Syracuse University Press, 2017).
Enright, Anne, *The wig my father wore* [1995] (London: Minerva, 1996).
Enright, Anne, *What are you like?* [2000] (London: Vintage, 2001).
Enright, Anne, *The pleasure of Eliza Lynch* [2002] (London: Vintage, 2003).
Enright, Anne, Interview with Maloney, in Maloney and Thompson (eds), *Irish women writers speak out*, pp. 51–64.
Enright, Anne, *Making babies: stumbling into motherhood* (London: Vintage, 2005).
Enright, Anne, 'Diary', *London Review of Books*, 29:9 (May 2007).
Enright, Anne, *The gathering* [2007] (London: Vintage, 2008).
Enright, Anne, 'What women want: Anne Enright', interviewed by Susanna Rustin, *Guardian* (15 March 2008).
Enright, Anne, 'Diary', *London Review of Books*, 33:4 (February 2011).
Enright, Anne, *The forgotten waltz* (London: Jonathan Cape, 2011).
Enright, Anne, '*The country girl* by Edna O'Brien – review', *Guardian* (12 October 2012).
Enright, Anne, Interview with Irene Gilsenan Nordin at Dalarna University (2013), www.youtube.com/watch?v=okr9xdfJ5e4 (accessed 29 June 2018).
Enright, Anne, 'Reflections on the independence referendum', *London Review of Books*, 36:17 (September 2014).
Enright, Anne, 'A return to the western shore: Anne Enright on yielding to tradition', *Guardian* (9 May 2015).
Enright, Anne, 'Antigone in Galway: Anne Enright on the dishonoured dead', *London Review of Books*, 37:24 (December 2015).
Enright, Anne, *The Green Road* (London: Jonathan Cape, 2015).
Enright, Anne, 'Diary', *London Review of Books*, 39:18 (September 2017).
Enright, Anne, 'The question of consent', in Mullally (ed.), *Repeal the 8th*, pp. 27–32.
Evason, Eileen, *Against the grain: the contemporary women's movement in Northern Ireland* (Dublin: Attic Press, 1991).
Felski, Rita, *The gender of modernity* (Cambridge, MA: Harvard University Press, 1995).
Felski, Rita, 'On confession', in Sidonie Smith and Julia Watson (eds), *Women, autobiography, theory: a reader* (Madison: University of Wisconsin Press, 1998), pp. 83–95.
Fischer, Clara and Mary McAuliffe (eds), *Irish feminisms: past, present and future* (Galway: Arlen House, 2014).
Foster, R. F., *Luck and the Irish: a brief history of change, 1970–2000* (London: Allen Lane, 2007).
Foster, R. F., *Vivid faces: the revolutionary generation in Ireland, 1890–1923* (London: Allen Lane, 2014).

Franks, Jill, *British and Irish women writers and the women's movement: six literary voices of their times* (Jefferson, NC: McFarland, 2013).
Fraser, Nancy, *Fortunes of feminism* (London: Verso, 2013).
Gray, Breda, *Women and the Irish diaspora* (London: Psychology Press, 2004).
Greenwood, Amanda, *Edna O'Brien* (Tavistock: Northcote, 2003).
Harte, Liam, 'Introduction', in Harte (ed.), *Modern Irish autobiography: self, nation and society* (London: Palgrave Macmillan, 2007), pp. 1–13.
Harte, Liam, *Reading the contemporary Irish novel* (Chichester: Wiley, 2014).
Hayes, Dermott, *Sinéad O'Connor: so different* (London: Omnibus, 1991).
Ingman, Heather, 'Edna O'Brien: stretching the nation's boundaries', *Irish Studies Review*, 10:3 (2002), pp. 253–65.
Innes, C. L., *Woman and nation in Irish literature and society, 1880–1935* (Hemel Hempstead: Harvester Wheatsheaf, 1993).
Jones, Ernest, *Sigmund Freud: life and work* (London: Hogarth Press, 1955), vol. 2.
Kennedy, Sinéad, 'Ireland's fight for choice', *Jacobin* (March 2018), www.jacobinmag.com/2018/03/irelands-fight-for-choice (accessed 30 June 2018).
Kipnis, Laura, *The female thing: dirt, sex, envy, vulnerability* (London: Profile Books, 2006).
Laing, Katherine, Sinéad Mooney and Maureen O'Connor (eds), *Edna O'Brien: new critical perspectives* (Dublin: Carysfort Press, 2006).
Leith, William, 'The life of Saint Sinéad', *Independent*, 29 November 1992.
Levine, June, *Sisters: the personal story of an Irish feminist* (Dublin: Ward River Press, 1982).
Lloyd, David, 'The memory of hunger', in Tom Hayden (ed.), *The Irish hunger: personal reflections on the legacy of the Famine* (Boulder, CO: Roberts Rinehart, 1997), pp. 32–47.
MacCabe, Colin, *The butcher boy* (Cork: Cork University Press, 2007).
Maloney, Catriona and Helen Thompson (eds), *Irish women writers speak out: voices from the field* (Syracuse, NY: Syracuse University Press, 2003).
Malouf, Michael, 'Feeling Éire(y): on Irish-Caribbean popular culture', in Diane Negra (ed.), *The Irish in us: Irishness, performativity, and popular culture* (Durham, NC: Duke University Press, 2006), pp. 318–53.
McAliskey, Bernadette (formerly Bernadette Devlin), 'Maiden speech to the House of Commons, 22 April 1969', https://api.parliament.uk/historic-hansard/commons/1969/apr/22/northern-ireland#S5CV0782P0_19690422_HOC_27 (accessed 23 June 2018).
McAliskey, Bernadette, 'Britain's youngest MP, Bernadette Devlin, gives a press conference', www.youtube.com/watch?v=XWOHgVS3E8M (accessed 23 June 2018).
McAliskey, Bernadette, 'Bernadette Devlin – Bogside barriers', www.youtube.com/watch?v=9n9SMYsT04g (accessed 23 June 2018).

McAliskey, Bernadette, *The price of my soul* (London: Pan Books, 1969).
McAliskey, Bernadette, 'Bernadette Devlin interview after Home Secretary Commons attack', www.youtube.com/watch?v=KLlpVQFdjCo (accessed 23 June 2018).
McAliskey, Bernadette, 'Bernadette Devlin delivers a proletarian protest', www.youtube.com/watch?v=3EKxowOFQP8 (accessed 23 June 2018).
McAliskey, Bernadette, 'Speech to Clár na mBan conference' (1994), in Bourke *et al.* (eds), *The Field Day anthology*, vol. 5, pp. 420–23.
McAliskey, Bernadette, 'Address to Bloody Sunday march' (2013), http:// thepensivequill.am/2013/01/end-impunity-bernadette-mcaliskey.html (accessed 23 June 2018).
McAliskey, Bernadette, 'Speech on the centenary of the Easter Rising' (2016), www.youtube.com/watch?v=J9QCArSU3-g (accessed 29 June 2018).
McAliskey, Bernadette, 'I am astounded I survived. I made some mad decisions', interview with Kitty Holland, *Irish Times* (22 September 2016).
McAliskey, Bernadette, 'A terrible state of chassis', Seamus Deane Honorary Field Day lecture (2016), www.youtube.com/watch?v=42yJcDQSsRQ (accessed 23 June 2018).
McAuliffe, Mary and Liz Gillis, *Richmond Barracks 1916: 'We were there' – 77 women of the Easter Rising* (Dublin: Four Courts Press, 2016).
McBride, Eimear, 'Introduction', in Edna O'Brien, *The country girls trilogy* (London: Faber, 2017), pp. ix–xvii.
McCafferty, Nell, *The Armagh women* (Dublin: Co-op Books, 1981).
McCafferty, Nell, *The best of Nell* (Dublin: Attic Press, 1984).
McCafferty, Nell, *A woman to blame: the Kerry babies case* (Dublin: Attic Press, 1985).
McCafferty, Nell, *Nell: a disorderly woman* (Dublin: Penguin, 2005).
McCann, Eamonn, *War in an Irish town* (London: Pluto Press, 1993).
McCann, Fiona, 'Writing by and about republican women prisoners', *Irish University Review*, 47, Issue supplement (November 2017), pp. 502–14.
McGahern, John, *The barracks* (London: Faber & Faber, 1963).
McGahern, John, *Memoir* (London: Faber & Faber, 2005).
McKay, Susan, 'Interview with Róisín McAliskey', in Bourke *et al.* (eds), *The Field Day anthology*, vol. 5, pp. 1533–6.
McKay, Susan, *Sophia's story* (Dublin: Gill & Macmillan, 2004).
McKay, Susan, *Bear in mind these dead* (London: Faber & Faber, 2008).
McKeown, Belinda, 'Review of Anne Enright, *The Green Road*: so Irish it's almost provocative', *Irish Times* (2 May 2015).
McLaughlin, Noel and Martin McLoone, 'Hybridity and national musics: the case of Irish rock music', *Popular music*, 19:2 (2000), pp. 181–99.
McLean, Stuart, *The event and its terrors: Ireland, famine, modernity* (Stanford, CA: Stanford University Press, 2004).
Meaney, Gerardine, *Gender, Ireland and cultural change* (London: Routledge, 2010).
Meaney, Gerardine, 'Waking the dead: Antigone, Ismene and Anne Enright's

narrators in mourning', in Bracken and Cahill (eds), *Anne Enright*, pp. 145–64.
Mitchell, Juliet, *Psychoanalysis and feminism* (Harmondsworth: Penguin, 1974).
Moi, Toril, *Simone de Beauvoir: the making of an intellectual woman* (Oxford: Blackwell, 1994).
Moi, Toril, *What is a woman? and other essays* (Oxford: Oxford University Press, 1999).
Moore, Thomas, *Irish melodies* (London: Longmans, 1873).
Mulhall, Anne, 'The spectral feminine in the work of Anne Enright', in Bracken and Cahill (eds), *Anne Enright*, pp. 67–86.
Mullally, Una (ed.), *Repeal the 8th* (London: Unbound, 2018).
Mullally, Una, 'Referendum shows us there is no Middle Ireland, just Ireland', *Irish Times* (26 May 2018).
Napier, Taura S., 'Pilgrimage to the self: autobiographies of twentieth-century Irish women', in Harte (ed.), *Modern Irish autobiography*, pp. 70–90.
Nolan, Emer, *Joyce and nationalism* (London: Routledge, 1995).
Nolan, Emer, *Catholic emancipations: Irish fiction from Thomas Moore to James Joyce* (Syracuse, NY: Syracuse University Press, 2007).
Nolan, Emer, 'Postcolonial literary studies, nationalism, and feminist critique in contemporary Ireland', *Éire-Ireland*, 42:1 and 42:2 (Spring/Summer 2007), pp. 336–61.
O'Brien, Conor Cruise, *States of Ireland* (Frogmore, Herts: Panther Books, 1974).
O'Brien, Edna, *A pagan place* [1970] (Harmondsworth: Penguin, 1971).
O'Brien, Edna, *Night* [1972] (London: Faber & Faber, 2014).
O'Brien, Edna, *Mother Ireland* (New York: Harcourt Brace Jovanovich, 1976).
O'Brien, Edna, *A fanatic heart: selected stories of Edna O'Brien* (New York: Farrar, Straus and Giroux, 1984).
O'Brien, Edna, *The country girls trilogy* (New York: Farrar, Straus and Giroux, 1986).
O'Brien, Edna, *The high road* (London: Weidenfeld & Nicolson, 1988).
O'Brien, Edna, 'Co Clare', in *32 counties: photographs of Ireland by Donovan Wylie, with new writing by thirty-two Irish writers* (London: Secker & Warburg, 1989), pp. 229–30.
O'Brien, Edna, *James Joyce* (London: Weidenfeld & Nicolson, 1999).
O'Brien, Edna, *Wild Decembers* [1999] (New York: Houghton Mifflin, 2001).
O'Brien, Edna, Interview with Thompson, in Maloney and Thompson (eds), *Irish women writers speak out*, pp. 197–205.
O'Brien, Edna, Interview with BBC *Newsnight* (November 2010), 'Irish writers on national shame and anger over bailout', news.bbc.co.uk/2/hi/9216037.stm (accessed 22 June 2018).
O'Brien, Edna, *Country girl: a memoir* (London: Faber & Faber, 2012).

O'Brien, Edna, *The little red chairs* (London: Faber & Faber, 2015).
O'Brien, Matthew J., 'Irish America, race and Bernadette Devlin's 1969 American tour', *New Hibernia Review*, 14:2 (Summer 2010), pp. 84–101.
O'Brien, Peggy, 'The silly and the serious: an assessment of Edna O'Brien', *The Massachusetts Review*, 28:3 (Autumn 1987), pp. 474–88.
O'Callaghan, Margaret, 'Women and politics in independent Ireland, 1921–68', in Bourke *et al.* (eds), *The Field Day anthology*, vol. 5, pp. 120–34.
O'Connor, Sinéad, *The lion and the cobra* (album) (Ensign/Chrysalis,1987).
O'Connor, Sinéad, *I do not want what I haven't got* (album) (Ensign/Chrysalis,1990).
O'Connor, Sinéad, *Universal mother* (album) (Ensign/Chrysalis,1994).
O'Connor, Sinéad, *Faith and courage* (album) (Atlantic, 2000).
O'Connor, Sinéad, *Sean-nós nua* (album) (Vanguard, 2002).
O'Connor, Sinéad, *Throw down your arms* (album) (Chocolate and Vanilla, 2005).
O'Connor, Sinéad, 'To Sinéad O'Connor, the Pope's apology for sex abuse in Ireland seems hollow', *Washington Post* (28 March 2010).
O'Connor, Sinéad, *How about I be me (and you be you)?* (album) (One Little Indian/RED, 2012).
O'Connor, Sinéad, *I'm not bossy, I'm the boss* (album) (Nettwerk, 2014).
O'Faolain, Nuala, 'Edna O'Brien', in *Ireland Today* (Bulletin of the Department of Foreign Affairs) (September 1983), pp. 10–13.
O'Faolain, Nuala, 'Irish women and writing in modern Ireland' [1985], in Bourke *et al.* (eds), *The Field Day anthology*, vol. 5, pp. 1601–5.
O'Faolain, Nuala, *Are you somebody?: the life and times of Nuala O'Faolain* (Dublin: New Island Books, 1996).
O'Faolain, Nuala, *Are you somebody?: the accidental memoir of a Dublin woman* [revised US edition of *Are you somebody?: the life and times of Nuala O'Faolain*] (New York: Henry Holt, 1998).
O'Faolain, Nuala, *My dream of you* (New York: Riverhead Books, 2001).
O'Faolain, Nuala, *Almost there: the onward journey of a Dublin woman* (London: Penguin, 2003).
O'Faolain, Nuala, *The story of Chicago May* (New York: Riverhead Books, 2005).
O'Faolain, Nuala, 'If I had my time back, I'd be somewhere other than in RTÉ before, during and after the hunger strikes', *Sunday Tribune* (19 August 2007).
O'Faolain, Nuala, Interview with Marian Finucane, RTÉ radio (April 2008), https://soundcloud.com/keessentials/nuala-ofaolains-interview-on (accessed 25 June 2018).
O'Faolain, Nuala, *Best love, Rosie* (Dublin: New Island Books, 2009).
O'Faolain, Nuala, *A more complex truth: selected writing* (Dublin: New Island Books, 2010).
O'Rahilly, Helen, 'As an emigrant, "Linger" wasn't about love, it was about Ireland', *Irish Times* (19 January 2018).

O'Toole, Fintan, 'Foreword', in O'Faolain, *A more complex truth*, pp. ix–xiv.
Fašeta, Senia, *Irish nationalist women, 1900–1918* (Cambridge: Cambridge University Press, 2014).
Pelan, Rebecca, 'Reflections on a Connemara Dietrich', in Laing *et al.* (eds), *Edna O'Brien*, pp. 12–37.
Peterson, Shirley, '"Meaniacs" and martyrs: sadomasochistic desire in Edna O'Brien's *The country girls trilogy*', in Laing *et al.* (eds), *Edna O'Brien*, pp. 151–70.
Reynolds, Simon and Joy Press, *The sex revolts: gender, rebellion and rock 'n' roll* (London: Serpent's Tail, 1995).
Robinson, Mary, 'Acceptance speech', 9 November 1990, www.president.ie/en/media-library/speeches/president-robinsons-acceptance-speech (accessed 21 June 2018).
Robinson, Mary, 'Inaugural speech', 3 December 1990, www.president.ie/en/media-library/speeches/address-by-the-president-mary-robinson-on-the-occasion-of-her-inauguration (accessed 21 June 2018).
Rockett, Emer and Kevin Rockett, *Neil Jordan: exploring boundaries* (Dublin: Liffey Press, 2003).
Rose, Jacqueline, *Women in dark times* (London: Bloomsbury, 2014).
Ross, F. Stuart, *Smashing H-Block: the rise and fall of the popular campaign against criminalization, 1976–82* (Liverpool: Liverpool University Press, 2011).
Ryan, Louise and Margaret Ward, *Irish Women and nationalism: soldiers, new women and wicked hags* (Newbridge, Co. Kildare: Irish Academic Press, 2004).
Ryan, Matthew, 'What am I like: writing the body and the self', in Bracken and Cahill (eds), *Anne Enright*, pp. 165–84.
Salome, Louis J., *Violence, veils and bloodlines: reporting from war zones* (Jefferson, NC: McFarland, 2010).
Scally, Robert, *The end of hidden Ireland: rebellion, famine and emigration* (New York: Oxford University Press, 1995).
Smyth, Ailbhe (ed.), *The abortion papers* [1992], vol. 1 (Cork: Cork University Press, 2015).
Smyth, Gerry, *Noisy island: a short history of Irish popular music* (Cork: Cork University Press, 2005).
Sweetman, Rosita, *On our knees* (London: Pan, 1972).
Target, G. W., *Bernadette: the story of Bernadette Devlin* (London: Hodder & Stoughton, 1975).
Tóibín, Colm, 'Introduction', Colm Tóibín (ed.), *The Penguin book of Irish fiction* (London: Viking, 1999), pp. ix–xxxiv.
Waters, John, 'Sinéad the keener', *Irish Times* (28 January 1995).
Waters, John, *Beyond consolation* (London: Continuum, 2010).
Weinstein, Laura, 'The significance of the Armagh dirty protest', *Éire-Ireland*, 4:3 and 4:4 (Fall/Winter 2006), pp. 11–41.

Wills, Clair, 'Women, domesticity and the family: recent feminist work in Irish cultural studies', *Cultural Studies*, 15:1 (January 2001), pp. 33–57.

Wills, Clair, 'Feminism, culture and critique in English', in Bourke *et al.* (eds), *The Field Day anthology*, vol. 5, pp. 1578–87.

Wills, Clair, *The best are leaving: emigration and post-war Irish culture* (Cambridge: Cambridge University Press, 2015).

Woolf, Virginia, *Three guineas* (New York: Harcourt, 2006).

Wulff, Helena, *Rhythms of writing: an anthropology of Irish literature* (London: Bloomsbury, 2017).

Wynne-Jones, Ros, 'It's not a crime to fall in love with an IRA man', *Independent* (31 May 1997).

Yeats, W. B., *Collected poems* (London: Macmillan, 1982).

Žižek, Slavoj, *Tarrying with the negative* (Durham, NC: Duke University Press, 1993).

Index

abortion 9, 58, 101, 122, 144, 165
  Eighth Amendment, repeal of 206,
    193–4n.26
  'Pro-life' (Eighth) amendment to the
    constitution 169, 193n.26
  'X' Case 19, 65, 150, 201–2
Adams, Gerry 38
Ahern, Bertie 204
'aisling' poetry see O'Connor, Sinéad
  and
Anglo-Irish Agreement (1985) 81
Anglo-Irish Treaty (1921) 81, 108
Antigone see Enright, Anne, 'Antigone in
  Galway'; McAliskey, Bernadette
  and;
Aosdána see O'Brien, Edna
Armagh Jail see McAliskey, Bernadette
  and

banking crisis (Ireland 2008) 38–9, 71,
  180, 204
Bardwell, Leland 133
Barthes, Roland 52
BBC (British Broadcasting Corporation)
  38, 119, 152, 173
Beauvoir, Simone de 2–3, 17, 26, 29,
  41–2, 65, 67–8, 130, 132, 135,
  136, 205
Beckett, Samuel 7, 15
Beethoven, Ludwig van 143
Belfast Agreement (1998) 38
  see also Good Friday Agreement
Benjamin, Walter 8
Berger, John 132, 134
Birmingham Six 150
Black, Mary 69
Black Panthers 98
Bloody Sunday (Derry 1972) see
  McAliskey, Bernadette and

Bogside, Battle of see McAliskey,
  Bernadette and
Boland, Eavan 17
Bono 64, 70
Bowen, Elizabeth
  The last September 17
Browne, Noel 124
Browne, Vincent 103
Bullingdon Club 133
Burning Spear (Winston Rodney) 63,
  64
Burntollet Bridge, Battle of see
  McAliskey, Bernadette and
Butler, Judith 42–3
Byrne, Gay see O'Faolain, Nuala,
  interview with

Carson, Johnny see McAliskey,
  Bernadette, appearance on
  Tonight show
Carter, Angela 166–8
Caruth, Cathy 53
'Celtic Tiger' 9, 38, 50, 129, 146, 153,
  165, 175, 179, 192, 204
Chichester-Clark, James 96
Chieftains, The
  The long black veil (album) 69, 70
child abuse see sexual abuse
Children of Lir 15, 59–60, 77n.12
Civil War
  American 69
  Irish 4
Clannad 50
Clare, County 17, 32, 120, 140, 153,
  156, 181, 182, 185
  see also Enright, Anne and; O'Brien,
    Edna and; O'Faolain, Nuala and
Colletta, Lisa 39
Condell, Sonny 57

INDEX

Condron, Neil
  Upon small shoulders (painting) 72
Connolly, James 95, 201
Constitution of the Irish Republic (1937) 4
Contraception, availability of in Ireland 4, 9, 81, 136, 169
Corless, Catherine 182, 183, 196n.75
  see also Mother and Baby Home, Tuam
Corrs, The 50
Coughlan, Patricia 38, 40
Craig, Harry 134
Cronin, Michael G. 30, 128
Cullingford, Elizabeth 59n.11, 61–2

Daily Mirror 85
Daley, Richard 97
Daly, Miriam 87
De Paor, Liam 123
De Valera, Eamon 127, 202
Devlin, Bernadette *see* McAliskey, Bernadette
Devlin, John 88
Devlin, Lizzie 88
divorce, availability of in Ireland 4, 9, 122, 169
Dodd, Luke 122–3
Donoghue, Denis 131–2, 143
Doolan, Lelia 93
  Bernadette: notes on a political journey (film) 89, 93, 95, 111
Downing Street Declaration 109, 117n.90
Drew, Ronnie 70
Dudley Edwards, Ruth 38
Duignan, May ('Chicago May') 116n.89, 120
DUP (Democratic Unionist Party) 107

Easter 1916 (Rebellion/Rising) 4, 5, 70, 81, 87, 103, 108, 182, 204
  centenary of, 72, 86, 181–2, 183
Edgeworth, Maria 17
Education Act of 1947 (UK) 89
Eighth Amendment *see* abortion
Emmet, Robert 83
Enright, Anne 1, 6, 7, 10, 17, 164–92, 200–5 *passim*
  Angela Carter and, 166–8
  background 164–6
  Clare (county) in writings of 181–2, 184–7, 188–9
  education 166
  employment at RTÉ 166
  feminism and 167, 171–2, 184, 192–3n.4
  hospitalisation 166

London Review of Books and 164, 175, 181
  writings
  'Antigone in Galway' 181–2, 183, 196n.75
  'A return to the western shore' 181–2, 184–6
  The forgotten waltz 165, 179–8
  The gathering 164, 165, 175–9, 181
  The Green Road 165, 181, 185–92
  Making babies, 164, 166–7, 168
  The pleasure of Eliza Lynch 171, 174
  What are you like? 171, 172
  The wig my father wore 173–4
Enya (Enya Ní Bhraonáin) 54, 67
European Economic Community 38
Evening Press, The 124

famine *see* Great Famine, The
Farmleigh Conference (2009) 75
Farrell, Mairéad 111, 116n.77
Felski, Rita 8–9, 151
feminism 1–12 *passim*, 201–3 *passim*
  see also Beauvoir, Simone de; Boland, Eavan; Enright, Anne and; Kipnis, Laura; McAliskey, Bernadette and; O'Brien, Edna and; O'Connor, Sinéad and; O'Faolain, Nuala and; Rose, Jacqueline; Wills, Clair
'Fifth province' 7
Finucane, Marian *see* O'Faolain, Nuala, interview with
Fitzgerald, Edward 108
Fontenoy, Battle of (and poem) 187
Foster, Arlene 107
Freud, Sigmund 11
Fry, Albert 155

Gardner, Helen 133
Gebler, Ernest 30, 33
Geldof, Bob 54, 67
George, Terry
  Some mother's son (film) 108
Goldenbridge (Industrial School) 160n.127
Good Friday Agreement 101, 145
  see also Belfast Agreement
Gonne, Maud 56, 108
Grant, John
  'Queen of Denmark' (song) 73
Great Famine, The 36, 53, 76n.5, 146, 153, 189
Great War, The 81
Greenberg, Clement 146
Greer, Germaine 59

INDEX

Gregory, Augusta
  Cathleen ni Houlihan (play) 17
Guardian 35, 119, 164, 181, 184

Harris, Eoghan 86
Harte, Liam 151, 176
Haughey, Charles J. 128, 129
H-Block (prison) *see* McAliskey, Bernadette and
Hillsborough (stadium disaster) 110
Hilton, Tim 132
Holland, Kitty 105
Holland, Mary 105
Holloway Prison 102
Horslips, The 54
House of Commons 81, 85, 95, 98
  see also Westminster

INLA (Irish National Liberation Army) 35, 101
International Criminal Court (The Hague) 37
IRA (Irish Republican Army) 57–8, 85, 86, 100, 101, 103, 111
  see also McAliskey, Bernadette and; O'Connor, Sinéad, Irish republicanism and
Irish Censorship Board, 19
Irish Literary Revival, 14, 187
Irish Parliamentary Party, 81
Irish Republican Socialist Party *see* McAliskey, Bernadette and
Irish Times 105, 119, 202

Jackson, Jesse 97
James II, King of England and Ireland 92, 187
James, Henry 130
Jordan, Neil
  The butcher boy (film) 61–2
Joyce, James 7, 19, 20, 40, 129, 137, 166, 170, 202–3
  biography of *see* O'Brien, Edna
  'The Dead' 173
  Dubliners 15, 17, 176
  A portrait of the artist as a young man 127
  Ulysses 16, 21

Karadžić, Radovan 34, 37
Kavanagh, Patrick 137
Kenny, Enda 182
Kent, Thomas 182–3
Kelly, Luke 69
Kettle, Arnold 123, 143
Kilmainham (jail) 103
King, Philip 57
Kipnis, Laura 37

Late late show (RTÉ) *see* O'Connor, Sinéad, appearance on; O'Faolain, Nuala, appearance on
Laureate for Irish Fiction 164
Laverty, Maura 17, 133
Lavin, Mary 17, 133
Lawless, Emily 186–8, 191
Lemass, Seán 127
Les misérables 148
Lincoln, Abraham 69
Lindsay, John 97
Lissadell (Co. Sligo) 108, 139
Livingston, Jennie
  Paris is burning 42
London Review of Books see Enright, Anne and
Low-Beer, John 134, 137
Lynott, Phil 54

McAliskey, Bernadette (formerly Devlin) 5, 7, 10, 80–112, 199–206 *passim*
  as Antigone 85, 99
  Armagh Jail and 102, 104–5, 109, 111, 115n.75, 115n.77
  attempted assassination of 87, 104
  background 83, 88–90, 101
  Bloody Sunday and 85, 98–100, 107, 110, 111
  Bogside, Battle of, and 93–4, 96
  Burntollet Bridge, Battle of, and 92
  campaign for civil rights and 5, 10, 81, 82–3, 91–3, 96–8
  election of 81
  feminism and 81–7 *passim*, 97, 104–5, 107, 111
  nationalism and 85–6
  Good Friday Agreement and 101
  H-Blocks and 102–7 *passim*
    hunger strikes 102–4, 106–10 *passim*
    protests 103–4, 106, 107
    Special Category Status in 102–3
  IRA (Irish Republican Army), and 100–1, 103
  Irish Republican Socialist Party and 101
  loss of seat 100
  maiden speech at parliament 95–7
  Máiréad Farrell killing and 111
  Markievicz, Constance, comparison with 81, 96
  Peace Process and 107, 108–9
  People's Democracy and 82, 92, 93, 106
  The price of my soul (memoir) 83, 100
  Robinson, Mary, comparison with 81–3 *passim*, 112
  socialism and 82, 84, 87, 88, 91

INDEX

McAliskey, Bernadette (formerly Devlin) (*cont.*)
  at Queen's University (Belfast) 82, 90–1
  visit to USA 97–8
McAliskey, Michael, 87, 100
McAliskey, Róisín 102, 109
McBride, Eimear 22
McBride, John 108
MacCabe, Colin 61
McCafferty, Nell 99–100, 105
  Nell (memoir) 135
  see also O'Faolain, Nuala, relationship with
McCann, Eamonn 82, 83, 97–8
McCarthy, Mary 152
McCourt, Frank
  Angela's ashes (memoir) 152–3
McGahern, John, 17, 19, 170
  Amongst women (novel) 127
  The barracks (novel) 16
  The dark (novel) 127
  Memoir 16
McGlinchey, Dominic 35
McKay, Susan 105
McLaughlin, Noel 66
Mac Liammóir, Michael 83
McLoone, Martin 66
Mac Réamoinn, Seán 123, 138
McSwiney, Terence 104
Magdalene women 182
Maher, Mary 105
Malouf, Michael 63, 83
Man Booker Prize 164
Mangan, James Clarence 187
Markievicz, Constance 6, 86–7, 108, 109, 116n.89, 201
  see also McAliskey, Bernadette, comparison with
Marley, Bob 63
Maudling, Reginald 85, 98
Meaney, Gerardine 177
Merriman Summer School 123, 138, 155
Moi, Toril 2–3, 67–8, 132, 202
Monty Python
  The life of Brian (film) 34
Moore, George
  Esther Waters (novel) 123
Moore, Thomas
  'The song of Fionnuala' 15–16
Morrison, Van 64
Mother and Baby Home, Tuam 165, 181–4
Mother Ireland 4, 17, 43, 97, 111, 140, 186, 187
Mother Ireland
  (documentary, Anne Crilly, dir.) 111
  (book) *see* O'Brien, Edna

Mulhall, Anne 172
Mullally, Una 206
Murphy Report (2009) 71
MTV (Music Television) 50

Napier, Taura S. 138–9
National Library (of Ireland) 120
New York Times, 38, 119, 151

O'Brien, Conor Cruise 86, 99, 183–84
  States of Ireland 85
O'Brien, Edna 13–43, 84, 119, 121, 125, 127, 136, 144, 147, 152, 166, 170, 171, 185, 199–206 *passim*
  Aosdána and 35, 40
  'Big House' and 17, 24
  Clare (county) in writings of 32–3, 35, 140
  feminism and 17, 22–3, 33–4, 39
  O'Faolain, Nuala and, comparison of viewpoints 140–1
  writings
    A Pagan Place 19
    Country girl: a memoir 18, 24, 28, 31, 39
    The country girls trilogy 17–19 *passim*, 22–8, 34, 45n.55, 46n.70, 124, 127, 133, 138, 140, 205
    Down by the river 19
    The house of splendid isolation 35
    In the forest 35, 46n.72, 149
    James Joyce (biography) 21
    The little red chairs 34, 37
    Mother Ireland 18, 26–8, 32, 41, 200
    Night 40
    Wild Decembers 35–6
O'Brien, Flann 137, 166
O'Brien, Peggy 33, 41
O'Callaghan, Margaret 6, 122
O'Connor, Frank 57
O'Connor, Maureen 39
O'Connor, Sinéad 1, 6–7, 10, 23, 38, 50–76, 119, 121, 164, 199–206 *passim*
  'aisling' poetry and 64
  albums
    Faith and courage (2000) 51, 60, 61–2, 64, 65
    How about I be me (and you be you)? (2012) 51, 71–2, 73, 74, 75, 199, 204
    I do not want what I haven't got (1990) 51, 56
    I'm not bossy, I'm the boss (2014) 51, 71, 72–3, 74

INDEX

The lion and the cobra (1987) 51, 54, 55–6, 67
Sean-nós nua (2002) 51, 63, 66, 68–9, 72
Theology (2007) 73
Throw down your arms (2005) 63–4
Universal mother (1994) 51, 59–61
background 52
Catholic church, relationship with 61–2, 65, 66–7, 71, 78n.13
death of mother 58
feminism and 51, 56, 59, 65–8 *passim*
Irish republicanism and 65, 78n.22
Late late show, appearance on 67
London, life in 57–8
Rastafarian influence 62–4
reggae influence 62–4
Robinson, Mary, contrast with 77n.10
Saturday Night Live, appearance on 50, 77n.11, 78n.17
Pope (John-Paul II), tearing image of 10, 50, 59, 63
songs
  'A perfect Indian' 59–60
  'Back where you belong' 74
  'Daddy I'm fine' 62
  'Dancing lessons' 62
  'Dense water deeper down' 73
  'Downpressor man' 65
  'Famine' 76n.5
  'Fire on Babylon' 59
  'The foggy dew' 69, 70
  'I am stretched on your grave' 57
  'I had a baby' 74
  'John, I love you' 59
  'Kyrié eléison' 62
  'The lamb's book of life' 64
  'Marcus Garvey' 64–5
  'No man's woman' 62
  'Nothing compares 2 U' 50, 56–7
  'Old lady' 73
  'Óró, sé do bheatha 'bhaile' 67
  'Paddy's lament' 69
  'The parting glass' 68
  'Queen of Denmark' 73
  'Reason with me' 75
  'Streetcars' 74–5
  'Take off your shoes' 74, 199
  'Thank you for hearing me' 59, 60
  'Three babies' 58–9
  'Troy' 56
  'Very far from home' 72
  'The Vishnu room' 73–4
  'War' 64, 65
  'The wolf is getting married' 73
  'You cause as much sorrow' 58
O'Donnell, Brendan 149

O'Donnell, Peadar 124
O'Faolain, Nuala 1, 6, 7, 10, 32, 42, 84, 119–56, 170, 198–206 *passim*
background 124–6
Clare (county) life in 120, 139–40
  in writings of 149, 153, 156
death of 119, 120–1
education 119, 123, 130
feminism and 120–3 *passim*, 127, 134, 137, 144, 147, 149–53 *passim*, 159n.118, 161n.161
nationalism and 85–6, 102
interview with Gay Byrne on the *Late late show* 10, 120, 135
interview with Marian Finucane 10, 121, 127, 155
Irish Times and 119
O'Brien, Edna
  commentary on 21–3
  comparison of viewpoints 42, 140–1
relationships and 131–4
  with Nell McCafferty 134–6, 145, 151
  with 'Terry O'Sullivan' (Tomás O'Faolain) 124, 127–8
RTÉ, working relationship with 119, 123, 138, 140–1, 143, 174
writings
  Almost there 122
  A more complex truth 148–9
  Are you somebody? 120, 123, 125, 127, 130–1, 132, 134–5, 138–40 *passim*, 150–2, 161n.164, 198
  Best love, Rosie 138
  'Irish women and writing in modern Ireland' 159n.118
  My dream of you 138, 146–7, 161n.170
O'Gorman, Colm 206
Oil Crisis (1972) 9
O'Malley, Grace 9
O'Neill, Terence 96
Open University 119, 143
Ó Riada, Seán
  Mise Éire 138
Osnabrück (Germany) 102
'O'Sullivan, Terry' *see* O'Faolain, Nuala
O'Toole, Fintan 142
Oxford University 119, 130, 132, 133, 152

Paisley, Ian 85
partition (of Ireland) 5, 6, 14, 81, 91, 122, 173, 201
Peace Process (Northern Ireland) 38, 100, 107, 109, 153

INDEX

Pearse, Patrick 83, 95, 103, 108
People's Democracy *see* McAliskey, Bernadette and
Pogues, The 54
Pope, John-Paul II *see* O'Connor, Sinéad and
Price, Dolours 110, 117n.92
Price, Marian 110, 117n.92
Prince, 50, 56, 57
Proclamation of the Republic (1916) 5
Proust, Marcel 130

rape *see* sexual abuse
Rastafarianism *see* O'Connor, Sinéad and
reggae *see* O'Connor, Sinéad and
Reynolds, Lorna 132-3
Rich, Adrienne 199, 201
Rilke, Rainer Maria 154
Robinson, Mary (President) 4-5, 7, 77n.10.
  see also McAliskey, Bernadette, comparison with
Rodney, Winston *see* Burning Spear
Rose, Jacqueline 30, 205
RTÉ (Raidió Teilifís Éireann) 10, 86, 119, 120, 121, 123, 138, 140, 143-4, 145, 166, 174, 203
  and censorship 86, 145, 205
  see also O'Faolain, Nuala and
Ryan, Louise 5
Ryan, Matthew 188
Ryan Report (2009) 71

Samuel, Raphael 123, 130
Sands, Bobby 102-4, 106
Sarraute, Nathalie 152
Saturday Night Live see O'Connor, Sinéad, appearance on
Sarsfield, Patrick 186
Sartre, Jean-Paul 132
Saville enquiry 110
Scally, Robert
  The end of hidden Ireland: rebellion, famine and emigration 146-7
Scullion 57
SDLP (Social Democratic and Labour Party) 100
Second World War 22
Section 31 (of the Broadcasting Act) 86
  see also RTÉ and censorship

sexual abuse 9, 19, 38, 50, 52, 61, 63, 65, 71-2, 74, 78n.17, 104, 105, 110, 116n.78, 122, 125, 141, 145, 149-50, 152, 161n.170, 165, 175-8, 201-2
Sheehy Skeffington, Hanna 104
Sinn Féin 38, 81, 85-6, 101, 103, 104, 106, 107, 109
Smyth, Gerry 66-7
Sterne, Laurence 166
St Patrick's Academy (Dungannon) 89

Thatcher, Margaret 57, 103
Tóibín, Colm 164, 166
Tone, Wolfe 108
Treaty of Limerick (1691) 186, 187
Trinity College Dublin 166
Turner, Martyn 202

UDA (Ulster Defence Association) 87, 104
University College Dublin 119
University of East Anglia 166
U Thant (UN Secretary-General) 97

Vietnam (War) 70
Vinegar Hill 88

Wall, Maureen 133
Ward, Margaret 5
War of Independence 24
Waters, John 121, 122
Westminster 81, 84, 91
  see also House of Commons
Wild Geese 186, 187, 191
William of Orange, King 187
Wills, Clair 37-8, 147
Woolf, Virginia 6
Wulff, Helena 174-5

'X' Case (1992) *see* abortion

Yeats, W.B. 7, 14, 15, 17, 20, 40, 54, 108, 137, 187, 191
  Cathleen ni Houlihan 17
  'No Second Troy' 56
  'On a political prisoner' 86-7, 108, 109

Žižek, Slavoj 141
Zola, Emile 132

Lightning Source UK Ltd.
Milton Keynes UK
UKHW012243270320
360995UK00003B/77